# Learning Analyt

M000170315

*Learning Analytics Explained* draws extensively from case studies and interviews with experts in order to discuss emerging applications of the new field of learning analytics. Educational institutions increasingly collect data on students and their learning experiences, a practice that helps enhance courses, identify learners who require support and provide a more personalised learning experience. There is, however, a corresponding need for guidance on how to carry out institutional projects, intervene effectively with students, and assess legal and ethical issues. This book provides that guidance while covering the evolving technical architectures, standards and products within the field.

**Niall Sclater** is an independent consultant based in Scotland. He is Affiliated Faculty at the Amsterdam Business School of the University of Amsterdam and was formerly Director of Learning and Teaching at The Open University, UK.

# Learning Analytics Explained

**Niall Sclater**

Routledge
Taylor & Francis Group

NEW YORK AND LONDON

First published 2017
by Routledge
711 Third Avenue, New York, NY 10017

and by Routledge
2 Park Square, Milton Park, Abingdon, Oxon, OX14 4RN

*Routledge is an imprint of the Taylor & Francis Group, an informa business*

© 2017 Taylor & Francis

*Library of Congress Cataloging in Publication Data*
Names: Sclater, Niall, author.
Title: Learning analytics explained / by Niall Sclater.
Description: New York ; London : Routledge, [2017]
Identifiers: LCCN 2016029240| ISBN 9781138931725 (hbk) | ISBN
9781315679563 (ebk) | ISBN 9781138931732 (pbk.)
Subjects: LCSH: Education--Research--Data processing. | Students--
Research--Data processing. | Data mining.
Classification: LCC LB1028.43 .S37 2017 | DDC 370.72--dc23
LC record available at https://lccn.loc.gov/2016029240

ISBN: 978-1-13893-172-5 (hbk)
ISBN: 978-1-13893-173-2 (pbk)
ISBN: 978-1-31567-956-3 (ebk)

Typeset in Times New Roman
by Integra Software Service Pvt. Ltd.

For Josie and Claudia

# Contents

viii   *Contents*

# Preface

My motivation for researching and writing this book is to attempt to answer the question 'What is learning analytics, and how can we make the best use of it?' For several years I have been working in the area, recently almost exclusively, and have encountered a mixture of intrigue and bewilderment about learning analytics from people across education. Many institutions have begun to deploy innovative educational products that use data about students and their learning to enhance education in various ways. The field has developed extremely quickly and a growing number of professionals are now investigating its different aspects and applications as part of a vibrant global community of researchers and practitioners.

Ask educators what learning analytics is, though, and a wide range of responses can be expected. Many of them recognise its potential to help solve some of the key challenges faced by their institutions but there is, unsurprisingly, a general lack of understanding of the different applications, logistics, technologies and deployment issues involved. There is, however, no shortage of knowledge available: the problem is that it is encapsulated in a large, dispersed and rapidly growing collection of journal and conference papers, articles and reports, not to mention the brains of people expert in each of its dimensions. Many of the publications are relatively impenetrable to a general audience, sometimes containing complex mathematical formulae or computer code. This book draws on the literature base, and the voices of experts in learning analytics, to provide what is intended to be a readable and informative summary of the area. It is aimed at individuals working or studying in universities and colleges who wish to gain a comprehensive understanding of the current practice and potential of this fascinating and multifaceted field.

## A Note on Spelling, Grammar and Terminology

For a while I have been completely immersed in the global literature and the worldwide academic community around learning analytics – and for much longer in the wider field of educational technology. I am thus used to continual variations in the spelling of English words, differing naming conventions for technologies and a variety of educational concepts and processes internationally. For this book I have settled somewhere mid-Atlantic, and have opted for the following:

- The use of UK spellings throughout except in quotations from other sources.
- Use of 'learning management system' (LMS) rather than 'course management system' or 'virtual learning environment' (prevalent in the UK).
- Use of 'student information system' (SIS) rather than 'student record system' (also common in the UK).
- The US terms 'faculty' and 'staff', where faculty are people primarily involved in teaching and research and staff mainly perform managerial or administrative functions. A faculty can, of course, also be an administrative unit within a university.
- The words 'instructor', 'lecturer', 'academic', 'teacher' and 'tutor' used more or less interchangeably.
- Use of 'educator' as a generic term for those involved in educating students at institutions.
- Retention of country-specific educational terms and concepts, such as 'freshman' (US), in case studies.
- 'Course', in the US sense, where in some other countries 'module' would be used – a unit of study that, combined with others, may lead to a qualification.

I refer to learning analytics in the singular, for example 'learning analytics is' rather than 'are', given its emergence as a 'thing' in its own right; most people now seem to use the singular too. However, I treat the word 'analytics' on its own as plural, for example 'the analytics tell us that'. I have also opted to use 'data' in the singular. Finally, the term 'learning analytics' is used throughout the book, rather than the much less frequently used 'learner analytics', which perhaps implies analysis of the learners only rather than the many aspects surrounding their learning.

# Acknowledgements

I would like to acknowledge the inspiration provided by colleagues at Jisc, especially Phil Richards for providing the opportunity to input to his visionary Effective Learning Analytics project. Many conversations and activities carried out with Paul Bailey and Michael Webb, as part of that project, have influenced the content of this book. Together with others at Jisc, including Rob Wyn Jones, Lee Baylis, Jo Wheatley, Myles Danson, Martin Hall, Shri Footring and George Munroe, they bring a wealth of experience and are tremendous company, wherever we happen to meet up.

The emerging learning analytics community is dynamic, altruistic and young (in spirit, anyway: some of us are getting a little long in the tooth). I have been touched by the willingness of busy people to share their thoughts and experiences and to provide input to the book, including the experts, listed in the introduction, whose voices I have incorporated throughout. Lindsay Pineda of Unicon gave detailed and insightful comments about the deployment section. The thoughts of Jisc's Andrew Cormack on the chapters covering legal and ethical issues were also most welcome. Sandeep Jayaprakash of the University of California, Berkeley, meanwhile, provided some useful input on data, metrics and predictive modelling. Various enjoyable discussions with Alan Berg of the University of Amsterdam and Doug Clow of the UK's Open University also helped to shape my thinking.

I would like to express my gratitude, too, to a number of vendors who have provided extensive information on their products, as well as helpful conversations around learning analytics in general: Richard Gascoigne of DTP SolutionPath, Richard Burrows of Blackboard International, Cheyne Tan of Civitas Learning International, Shady Shahata of D2L, Alison Pendergast of Acrobatiq, Steve Sapseid of BME Solutions, Ben Stein of Hobsons and Sabrina Fuchs of CogBooks.

Finally, a special thank you is due to Liliana Torero Fernandez, who put up with months of poor communication and lack of attention to domestic duties. When I occasionally emerged from my writing – muttering, no doubt, some obscure fact about learning analytics – it was invariably to a plate of her fine cuisine.

# Abbreviations

| | |
|---|---|
| API | application program interface |
| BI | business intelligence |
| EDM | educational data mining |
| GPA | grade point average |
| IPR | intellectual property rights |
| IT | information technology |
| LAK | International Conference on Learning Analytics and Knowledge |
| LMS | learning management system (also known as virtual learning environment) |
| LRS | learning record store |
| MOOC | massive open online course |
| PMML | Predictive Model Markup Language |
| ROI | return on investment |
| SIS | student information system (also known as student record system) |
| SoLAR | Society for Learning Analytics Research |
| VLE | virtual learning environment |
| xAPI | experience application program interface |

# Introduction

The literature base surrounding learning analytics is large and varied, reflecting the multiple disciplines from which it is derived and the diverse backgrounds and interests of those developing the area. In this book, I attempt to summarise the field: what researchers are investigating and what institutions are doing to enhance education with the ever-increasing sources of data they have at their disposal about students and their learning contexts. The book is divided into six parts: background, applications, logistics, technologies, deployment and future directions.

## Part I: Background

In Part I, I discuss how learning analytics has emerged in recent years and how it is being built on a foundation of other well-established disciplines. I also uncover the personal motivations for involvement in the field of a panel of experts on learning analytics interviewed for the book and their perceptions of what interests institutions most about this area.

## Part II: Applications

In this part, I look at the main uses of learning analytics that have emerged so far. These include early alert and student success, the area that has captured most attention due to its potential to improve retention and grades. This, of course, can have a direct impact on the finances of institutions, particularly those with a serious attrition problem. Course recommendation is the next major area of activity to be covered: these systems attempt to guide a student regarding what course to take next. I then discuss adaptive learning systems, which build on a long tradition of intelligent tutoring but are now incorporating new data sources. Some institutions are now adopting them on a large scale. The other main and, to date, largely underexploited, application area covered is curriculum design. Learning analytics is enabling educators to enhance educational provision, responding to issues as they arise during a course. It can also facilitate subsequent refinement of the learning content and activities for future cohorts and provide insight for the development of new courses.

## Part III: Logistics

Part III, on logistics, examines in depth the areas that need to be tackled when carrying out learning analytics. A chapter on data describes the main data sources for learning analytics, and the processes that need to be undertaken to prepare the data. I then look at the metrics that can be developed to measure aspects of engagement, and some of the techniques used for predicting the academic attainment of students, or their likelihood of withdrawal. Visualisation of the analytics warrants a chapter in itself as it is essential for making sense of the data. One of the themes of this book is that there is little point in carrying out learning analytics unless something is done as a result. The next chapter therefore covers intervention: the actions taken by faculty or staff based on the data. Students, too, can make their own interventions and, in the final chapter of this part, I discuss the provision of analytics directly to learners.

## Part IV: Technologies

The first chapter in this part describes the architecture of a typical institutional learning analytics deployment, outlining the different components that might be required. The next chapter delves into the emerging specifications and standards in the area, which should help to build the market for learning analytics, providing some assurance to institutions that they will not be locked into the products of one provider indefinitely. I then outline some of the systems that have become available, particularly in the area of predictive analytics, showing how vendors of different types of platform are competing for a share of a rapidly growing market.

## Part V: Deployment

Here I examine the key organisational areas to be considered by institutions wishing to deploy learning analytics. Institutional readiness is a subject that has already received reasonable coverage in the literature and is clearly important for organisations to assess at an early stage. I also look more closely at aspects of project planning that are likely to be required for large-scale implementation. The following chapter introduces the many ethical issues that have been raised in relation to learning analytics, to which institutions would be well advised to consider their response. Two further chapters follow, on areas that have both a legal and ethical dimension: the first on the need for transparency around analytics processes and obtaining consent from students for the use of their data; the second on issues around privacy and data protection. All of these aspects are important for reasons ranging from attempting to reduce objections from stakeholders to preventing legal action against the institution.

## Part VI: Future Directions

In the final part, I outline three of the techniques that are being deployed increasingly in learning analytics, namely the analysis of discourse, social networks and emotions. These are some of the most intriguing areas of current research; their use, especially when combined with other methods, promises greater insight into aspects of that fascinating yet still somewhat elusive phenomenon: learning.

## Expert Voices

As well as immersing myself in the growing number of publications around learning analytics as I researched this book, I was interested to tap directly into the thinking of some of the leading thinkers in the area around the world, the people who are the driving force behind its development. To this end, I carried out semi-structured interviews with 20 of them, and have incorporated their voices at the end of each section of the book:

- **Josh Baron**, Open Education Ambassador at Lumen Learning; Member, Board of Directors, Apereo Foundation.
- **Alan Berg**, Chief Technical Officer of the Center of Job Knowledge Research, Amsterdam Business School, University of Amsterdam; Board Member, Apereo Foundation.
- **Professor Simon Buckingham Shum**, Professor of Learning Informatics; Director of the Connected Intelligence Centre at the University of Technology Sydney.
- **Dr Doug Clow**, Senior Lecturer at the Institute of Educational Technology, Open University, UK.
- **Professor Shane Dawson**, Professor, Learning Analytics and Director, Teaching Innovation Unit, University of South Australia; Founding Executive Committee Member, Society for Learning Analytics Research.
- **Dr Rebecca Ferguson**, Senior Lecturer at the Institute of Educational Technology, Open University, UK; Executive Committee Member, Society for Learning Analytics Research; Principal Investigator of the Learning Analytics Community Exchange project; Principal Investigator of the Learning Analytics for European Educational Policy project.
- **Professor Dragan Gašević**, Professor and Chair in Learning Analytics and Informatics at the University of Edinburgh; President of the Society for Learning Analytics Research; Founding Editor of the *Journal of Learning Analytics*; General Chair of the International Conference on Learning Analytics and Knowledge 2016.
- **Dr Mark Glynn**, Head of Teaching Enhancement Unit, Dublin City University.
- **Dr Jeff Grann**, Academic Director of Assessment and Learning Analytics at Capella University, Minnesota; Member of the Higher Education Institutional Executive Board, IMS Global Learning Consortium.
- **Dr Cathy Gunn**, Associate Professor and Deputy Director, Centre for Learning and Research in Higher Education, University of Auckland; life member and former President of the Australasian Society for Computers

in Learning in Tertiary Education (Ascilite); Principal Investigator / Project Leader: Building an Evidence-Base for Teaching and Learning Design using Learning Analytics.

- **Dr Kirsty Kitto**, Senior Research Fellow, Queensland University of Technology; Founding Member of Board of Directors, Data Interoperability Standards Consortium.
- **Dr Leah Macfadyen**, Program Director, Evaluation and Learning Analytics at the Faculty of Arts, University of British Columbia; Executive Committee Member of the Society for Learning Analytics Research.
- **Professor Timothy McKay**, Arthur F. Thurnau Professor of Physics, Astronomy and Education at the University of Michigan; Director of the Digital Innovation Greenhouse; former Chair of the Learning Analytics Task Force, University of Michigan; Instructor, Practical Learning Analytics MOOC.
- **Dr Mark Milliron**, Co-Founder and Chief Learning Officer, Civitas Learning; previously Deputy Director of the Bill and Melinda Gates Foundation; previously Vice President, Education and Medical Practice, SAS.
- **Dr Stefan Mol**, Assistant Professor in Organisational Behavior, Amsterdam Business School, University of Amsterdam.
- **Dr Abelardo Pardo**, Senior Lecturer in the School of Electrical and Information Engineering at the University of Sydney; Executive Committee Member of the Society for Learning Analytics Research.
- **Dr Bart Rienties**, Reader in Learning Analytics at the Institute of Educational Technology, Open University, UK.
- **Professor Stephanie Teasley**, Research Professor in the School of Information at the University of Michigan; Member, Learning Analytics Task Force, University of Michigan; President Elect of the Society for Learning Analytics Research.
- **Dr John Whitmer**, Director for Analytics and Research, Blackboard.
- **Dr Alyssa Wise**, Associate Professor of Educational Communication and Technology, Steinhardt School of Culture, Education, and Human Development, New York University, New York; Executive Committee Member and Treasurer for the Society for Learning Analytics Research; Associate Editor of the *Journal of Learning Analytics*; General Chair of the International Conference on Learning Analytics and Knowledge 2017.

I start by asking the experts what their personal interest is in learning analytics. As could be expected with people from such wide-ranging backgrounds, they have a variety of drivers for involvement in the area. However, there is also a lot of common ground. All of them, including the representatives from the commercial world, have a strong background in higher education. There is an ever-present realism in their comments about the barriers to progress at institutions and the risks that institutions face if the field is not developed with great attention to the ethical dimension and the needs of the learner.

   Like many people working in education, though, the interviewees appear to be driven by a belief in education's potential to transform lives: a constant theme in the conversations is that learning analytics is a key area that can and will improve things for learners. This vision is perhaps founded on an underlying technological utopianism, which is apparent among most of the experts: a belief that the appropriate use of technology will lead to better education than that which institutions are currently providing. The many case studies mentioned throughout the book, drawn from colleges and universities across the world, also demonstrate the huge efforts being made by innovative researchers, practitioners and vendors to develop the field. It can be assumed that the majority of these are also driven by their own personal belief in the potentially transformative nature of the technologies and associated practices.

# Part I
# Background

# 1   The Evolution of a New Field

Online and mobile technologies are facilitating the accumulation of vast amounts of data across business, industry, government and other areas of human endeavour. We have become dependent on the internet as a source of information for most of what we need to know, for access to entertainment, for communication with others, for purchases and banking and for carrying out our work. As our lives become increasingly intertwined with technology, we are generating huge quantities of 'digital exhaust' through the use of internet-connected extensions of ourselves: devices such as smartphones, tablets, laptops, e-book readers and fitness trackers.

The use of analytics to process and help interpret this data is enabling organisations to develop better insight into people's activities and to optimise organisational processes and outputs. Business intelligence, as this area is often known, is now essential for the survival and expansion of commercial organisations and an increasingly essential tool in other sectors. Insurance providers, for instance, offer discounts to customers prepared to install devices in their cars that monitor the safety of their driving. Meanwhile, in medicine, analytics identify the spread of disease across populations and help agencies to target interventions more rapidly.

In universities and colleges, data has until recently often been stored on paper in filing cabinets and in a wide variety of different formats,[1] sometimes residing on spreadsheets on a teacher's or administrator's machine. However, large, more easily accessible datasets increasingly exist about learners, their learning activities and the environments in which they study. Educators are beginning to understand how to exploit this to help solve some of the challenges faced by their institutions. Analytics about learning promises to enhance many aspects of the educational experience through the use of data about students and their learning contexts.

This chapter outlines how the field of learning analytics is evolving: what the drivers are for institutions and which existing fields of enquiry are contributing to it. I discuss some of the definitions for learning analytics and to what extent it can be differentiated from other closely related fields. Finally, I look at what the main current focusses of investigation are and how the worldwide community of researchers, practitioners and vendors is (at least sometimes) working together to build the new domain of learning analytics.

## The Opportunities Presented by Big Data and Analytics

Access to the internet has become an important aspect of education – an essential part of it if learners are to become effective citizens and employees in a world organised digitally. Institutions offer many courses in blended or fully online modes and it is increasingly unlikely that a university student will complete a degree programme without carrying out some studies using web-based tools. The internet has encouraged the growth of for-profit online colleges in the US,[2] and massive open online courses (MOOCs) provide online education to millions more learners globally.

As students navigate online learning systems, they leave 'digital footprints', or traces of their activities. Clearly, the more learning that takes place online, the more data is likely to be accumulated. Meanwhile, other aspects of student activity are being recorded continually, such as their presence on campus, their attendance at lectures, their use of library facilities and their submission of assignments. These multiple sources of information enable the development of a much richer view of student behaviour than has been possible before, helping institutions to identify opportunities to improve courses, to personalise the study experience for individual learners and to assist those identified by the systems as academically at risk.

## Data-Informed Decision Making

The growth of big data – datasets that are beyond the ability of traditional software to capture, store, manage and analyse[3] – is driving the development of the tools and methods of learning analytics.[4] While there are problems with the reliability of some of this data, it can generally be collected cheaply[5] or is already being gathered by the systems that the students are using. Analysing learners' experiences of education has traditionally been carried out using questionnaires and interviews with limited numbers of students. Using the data accumulated by students during their normal study activities is less intrusive than these research methods and provides a more continuous, uninterrupted and complete picture of study activities.[6]

Traditionally, most of the decisions made in educational institutions by faculty, staff and administrators have been based on intuition, anecdotes or presumptions. Formulating a hypothesis and then attempting to prove or disprove it can be a time-consuming process, limited by the quality of the research question. Empirical educational research, until recently, has been designed to answer a single question: which of two approaches works better?[7] Decisions on how to enhance education are likely to have better results if they are founded on data, facts and statistical analysis.[8, 9] This is not to suggest that human qualities such as experience, expertise and judgement should be entirely replaced but they should be supplemented by analytical techniques where appropriate.[10]

As education moves increasingly online, teachers may lack the visual clues that helped them to identify students who were insufficiently challenged, bored, confused or who were failing to attend:[11] the use and interpretation of learning activity data thus becomes key for those teaching online. Data can help highlight issues in ways that were not previously possible and its use can encourage a philosophy of continuous improvement.[12] Patterns and trends can be identified and the merits of different options can be weighed up.[13]

Cooper suggests that analytics can help us to answer questions of information and fact, such as 'What happened?' or 'What is happening now?' and 'Where are trends leading?' He differentiates these from questions of understanding and insight such as 'How and why did something happen?' or 'What should we do next?' and 'What is likely to happen?'[14] Colleges and universities that fail to ask such questions and to learn from the increasingly valuable data being accumulated about their learners risk being left behind by more innovative institutions, which offer better and more personalised education to their students.

## Pressures on Institutions

The need for more effective decision making at all levels of institutions is given impetus by a wide range of pressures affecting education, particularly greater student numbers. In an era of accountability and liability, there is a requirement for better measurement and quantification of many educational processes.[15, 16] Institutional budgets are more and more stretched and there is a need for evidence-based prioritisation of spending. Meanwhile, students who pay for their education will increasingly and justifiably expect to be able to see evidence that their fees are being spent appropriately.

Simultaneously, there is increased government scrutiny of issues such as retention and the equality of educational provision for minority groups. In the US, high student attrition levels are a focus of the Department of Education, and a number of for-profit institutions have been targeted for poor retention rates and for receiving financial aid for students who subsequently withdraw.[17] In the UK, the government-imposed Teaching Excellence Framework requires universities to measure aspects of their teaching provision in order to ensure quality, value for money and, ultimately, the employability of graduates.[18] The concerns of Western governments that their economies are falling behind the rising nations of Asia is captured in an Australian review of higher education, which identifies the link between educational attainment and economic productivity. The document also sets targets for improving retention and completion rates for indigenous students and those from low socio-economic backgrounds.[19]

Poor retention rates affect institutions in numerous ways, as well as broader society and countries' economic progress. The financial impact resulting from the loss of income from student fees, in particular, can be significant. The cost of recruiting the students may have been wasted and revenues from catering outlets and student accommodation can also be affected.[20] The personal impact on a student who has dropped out can, of course, be dramatic as well. Apart from feelings of failure and the loss of self-esteem, job prospects may be adversely impacted and debt may have been accrued that is never paid off. There are strong correlations between academic achievement and higher income levels.[21] Graduates tend to have higher status jobs, be healthier and live longer. They may also be more likely to rate their former institutions highly, leading to improved reputation and enhanced recruitment possibilities.

## Influences

Key contributing disciplines to learning analytics are computer science, education and statistics.[22] Dawson and colleagues analysed contributions to the International Conference on Learning Analytics and Knowledge (LAK), for example, and discovered that approximately 51% of papers were from computer scientists whereas 40% of authors had a background in education.[23] Theory and methodologies are drawn from disciplines as varied as psychology, philosophy, sociology, linguistics, information science, learning sciences and artificial intelligence.[24] Learning analytics draws on web analytics to help make sense of the data created in log files of users' access to websites.[25] Other methods deployed include social network analysis, predictive modelling and natural language processing – all fields of enquiry in their own right. Demonstrating the connections between learning analytics and other disciplines, for example, was an international conference in the well-established field of computer supported collaborative learning, which had nine papers, three posters and an invited session with 'learning analytics' in their titles.[26]

Clow argues that this eclectic approach facilitates rapid development of the field and the ability to build on established work. However, it means that learning analytics currently lacks its own coherent epistemology and established approaches.[27] Contributors to the key conferences in learning analytics and associated areas are, though, increasingly using theories from learning sciences to guide their selection of methods.[28]

## A Confusing Mix of Disciplines and Terminology

Given the recent emergence of learning analytics as a field and its multi-disciplinary origins, it is hardly surprising that there is confusion about what exactly it is and how it is differentiated from related areas. Analytics can refer to:

- a specific topic, such as health analytics;
- the aim of the activity, for instance predictive analytics;
- the data source, for example Google Analytics.[29]

*Analytics* itself has been defined as:

> the analysis of data, typically large sets of business data, by the use of mathematics, statistics and computer software.[30]

Campbell *et al.* suggest that analytics is considered as 'the practice of mining institutional data to produce "actionable intelligence"',[31] implying that taking action as a result of the insight is also key.

*Business intelligence* is often used synonymously with the term analytics. Although first recorded in 1958, it gained prominence after Gartner used it in 1989, in reference to the creation of management reports by extracting data from systems and organising it into more easily understandable formats. Business intelligence systems now incorporate dashboards and more sophisticated, customisable visualisation tools.[32]

*Academic analytics*, apparently first used by WebCT (now Blackboard)[33] was adopted by Goldstein & Katz in 2005 to describe the implementation of business intelligence in higher education. They recognise that the term is problematic, as it implies that administrative uses of analysis are not included.[34] Ironically, the term has come to be used, particularly in the US, primarily for analysing higher-level administrative functions in universities, such as recruitment, whereas *learning analytics* is used more for aspects of learning and the educational experience of students.

Learning analytics is also related to *action research*. Both attempt to improve education through cyclical investigations. Action research projects can be labour-intensive, though, and usually attempt to address an issue arising from teaching practice, often using qualitative methods. Learning analytics, in contrast, is based mainly on quantitative methods and may draw conclusions from already-collected data.[35, 36]

Numerous commentators have attempted to define *learning analytics* but the first LAK conference in 2011 described it as:

> the measurement, collection, analysis and reporting of data about learners and their contexts, for purposes of understanding and optimising learning and the environments in which it occurs.[37]

This has become the most frequently quoted definition of learning analytics; it seems to incorporate the *raison d'être* of the field, as is being discussed in research papers and implemented in practice. However, this rapidly evolving discipline may refuse to hold to a permanent definition and is likely to be refined over time. Given the fact that learning and the environments in which it occurs are so varied and dynamic, the objectives and applications of learning analytics are still in a state of flux.[38] Ferguson has pointed out that this definition covers most educational research, but that it is usually qualified with the fact that it draws on pre-existing machine-readable big data.[39] Elias adds that learning analytics minimises the delay between the capture of data and its use. It thus enables services to be targeted at students, based on current data, rather than using information from previous periods to inform improvements.[40]

One completely different way to think of learning analytics, suggested by Duval & Verbert, is as an application of the 'quantified self' movement,[41] where people seek to measure aspects of their activities or performance through devices such as fitness trackers. From the learners' perspective, if they are provided with useful dashboards and apps, this may be quite appropriate. However, this can only ever be part of the story, as most applications of learning analytics are directed currently towards institutions rather than students and the data is useful in aggregated formats across cohorts, as well as for individuals.

The related area of *educational data mining* (EDM) arose at about the same time as learning analytics but has its own research community. Data mining uses statistics and algorithmic techniques in 'a kind of speculative prospecting for riches'[42] on the pre-existing data generated by users, to help understand students and the settings in which they learn.[43] Unlike other forms of data mining, EDM takes into account pedagogical aspects of the learner and the system.[44]

EDM can be regarded as a set of techniques that learning analytics initiatives can deploy. Whereas EDM focusses on data-mining techniques such as clustering and classification, learning analytics brings in other methods such as statistical software, social network analysis and visualisation tools.[45] EDM compares different automated techniques; in learning analytics, which adopts a more holistic framework, human judgement is often used to interpret the analytics and take action.[46, 47] Romero & Ventura argue that learning analytics, academic analytics and EDM are all fundamentally part of the same research area and community, with different viewpoints regarding the same issues.[48] Piety *et al.* suggest that they should be grouped under the discipline of *educational data sciences* and that they have five features in common:

- rapid evolution indicative of a broad sociotechnical movement;
- boundary issues indicating commonality;
- disruption in evidentiary practices;
- questions about visualisation, interpretation and culture;
- issues around ethics, privacy and information architecture.

They believe that working in this new combined field will increasingly require a combination of technical and social skills and an understanding of engineering and educational issues.[49]

## Focus of Activity

Another way of conceptualising the developing arena of learning analytics is to examine the areas of activity that are engaging researchers and practitioners. Sin & Muthu analysed 45 papers in the field, which they identified via Google Scholar and found that researchers were concentrating on three major areas. First, there were introductory articles about learning analytics, including its concepts, challenges and its impacts on education. This category also included works that emphasised the importance of learning theory and design and ethics frameworks. The second area concerned EDM techniques for enhancing learning analytics and communication between the two communities. It also covered visualisation. Third, the use of analytics in social settings and in MOOCs was discussed, often supporting constructivist learning theories.[50]

Ochoa and colleagues analysed contributions to the third LAK conference, which took place in 2013. They found the most frequently used words in the papers to be: students, data, analytics, learning, use, activity and education, which, they suggest could form a definition for learning analytics: 'use of student and activity data to improve learning and educational processes'. They put the papers into six categories: visualisation, behaviour analysis, social learning analytics, applications, challenges and definitional.[51]

Papamitsiou & Economides' rigorous survey of empirical studies into learning analytics and EDM found that most investigations were around student behaviour modelling and predictions of their performance. Most were based on LMS data but cognitive tutoring systems, MOOCs and social platforms were also covered. The authors examined demographic factors, grades, portfolios, engagement, enrolment and moods, as factors in predicting academic performance. Key issues were the identification of disconnected students and the prediction of withdrawal.[52]

Dawson *et al.* contributed further to analyses of the literature around learning analytics. They found that the most commonly cited papers were more conceptual than empirical, suggesting, they felt, that researchers were still attempting to define the domain. As the need to do this reduces, they believe, studies are likely to become more rigorous. Some of the documented techniques used for carrying out learning analytics were analysed by Khalil & Ebner, who found, in their survey of 91 relevant papers, that data-mining techniques were the most used and statistics and mathematical techniques the second most used. Text mining, semantics and linguistic techniques also appeared. Social network analysis was less prominent in the papers they reviewed.[53]

Researchers are naturally inclined to explore exciting new domains. However, the overwhelming interest among institutions in learning analytics to date has been around predictive analytics and the identification of students at risk of academic failure or withdrawal. Vendors, too, have understandably concentrated on developing products in this space. Many initiatives in the area of early alert and student success are documented in the literature and reported in this book. Institutions are also deploying course recommender tools and adaptive learning platforms and using analytics in various ways to enhance the curriculum.

## Developing the Community

The community around learning analytics involves researchers, teachers and other personnel from educational institutions, vendors and a few staff from membership organisations such as Jisc in the UK and EDUCAUSE in the US. Dialogue between these different groups is essential in order to ensure the development of appropriate tools, technologies, methodologies and practices. The current gap between researchers, vendors and the end users of their products is a challenge: there is little connection between the empirical research carried out in universities and the commercial software tools being developed.[54]

Learning analytics requires bringing people with high levels of technical expertise together with others who understand pedagogy and educational processes. A number of organisations have attempted to develop a community through conferences and other activities.[55] A series of workshops on EDM began in 2005 and evolved into an annual conference in 2008. The first LAK conference took place in 2011.[56] This event was specifically aimed at encouraging dialogue between technical, pedagogical and social domains.[57] Core values that some in these fields would like to see promoted are: 'high quality, inclusiveness, openness, transparency and multidisciplinarity'.[58]

The Society for Learning Analytics Research (SoLAR) was created in 2011 and took over the organisation of future LAK conferences.[59] An analysis of presentations from the 2013 LAK conference showed that 128 authors came from academic institutions, eight from research centres and seven from companies, demonstrating that this is primarily a research-oriented conference. A practitioner track added subsequently has, however, attracted others to the event. The 2013 conference was dominated by researchers from the US (51 authors), UK (20), Germany (18), Greece (9) and the Netherlands (9), with very few contributors from developing nations. There was a considerable level of international collaboration among authors, with 30% of papers written by authors affiliated with institutions across more than one country.[60] The 2016 conference in Edinburgh continued to be dominated by papers from authors based in the US and Europe, with a few contributions from Australia and Asia.

The *Journal of Educational Data Mining* was founded in 2009 and SoLAR began publishing the *Journal of Learning Analytics* in 2014, to complement its annual conferences. Special issues on learning analytics have appeared in various journals in the educational technology and other arenas. The European Commission has funded projects to develop the field; EDUCAUSE has a series of publications in the area; and other national agencies such as Jisc in the UK, SURF in the Netherlands and the Australian government's Office for Learning and Teaching organise collaborations and events and fund research and development activities to promote learning analytics. Meanwhile, the influential New Media Consortium's Horizon Report has for several years discussed learning analytics as an important area for institutions to embrace.[61]

## Further Evolution of the Field

Where learning analytics goes next could, perhaps, be predicted from empirical analyses of the literature and citations by predictive analytics experts. Siemens suggests that it will continue to establish its own distinct identity and this appears to be happening, with considerable interest expressed in the field across education.[62] He does, however, argue, with colleagues Gašević and

Dawson, that analytics tools which are not informed by learning theory are unlikely to achieve effective adoption. Learning analytics, they suggest, needs to ground its activities within existing educational research.[63] Chatti *et al.* propose that learners should be at the centre of analytics processes and that future studies will emphasise their role by empowering them to reflect on and act upon feedback, while helping teachers to intervene more quickly when things are going wrong.[64]

In Chapter 2, we hear directly from some of the most influential individuals in the field about their own personal motivations for involvement in learning analytics and what they believe are the drivers for institutions.

## References

1 Baker, R. S. J. d., 2014, Educational Data Mining: An Advance for Intelligent Systems in Education, *IEEE Intelligent Systems*, 29(3), pp. 78–82.
2 Picciano, A. G., 2012, The Evolution of Big Data and Learning Analytics in American Higher Education, *Journal of Asynchronous Learning Networks*, 16(3), pp. 9–20.
3 Manyika, J. *et al.*, 2011, *Big Data: The Next Frontier for Innovation, Competition, and Productivity*, McKinsey Global Institute.
4 West, D. *et al.*, 2015, *Learning Analytics: Assisting Universities with Student Retention Final Report 2015 (Part 1)*, Australian Government Office for Teaching and Learning.
5 Piety, P. J. *et al.*, 2014, Educational Data Sciences – Framing Emergent Practices for Analytics of Learning, Organizations, and Systems, *LAK14: Proceedings of the Fourth International Conference on Learning Analytics and Knowledge*.
6 Greller, W. & Drachsler, H., 2012, Translating Learning into Numbers: A Generic Framework for Learning, *Educational Technology and Society*, 15(3), pp. 42–57.
7 Baker, Educational Data Mining: An Advance for Intelligent Systems in Education.
8 Campbell, J. P. & Oblinger, D. G., 2007, *Academic Analytics*, EDUCAUSE.
9 Bichsel, J., 2012, *Analytics in Higher Education: Benefits, Barriers, Progress, and Recommendations*, EDUCAUSE Center for Applied Research.
10 Picciano, The Evolution of Big Data and Learning Analytics in American Higher Education.
11 Ferguson, R., 2012, Learning Analytics: Drivers, Developments and Challenges, *International Journal of Technology Enhanced Learning*, 4(5/6), pp. 304–317.
12 Bichsel, *Analytics in Higher Education: Benefits, Barriers, Progress, and Recommendations*.
13 Campbell & Oblinger, *Academic Analytics*.
14 Cooper, A., 2012, A Brief History of Analytics, *Jisc Cetis Analytics Series*, 1(9).
15 Campbell, J. P. *et al.*, 2007, Academic Analytics: A New Tool for a New Era, *EDUCAUSE Review*, 42(4), pp. 40–57.
16 Clow, D., 2013, An Overview of Learning Analytics, *Teaching in Higher Education*, 18(6), pp. 683–695.
17 Picciano, The Evolution of Big Data and Learning Analytics in American Higher Education.
18 Department for Business Innovation & Skills, 2016, *Success as a Knowledge Economy: Teaching Excellence, Social Mobility and Student Choice*.

19  Bradley, D. *et al.*, 2008, *Review of Australian Higher Education: Final Report*, Australian Government.
20  Campbell & Oblinger, *Academic Analytics*.
21  Ibid.
22  Romero, C. & Ventura, S., 2013, Data Mining in Education, *Wiley Interdisciplinary Reviews: Data Mining and Knowledge Discovery*, 3(1), pp. 12–27.
23  Dawson, S. *et al.*, 2014, Current State and Future Trends: A Citation Network Analysis of the Learning Analytics Field, *LAK14: Proceedings of the Fourth International Conference on Learning Analytics and Knowledge*.
24  Ibid.
25  Buckingham Shum, S. & Ferguson, R., 2011, *Social Learning Analytics*, Knowledge Media Institute.
26  Gašević, D. *et al.*, 2015, Let's Not Forget: Learning Analytics are about Learning. *TechTrends*, 59(1), pp. 64–71.
27  Clow, An Overview of Learning Analytics.
28  Baker, R. S. J. d. & Siemens, G., 2014, Educational Data Mining and Learning Analytics. In: *The Cambridge Handbook of the Learning Sciences*, Cambridge University Press, pp. 253–274.
29  van Barneveld, A. *et al.*, 2012, Analytics in Higher Education: Establishing a Common Language, *EDUCAUSE Learning Initiative*, paper 1, January.
30  Dictionary.com, www.dictionary.com/browse/analytics?s=t (accessed 29 September 2016).
31  Campbell, J. P. *et al.*, 2007, Academic Analytics: A New Tool for a New Era, *EDUCAUSE Review*, 42(4), pp. 40–57.
32  Cooper, A Brief History of Analytics.
33  Baepler, P. & Murdoch, C. J., 2010, Academic Analytics and Data Mining in Higher Education, *International Journal for the Scholarship of Teaching and Learning*, 4(2), article 17.
34  Goldstein, P. J. & Katz, R. N., 2005, *Academic Analytics: The Uses of Management Information and Technology in Higher Education*, EDUCAUSE Center for Applied Research.
35  Dyckhoff, A. L., 2011, Implications for Learning Analytics Tools: A Meta-Analysis of Applied Research Questions, *International Journal of Computer Information Systems and Industrial Management Applications*, 3, pp. 594–601.
36  Chatti, M. A. *et al.*, 2012, A Reference Model for Learning Analytics, *International Journal of Technology Enhanced Learning*, 4(5/6), pp. 318–331.
37  *LAK11: 1st International Conference on Learning Analytics and Knowledge*, https://tekri.athabascau.ca/analytics/ (accessed 29 September 2016).
38  West, *Learning Analytics: Assisting Universities with Student Retention Final Report 2015 (Part 1)*.
39  Ferguson, Learning Analytics: Drivers, Developments and Challenges.
40  Elias, T., 2011, *Learning Analytics: Definitions, Processes and Potential*, https://landing.athabascau.ca/file/download/43713 (accessed 29 September 2016).
41  Duval, E. & Verbert, K., 2012, Learning Analytics, *Eleed*, issue 8.
42  Baepler & Murdoch, Academic Analytics and Data Mining in Higher Education.
43  International Educational Data Mining Society, www.educationaldatamining.org/ (accessed 29 September 2016).
44  Romero, C. & Ventura, S., 2007, Educational Data Mining: A Survey from 1995 to 2005, *Expert Systems with Applications*, 33, pp. 135–146.
45  Chatti, M. A. *et al.*, A Reference Model for Learning Analytics.

46 Papamitsiou, Z. & Economides, A. A., 2014, Learning Analytics and Educational Data Mining in Practice: A Systematic Literature Review of Empirical Evidence, *Educational Technology and Society*, 17(4), pp. 49–64.
47 Romero & Ventura, Data Mining in Education.
48 Romero, C. & Ventura, S., 2015, Review of the book J. A. Larusson, B. White, eds, Learning Analytics: From Research to Practice, *Technology, Knowledge, and Learning*, 20, 357–360.
49 Piety *et al.*, Educational Data Sciences – Framing Emergent Practices for Analytics of Learning, Organizations, and Systems.
50 Sin, K. & Muthu, L., 2015, Application of Big Data in Education Data Mining and Learning Analytics – A Literature Review, *ICTACT Journal on Soft Computing*, 5(4), pp. 1035–1049.
51 Ochoa, X., *et al.*, 2014, Analysis and Reflections on the Third Learning Analytics and Knowledge Conference (LAK 2013), *Journal of Learning Analytics*, 1(2), pp. 5–22.
52 Papamitsiou & Economides, Learning Analytics and Educational Data Mining in Practice.
53 Khalil, M. & Ebner, M., 2016, What is Learning Analytics about? A Survey of Different Methods Used in 2013–2015, *Proceedings of Smart Learning Conference*, pp. 294–304.
54 Siemens, G., 2012, *Learning Analytics: Envisioning a Research Discipline and a Domain of Practice*, ACM, pp. 4–8.
55 Siemens, G. & Gašević, D., 2012, Guest Editorial – Learning and Knowledge Analytics, *Educational Technology and Society*, 15(3), pp. 1–2.
56 Baker, R. S. J. d., 2012, Learning, Schooling, and Data Analytics. In: M. Murphy *et al.*, eds, *Handbook on Innovations in Learning*, Information Age Publishing, pp. 179–190.
57 Siemens, G. & Baker, R. S. J. d., 2012, Learning Analytics and Educational Data Mining: Towards Communication and Collaboration, *LAK12: Proceedings of the Second International Conference on Learning Analytics and Knowledge*.
58 Gašević, D. *et al.*, 2015, Learning Analytics – A Growing Field and Community Engagement, *Journal of Learning Analytics*, 2(1), pp. 1–6.
59 Siemens, G., 2014, The *Journal of Learning Analytics*: Supporting and Promoting Learning Analytics Research, *Journal of Learning Analytics*, 1(1), pp. 3–4.
60 Ochoa *et al.*, Analysis and Reflections on the Third Learning Analytics and Knowledge Conference (LAK 2013).
61 Johnson, L. *et al.*, 2016, *The NMC Horizon Report: 2016 Higher Education Edition*, New Media Consortium.
62 Siemens, G., 2013, Learning Analytics: The Emergence of a Discipline, *American Behavioral Scientist*, 57(10), pp. 1380–1400.
63 Gašević *et al.*, Let's Not Forget: Learning Analytics are about Learning.
64 Chatti *et al.*, A Reference Model for Learning Analytics.

# 2 Expert Motivations

I wanted to discover, from the 20 experts in learning analytics I interviewed, what is motivating individuals working in the field, as well as what they perceive to be the main institutional drivers for learning analytics.

## Understanding the Learning Process

The most frequently expressed personal interest is to improve understanding of how learning takes place. For Doug Clow, Senior Lecturer at the UK's Open University, learning analytics is:

> a way of getting more insights into what's going on in the learning process in a non-intrusive way, and I think that's really interesting and exciting, and something I've wanted to get at since I started off being interested in technology in education.

Cathy Gunn, Associate Professor at the University of Auckland, sees the potential of learning analytics to:

> add a whole new layer of depth and credibility to educational research, providing teachers with more reliable feedback on the assumptions they make about learners and the decisions they make when they design courses and learning activities.

John Whitmer, who, before moving to Blackboard as Director for Analytics and Research, had a background of managing the deployment of academic technologies at scale, suggests that:

> we put a lot of attention into creating and successfully deploying technology, but rarely do we have the resources to evaluate the impact – that is, whether what we do makes a difference, and how much, and if we deliver programs in different ways, whether these differences affect impact on learning. Conventional research is often conducted with a 'black box' approach in terms

of technology interventions; with this approach the best you can do is compare two courses. What we don't know from that research is what actually happens while the student is interacting – which is to me the most important and the most valuable part … learning analytics allows us to see whether our interventions make a difference and in what ways they make a difference – in ways we've never been able to do before.

Dragan Gašević, Professor and Chair in Learning Analytics and Informatics at the University of Edinburgh, differentiates learning analytics from other forms of educational research because it:

allows us to understand learning as a dynamic process rather than a series of snapshots … we can be much closer to the decisions that learners are making, and based on that we can have a much more complete picture about learning.

Meanwhile, Mark Milliron, Co-Founder and Chief Learning Officer of Civitas Learning, suggests that:

we have more signals at our disposal than ever before to understand the journeys that students go on when they go through higher education. The digital signals are footprints, and if you pull those together you have a good understanding of the journey they go on, where they struggle, where they succeed, what drives acceleration, what actually slows them down, what knocks them off the path.

Several participants note that learning analytics enables us to understand learning in a much more nuanced, fine-grained way than has previously been possible. Meanwhile some of them are researching particular types of learning. Rebecca Ferguson, Senior Lecturer at the Open University, is interested in studying:

how people learn together online, and learning analytics gives us a way of looking at that, and it gives us a way of supporting that and of moving that forward – which we perhaps didn't have before.

## Enhancing Learning

Understanding the learning experience is not enough for most of the experts: they also want to do something to improve it, based on that understanding. What excites Doug Clow

is being able to see which learning resources, what parts of learning are learners having real trouble with, and being able to do something about that.

Stephanie Teasley, Research Professor in the School of Information at the University of Michigan, says she has been doing research on learning for a long time and [I] have always been very interested in doing very close analysis of behaviour to understand what aspects of the learning experience are most closely tied to cognitive gains.

Simon Buckingham Shum, Professor of Learning Informatics at the University of Technology Sydney, suggests that we should rethink how we find the evidence for learning in a 'fast, complex, turbulent world' and says:

learning analytics, with its ability to track so many more variables than traditional assessment, seems to me to be an exciting opportunity to shift practice and put it on a really firm empirical basis and evidence base.

Simon also articulates an intrinsic motivation that is likely to be driving many others working in educational technology:

I'm really fascinated about whether essentially we can be smarter because computers are working with us and augmenting our limited capacities to deal with complexity. Doug Engelbart's one of my heroes!

Kirsty Kitto, Senior Research Fellow at Queensland University of Technology, believes that learning analytics should be learner centred and

needs to be about helping learners and instructors to understand their own processes more fully, and to improve them and to learn things about themselves.

She suggests that it is difficult for people to understand enough about data to know what they want from it:

If I ask students or instructors, 'What do you want?' students, without fail, tell me, 'I want to know where I am compared to the rest of my cohort.' And instructors, almost always the first thing they say is, 'How many students watched my video?' I think that's really really boring. So my personal interests are about how can I prime people to understand what's possible, and then empower them to develop things that they find interesting.

For Josh Baron, Open Education Ambassador at Lumen Learning, learning analytics potentially provides solutions to some of the wider challenges in education, not just surrounding the learning process:

what's really driven me in my career around education has been transforming teaching and learning in really deep and fundamental ways.

[Learning analytics holds the potential to impact] on the learning experience but also on the whole business model and economics of education, and some of the real challenges that I think are facing, particularly higher education, at the moment.

## A Fascination with Data

A number of the experts are intrigued by data itself, as well as the potential for using it to enhance learning. Leah Macfadyen, Program Director of Evaluation and Learning Analytics at the University of British Columbia, is one of these:

> What got me into analytics was a data interest. But I'm really fascinated by the patterns that show up in data, especially from online courses and systems, and, at the point where we first had access to some of the data from our LMS, that was really exciting to start to be able to try to figure out whether any of it meant anything and to look at these really fascinating patterns and network diagrams of who was talking to who, and it revealed stuff that we couldn't see in any other way, and I think that's probably been the driver for all of my work since … Data like this doesn't reveal everything but it reveals something – so we ignore it at our peril.

Stephanie Teasley similarly describes how she had spotted the potential of the extensive datasets being collected at the University of Michigan:

> When I started doing work here at Michigan involving our LMS I realised that that system kicked out a lot of data about clicks – click-level data – and I had at my fingertips essentially data about everything that students and instructors did on every course on our campus because we have pretty deep penetration of our LMS … All that data was just here on the campus and nobody was looking at it, and I thought here was an educational technology that became infrastructure far quicker than any other educational technology I've ever seen in my career – and furthermore it produced a data trail. So the scope of it now went to tens of thousands of students and hundreds of courses and different instructors, different disciplines, different kinds of courses, different levels … And it gave me an opportunity to look into behaviours that we hadn't really been able to capture before … so: what students opened, when they opened it and who opened them, and how many were on the website, and that kind of thing. But it started to offer me a viewpoint into pretty fine-level behaviour at a very large scale, and I just had never had that opportunity before in my career, and I thought that was incredibly exciting.

Timothy McKay, Arthur F. Thurnau Professor of Physics, Astronomy and Education, also at Michigan, explains his own journey and motivations for his involvement in learning analytics:

I'm really a data scientist. I spent 25 years doing cosmology, big data cosmology, working on hundreds of millions of galaxies and developing techniques for drawing inference from observational datasets ... And then in the mid-2000s I became even more involved in education ... and started thinking about and looking at the progress of students through campus. I realised at that time that the University possessed a very rich quantity of data about every one of these students, and it was in a quite accessible form. We built a data warehouse here on campus in 1996, and all the standard student record data at least is, in a certain sense, easily accessible in that database. So you could gather a lot of data quickly and you could look for patterns in it and try to understand what was going on in campus much better. So we started to do that, first, initially with very narrow and local questions that we had about my own physics classes for example, and then that gradually grew. It has since become, it seems to me, a very great opportunity for us to understand what we're doing on our campuses, eventually to be able to improve what we do.

For Alyssa Wise, Associate Professor of Educational Communication and Technology at New York University,

the real drive is turning all this abundant data that is being generated and could be generated into useful, actionable insight ... There's a nice relationship between when data becomes available, and realising new questions you can ask – so I don't think it's just about using data to answer the questions you already have, but also for question generation.

## Personalisation

Personalisation of the learning experience is mentioned by several of the participants. Bart Rienties, Reader in Learning Analytics at the Open University, believes that:

most teaching ... teaches the average student, while there are a large number of students who are not the average student. And the reason that I really like learning analytics is that it provides the opportunity to provide personalised learning – so for students who are struggling slightly it gives them a slightly slower pace or a slightly different version of education, while the better or the excellent students get the opportunity to really go at it ... and not be stalled by the average Joe that doesn't really want to move as fast.

Timothy McKay is also fascinated by the possibilities of using learning analytics to provide more personalised learning:

We created a university, like we have, in the twentieth century, basically by industrialising. We set up a system in which the students are assumed to be more or less the same, and given the same kinds of treatment, and it wasn't a dreadful failure – we educated more than a million people in the twentieth century – but it's obviously not optimal either. So I would like to see us go from where we are now ... to a twenty-first century model, which is very much more personalised, able to interact with each individual in ways that are deeply responsive to their individual state, to their background, to their current state, their future goals, everything. We should never be interacting with students as if they are all the same.

Timothy believes this challenge will occupy him personally for the next few years. Two other participants mention the possibility of learning analytics providing better personalised education for specific minority groups. Alan Berg, Chief Technical Officer, Centre of Job Knowledge Research at the University of Amsterdam, has a personal interest:

I've got creative sons that have concentration problems but high IQ, so traditional learning approaches don't work for these sorts of people ... learning disabilities are severely under-reported, and I think learning analytics is a mechanism for dealing with that.

Mark Milliron, meanwhile, is particularly concerned with helping first-generation students to be more successful:

My own theory is that second, third, fourth generation students are scaffolded by the stories of the people who came before. If they get stuck, someone can come and help them. We now have a lot of first generation students who don't have the same kind of social networks. Learning analytics at their best, and I'm broadly defining learning analytics, can help that student understand the next set of choices they can make. We can help scaffold the student at that stage – part of the scaffolding by the way is to engage them when it's time to get tougher – it's not about spoon-feeding them – it's about getting them the right resources at the right moment and helping them in a way that most students in second, third, fourth generation are being scaffolded anyway.

To illustrate the possibilities of personalisation for disadvantaged groups, he draws an analogy with shopping for clothes:

I always juxtapose the difference between one-size-fits-all clothes, then being able to go into a store where they have small, medium, large. Then you go into a place where they have custom tailoring. That typically is the purview of the rich and I would argue that learning analytics at its best allows us to bring custom tailoring to everybody. A lot of students end up in learning situations getting a one-size-fits-all approach.

## Education and the Labour Market

Dr Stefan Mol, Assistant Professor of Organisational Behaviour at the Amsterdam Business School of the University of Amsterdam, has been investigating how higher education can meet the needs of industry, as part of the EU-funded Eduworks project.[1] With a background in industrial and organisational psychology, Stefan became interested in the possibilities of 'enhancing matchmaking between the individual, education and the labour market' through using data about learners. He notes that learning analytics focusses a lot of attention on retention and grades, but

> I don't think we're training our students to get good grades or to be retained: I think ultimately we have a role, especially public institutions, in creating or helping people to be employable on one side, but also to be happy, to fulfil a function in society – and I'm interested from a research perspective in defining that criterion space and pitting predictors against it so that we can influence outcomes that transcend the education to labour market divide.

## Involvement in a New, Interdisciplinary Field

Several of the interviewees discuss the interdisciplinary nature of the field and how they find that particularly stimulating. Abelardo Pardo, Senior Lecturer at the University of Sydney, is one of these:

> learning analytics appears to be an area that tries to combine psychology, educational psychology, educational theory, technology – and I have the feeling that is the right way of approaching such a complex problem as improving our learning experience.

Shane Dawson, Professor of Learning Analytics at the University of South Australia, similarly, finds that:

> What I really like is the interdisciplinary approach to it. You can't really resolve a lot of the larger, more conceptually and methodologically complex questions that learning analytics tries to address without a multidisciplinary approach. And I really like that – that you bring teams together with all different perspectives – it creates passion, friction, arguments and creativity.

While some of the researchers state the benefits of working with experts from other disciplines, Rebecca Ferguson is interested

> to see how a new field of study develops, and develops out of a lot of really closely related fields of study, and how it pulls itself together.

She also wants to observe how learning analytics is developing across a much broader context than just a single institution:

> So one of the things I've done is stepped back and looked at how it implements across a university, and then how does it work across a series of universities. What I'm doing now is looking at how it impacts on policy. What do governments do, what can regions do to make this happen, and why won't it happen if they don't take any action? So there's that looking into the future and seeing how it can affect things on a big scale, so I find that interesting.

However, all the necessary expertise in the research community does not yet appear to be closely integrated enough. Stephanie Teasley is impressed by the openness of the learning analytics community but would like to see a closer alliance between those who work with big data and the people who understand learning theory:

> Learning scientists are often very theory-driven and don't necessarily understand what to do with massive amounts [of data] …

Jeff Grann, Academic Director Assessment and Learning Analytics at Capella University, is also interested in bringing

> the techniques of data science to the educational context, which hasn't benefitted from those insights and techniques yet. So if those two could be aligned that would hopefully in the future make education much more meaningful and effective for meeting students' goals.

Shane Dawson believes, too, that members of the emerging learning analytics community could benefit from the input of other subject communities:

> They're selfless, fantastic people who are always willing to share ideas and opportunities with you. That you don't always come across in other groups. The sense that it's growing, the philosophy that it's developing: it's a very positive, a fantastic community. But I think a functioning community is also one that's very critical of itself. And I think there are people who are not in this community and offer different perspectives and ideas.

## Institutional Motivations

Understanding the wide range of individual motivations of prominent researchers in the field is helpful, but there is often a tension between personal interests and institutional drivers. I also ask the experts what aspects of learning analytics they think institutions are going to be most interested in. Here there is a degree of consensus, with almost all of the interviewees mentioning the institutional imperative to improve retention or graduation rates (though not necessarily at their own institutions). Doug Clow expresses it frankly:

> Pass rates and drop-out – because that's the bottom line. That's the easy sell into institutions ... Learning analytics gives you ways of getting hold of what's driving that and potentially what you can do about it.

The connection with the bottom line is noted by several of the experts. Mark Glynn, Head of the Teaching Enhancement Unit at Dublin City University, says:

> Institutions, by their nature, are influenced by money ... they are a business at the end of the day, so they're after ways in which they can use data to save students.

Josh Baron discusses the growing political imperative, particularly in the US, to improve graduation rates:

> Hey, if you can get even 1 or 2% more of your students to graduate on time, that's a huge cost saving. And also, just from a political standpoint, the amount of pressure coming both from the press as well as government agencies to address things like retention and completion rates is tremendous. So I think that's where everyone is jumping first. I think hopefully they'll find that to be successful and that will lead them to want to do more with this technology – but right now that's where I see a lot of people particularly focused.

Stephanie Teasley believes that the current pressures on education in the US are driven, to a large extent, by requirements for testing and measures of performance. She points out that higher education has become a political issue, that there are growing concerns that it is for the elite and is exacerbating the divisions in society:

> So what I think institutions at the higher level are interested in is how this data can be mined to better understand what they are doing ... how that can become more effective [and] more efficient, how can they use those numbers to show why students want to come to their institution instead of another institution, and, frankly, for the public to justify why the state should continue to support their institution.

Stephanie's colleague, Timothy McKay, adds that, even within the US, institutions vary enormously. While his own university, Michigan, has a relatively high graduation rate of 92%, many other institutions have much lower rates and their priority is to improve these. Mark Milliron meanwhile does not specifically mention early alert systems for students at risk but notes that:

in the US there's a lot of interest around pathway analytics and helping students to navigate higher education in ways that are going to allow them to be more successful ... There's [also] a lot of interest in subjects like STEM or math in how they can help students to make the most of their learning journeys.

Jeff Grann also notes the political context in the US being an issue for institutions, but thinks that learning analytics could help:

I think if government and society had more confidence in higher ed., being attentive to their effectiveness through these techniques, a lot of goodwill would be established – and trust that's increasingly being lost.

From an Australian perspective, Shane Dawson notes institutions' current focus on retention but adds that:

Education is a business now, so I think senior management is interested in the point of differentiation that learning analytics can bring to their organisation.

Shane suggests that if it can be shown that learning analytics is being used to enhance learning, it will feed into a virtuous circle, attracting better students, which in turn will improve graduate employability, leading to greater prestige for the university. Abelardo Pardo also sees:

a direct connection with the bottom line ... But ... once we make some inroads on retention, I think the next aspect that institutions will tune into is the quality of the learning experience ... things like taking care of the students throughout the institution, their transition during the first year, how they integrate in the social environment of the university. These are the types of things learning analytics can also detect ... and probably institutions will jump into that – very quickly.

Kirsty Kitto also believes that institutions are most interested in what makes money, but suggests that innovations such as personal learning record stores could prove financially viable:

so if you're in a university that can be seen as outputting students with a very fine profile that they can use to go and get jobs because they can show evidence of skills and capabilities well beyond their CV, there's a business case for that. In fact there's a whole ecosystem around service providers that you'd need to have to run that ... If you could get that up and running there's a lot of money to be made in that area.

John Whitmer finds that improving retention is the major focus area in the institutions he is working with, however he also notes a growing interest in:

more strategic and larger scale questions related to course design or overall curriculum improvement. These are at the administrative level: if we want to increase something across an institution, how can we use analytics to evaluate the effectiveness and success of our practices? I'm seeing people ask about these questions – we're mostly focused on course level success but to aggregate up at a higher administrative level, at higher levels of abstraction – to tease that out is exciting. The challenge with that is that the analytics that we have right now – what we've seen in the research so far – is that there's so much course-level variation that it's very hard to abstract above an individual course because most of our analysis so far is looking at comparisons between students within the same class.

Whether improving retention is the primary aim for learning analytics is very much dependent on the institutional context. Dragan Gašević's institution, the University of Edinburgh, like Michigan, does not have high attrition rates. He is concerned, however, that funding models, rather than enhancing learning, can drive institutional policy, not always in the best interests of students:

Institutions where they have many, say, first in family and also other types of students, will probably be primarily interested in retention. I fear that some institutions may be primarily interested in improving student satisfaction rather than ... improving the student experience. I think at this stage the level of interest that institutions are taking is primarily around student grades and satisfaction – and that is almost exclusively driven by the funding models.

Bart Rienties at The Open University believes that:

we're very much focused on just predicting who's at risk; the next real step is what can you do with analytics ... It's great to be able to predict that in Week 14 we lose 10% of our students from a particular background but what do you do in Week 10 ... and how can you then change the pedagogy in Week 10 to make sure that no-one next year drops out?

Bart's colleague, Rebecca Ferguson, also notes the major interest institutions have in improving retention, but believes that:

they're going to be a lot more cynical about other areas, and they're going to need more persuasion ... I think they're going to be deeply suspicious of anything which gives them a huge amount of data to understand ... The areas around learning analytics they're going to be interested in are the ones they can implement easily and with fairly low overheads to keep them maintained, and that they can see some clear benefit in financial terms.

Alyssa Wise comes at the issue from a slightly different angle. She thinks that:

> institutions right now are most interested in doing what they can with the data they already have ... I think the clever, forward-looking institution is going to say, hey, if we take a step back right now, and think carefully about how we're collecting data ... I think they'd be way ahead of the game.

She also differentiates the interests of researchers from those of institutions:

> I think what institutions will be interested in isn't necessarily with the research – it's putting things into practice ... So I would encourage the notion of perpetual beta and low stakes analytics rollouts, which I think that there will be interest in.

Leah Macfadyen sees more potential with smaller-scale learning analytics initiatives:

> Over time I've increasingly come to think that actually it's the big institutional implementations that are the real problem, or at least are the most difficult to implement, and the areas where I, and I think, other people are having the most success are in small-scale, targeted solutions that are meeting expressed needs.

Her institution, the University of British Columbia, does not have a particular problem with retention either – and this has an impact on institutional attitudes to learning analytics:

> In the early few years of learning analytics literature and research, let's say five to eight years ago, the projects that we heard about tended to be early alert systems, about the Signals Project at Purdue, and basically systems that were envisioned at the institutional level to flag at-risk students. When I talk to people at this institution about that they're not interested because, rightly or wrongly, this institution doesn't perceive itself to have a problem.

Leah also contrasts the situation in Canada with that of many US institutions:

> We certainly don't have an attrition problem like schools in the United States. We have a pretty high completion rate, and we don't have the kind of under-served minority group problem that the United States has either. To the extent that senior leaders were at conferences, and heard about early alert systems, they thought that that's what learning analytics is, it's all about catching failing students ... so it's not useful for us. And I think that's been quite a barrier for people like me to get past – to say 'No! That's just one piece of work that's been ongoing – here's all the other things we

can do', and it's only really been gaining any ground for me at the small scale level, working with a particular department or a particular committee to provide solutions that really work for them for the problem that they're struggling with.

These fascinating insights illustrate how the drivers for learning analytics vary widely and are influenced not just by the institutional context and the nature of the student cohort but by other factors such as national funding regimes and political situations. The scene is thus set for the rest of this book: addressing retention is the primary driver for many institutions in their deployment of learning analytics. However, the huge datasets that are increasingly being accumulated on students and aspects of their learning have many other potential applications in enhancing education. These are being explored by researchers and examined by institutions as ways of addressing a wide variety of challenges relating to their educational missions.

## Reference

1  Eduworks: www.eduworks-network.eu/ (accessed 30 September 2016).

# Part II
# Applications

# 3 Early Alert and Student Success

The most widespread application of learning analytics is the early identification of students predicted to be at risk of failure or withdrawal. Predictive models can be built using historical data about the activity of previous students. These suggest, often with a high degree of accuracy, whether a current student is at risk or not, based on that student's own patterns of activity. This 'actionable intelligence' can then lead to an intervention of some kind with students in an attempt to change their behaviour and improve their chances of academic success. The financial implications of reducing attrition make investment in early alert systems extremely attractive to senior management in institutions where dropout is a serious problem.

Measures of student success include retention, completion and graduation rates.[1] However, for universities and colleges that do not have significant problems with attrition, the enhancement of overall academic achievement (e.g. improvements in final degree classifications) or student satisfaction can be important goals, assisted by the use of a system that provides early information on student engagement and grade predictions.

One of the key assumptions of 'student success', 'early alert' or 'early warning' systems, as they are variously known, is that data collected about student engagement is a proxy for how well they are learning. This usually comes from use of the LMS and other web-based applications such as library systems. It can be supplemented with data about learners' physical presence on campus using attendance monitoring or Wi-Fi access. Information on student achievement from formative and summative assessments can also be important. Combining data about what students are doing with data about who they are and what they have done in the past can give a stronger indication of their likely academic achievement than simply looking at their current activity. The more data sources there are to draw on, the more accurate the predictions may turn out to be.

There are various challenges, however, to note with this approach:

- Most institutions do not use their LMS in a consistent way and many of their courses may make little use of online tools and resources. Thus data on student participation may be limited and only of use in the courses where LMS usage is a core part of the learning design.[2,3]

- Students may carry out much of their learning, including collaboration with other learners, using systems where usage data cannot be accessed by the institution, such as social networking sites.
- Participation in learning activities, as recorded in the data collected through various systems, does not mean that any learning is actually taking place, although this can be inferred.
- The highest levels of engagement do not necessarily correlate with the best results: the most engaged students may be academically struggling but simply working harder to try to improve their performance.[4]
- Predictions can be very accurate overall but they are still only predictions – there are many reasons why an individual student might perform differently from what is predicted. Withdrawal or poor performance may, for example, be caused by time conflicts with paid employment, health issues, childcare responsibilities, transportation difficulties or financial issues – all of which are outside the institution's control.[5]
- In principle, adding further data sources may enhance the predictive model but the additional data may only make a marginal difference, not justifying the cost of collecting it – for instance, if installing an attendance-monitoring system across a campus only increases the predictive accuracy of the model by 0.5%.

Despite these reservations, many studies confirm that students who engage *more* are likely to perform *better*. This is not surprising: educators have always known that more engaged students are likely to be more successful.[6] The point is that by using the data to identify less engaged students, something might be able to be done to improve their engagement before it is too late. Signs that a student may be at risk include failing to attend classes or participate in discussion forums, late or incomplete assignments, or significant changes in behaviour or academic performance.[7] In many circumstances automated systems can identify these factors more quickly and accurately than busy humans can.

### Signals at Purdue University

Probably the most frequently cited institutional deployment of learning analytics for early alert and student success is the Signals project at Purdue University in Indiana. Research showing considerable enhancements to both student achievement *and* retention has been widely hailed in the educational media. It has also galvanised action in the sector and been the inspiration behind a number of learning analytics products and many initiatives in other institutions.

Signals is based on the idea that students do not have a good understanding of how they are progressing in their courses. A lack of assessments during the course may mean that they only know where they are when they see their final grade. By the time they do realise that they are not progressing well it may be too late to withdraw from the class so they end up failing. Signals therefore aims to help students understand their progress early enough to seek help and either increase their likely grade or withdraw from the module and take something else.

At an institutional level, the aim is to enhance overall retention and graduation rates. Purdue developed its approach to 'early warning systems', which show at-risk students over a number of years, initially capturing on paper-based forms the views of staff on which of their students were at risk. While considered helpful, the warnings often came too late to be effective and the approach did not help students to change their behaviours adequately. Meanwhile the warnings sent to students were too general and not specific enough to the course they were taking.

While there were other early warning systems on the market, they were based on demographic, personal and grade data and did not take into account students' behaviour and efforts on their courses. These systems could become self-fulfilling prophecies by labelling students as at-risk based on certain characteristics such as low income or being the first in their family to attend higher education. Signals reduces this bias by incorporating dynamic data on performance and behaviour, data that is considered essential in being able to predict academic success. The resulting analytics aims to produce actionable intelligence, providing detailed support materials and positive steps for students to take.

Signals takes data about attendance and students' use of the LMS, together with grade information held in their LMS gradebook. The product is 'behaviourally based': more weight is given to interaction with the LMS and 'help-seeking behaviour' than on past academic performance. No evidence has been identified in the literature for this weighting and how it was decided – possibly because this is seen as proprietary information, which is core to what is now a commercial product. Other studies have shown that past performance is a strong indicator of future academic success. The Purdue researchers assert however that 'a student with average intelligence who works hard is just as likely to get a good grade as a student that has above-average intelligence but does not exert any effort'.

Signals aimed to avoid the problems of early warning systems that flag up at-risk students after mid-term grades are issued – generally too late to make a difference. These also often require attendance data to be captured, which is difficult to ensure in large lectures. Meanwhile, Signals is argued to be less labour intensive and costly than other systems where students bring frequent grade reports to academic advisors with the hope of improving their grades. Help-seeking behaviour, such as visiting a professor or attending a review session, is an indication of effort shown outside of the class and so it is regarded as important. A key part of the philosophy is to allow students to compare what they are doing with what others are doing and to show how these activities (such as submitting assignments or attending help sessions) correlate with success.

Signals mines data from the SIS, the LMS and the gradebook. This is then transformed and processed to produce a 'traffic-light' indicator showing how at risk each student is considered to be. A range of interventions can then be taken by the instructor. The predictive algorithm has four components:

- Performance – based on points earned on the course so far.
- Effort – interaction with the LMS compared with other students.
- Prior academic history – including high school GPA and standardised test scores.
- Student characteristics – for example, age or credits attempted.

These components are weighted and fed into the algorithm which produces the appropriate traffic signal. Red indicates a high likelihood of being unsuccessful, yellow potential problems and green a high likelihood of success.

Student using Signals tend to seek help earlier and more frequently and to perform better academically. The interventions taken and evaluations of how successful they are, are discussed in Chapter 11.[8, 9]

Essa & Ayad criticise the traffic-light approach on the basis that the three-level indicator simply does not provide enough data to the educator to allow meaningful intervention.[10] In some institutions, though, this is merely a prompt to the instructor, who can then delve into further analytics regarding students at risk, before deciding whether or not to intervene. Believing that the traffic signal is an accurate representation of a student's level of academic risk may also be problematic. Liu *et al.* found that the signals in the *Engagement Analytics* plug-in for the Moodle LMS did not accurately reflect ultimate student performance: high proportions of students given green lights subsequently achieved a final grade of below 50. However, the 'total risk' rating also provided by the tool, based on assessment, forum and login activities, was found to be a much more meaningful predictor of performance.[11]

### Student 'Wellness' as the Basis for Intervention at the University of New England

At the University of New England in Australia the *Automated Wellness Engine* draws information from eight institutional systems and analyses this against 34 risk indicators. These include students' own assessment of their wellbeing as indicated through emoticons they select to represent their mood. Members of the student support team monitor daily 'wellness' reports and contact students using email, social media tools and telephone. Meanwhile, weekly reports are sent to schools or units to gain an overall assessment of their students' wellbeing.

In one study of the use of the engine in an online course three particular behaviours were identified:

- No (or limited) access to learning content in the first two weeks of the course.
- Non-participation in early learning activities.
- No access to assessment tasks two weeks before the due date.
- Non-completion or low grades in an early assessment task.

Ninety out of the 248 students enrolled in the course met at least one of these behaviours and were contacted through a personalised email sent by their lecturers inviting the students to contact them to discuss any problems they might be experiencing. Fifty-five of these went on to complete the course successfully.

While impacts on retention and achievement were not conclusive from this study, over 90% of students believed that the interventions helped to increase their engagement and keep them on track. Students who did not receive an intervention were also surveyed and rated their learning experience lower than those who were contacted.[12, 13]

## Models to Predict Student Success

Many studies have been conducted to identify the variables that lead to student success. One example is at the University of Central Florida, where predictors of non-success were calculated by examining the records of 258,212 students. The factors examined included modality (online, face-to-face, blended, etc.), class size, gender, ethnicity, age, high-school grade point average (GPA) and cumulative GPA achieved while at the university. In this example, none of the variables assessed, except cumulative GPA, make any substantial difference to the predictive power of the model.[14] Other studies confirm, perhaps unsurprisingly, that the cumulative number of points earned is the best predictor of academic success.[15] These demonstrate that *what you do* while at university or college is much more important than *who you are*.

As learning migrates to online environments, it is becoming increasingly feasible to measure student activity to predict academic achievement with greater accuracy. Whitmer and his colleagues, for example, identified a direct positive relationship between students' use of the LMS and their final grade. They had expected this result but were surprised how direct it was.[16] Morris *et al.*, as far back as 2005, analysed 300,000 activities carried out by 423 students over three semesters for three courses and documented participation through 'frequency variables' – number of content pages viewed, number of original posts and number of follow-ups – and four 'duration variables': time spent viewing content, reading discussions, creating original posts and creating follow-up posts. They found that 'completers' (those obtaining a C grade or better) had significantly higher frequency and duration of participation. Their conclusion is that, although this appears to be 'documenting the obvious', such research is essential in understanding how students, faculty, course content and learning design interact, helping to discover what is successful student behaviour and how it can be encouraged.[17]

In another key study, Macfadyen & Dawson identified 15 variables that were significantly correlated with the final grade achieved. They found that 'total number of discussion messages posted', 'total number of mail messages sent' and 'total number of assessments completed' explained more than 30% of the variation in final grade.[18]

## Validity of the Models

Knowing how valid the predictive models are and to what extent they successfully predict attrition and academic achievement, is clearly essential if investment is to be made in early alert and student success systems. Many implementations test the models thoroughly against historical data from the institution. Much of the work in developing the models concerns the weighting of risk factors and adjustment of parameters to optimise the match with student behaviour. There is also considerable investment in extracting and cleaning the data from different sources. Generally, the greater the range of data sources and the more options tested, the more valid the resulting models, though research shows consistently that some data sources make minimal impact on the predictions.[19, 20]

At the New York Institute of Technology, recall of the predictive model is 74%; in other words, approximately three out of every four students who do not return to their studies the following year had been predicted as at risk by the model. This high recall factor is reported to be due to the choice of model, careful testing of alternatives and the inclusion of a wider range of data than similar models: financial and student survey data were included, as well as pre-enrolment data.[21]

Although many institutions have created their own specific models rather than adopting those developed elsewhere, a key finding of the Open Academic Analytics Initiative led by Marist College is that the predictive models developed at one institution can be transferred to very different institutions while retaining most of their predictive abilities. The researchers at Marist do recognise, though, that customising predictive models using local data may enhance their predictive potential.[22] Other researchers have shown that predictive models that are tailored to individual courses can increase the accuracy considerably,[23] and that knowledge of the pedagogical intent and the learning design is essential in ascertaining the indicators that meaningfully represent student activity.[24]

## Effectiveness of the Interventions

Student engagement has been shown in many studies to correlate positively with academic success but there is less evidence to date of the effectiveness of interventions on the basis of this intelligence. A report by the Society for Learning Analytics Research (SoLAR), funded by the Australian government's Office for

Learning and Teaching,[25] contains ten brief case studies from some of the most prominent learning analytics initiatives in Australia, the US and the UK. Few of these projects yet claim any significant impact from learning analytics – and many are still at early stages of implementation. One exception is Queensland University of Technology's early intervention programme, which the report states 'has resulted in significant improvements in retention for those students who have been successfully contacted'. However no data is provided to back up this claim.

## Identifying Success Factors and Evaluating Interventions at Rio Salado College

At Rio Salado College, a community college in Arizona, a project was carried out to identify factors that lead to success in online learning. A successful outcome was defined as a grade of C or higher, an unsuccessful outcome as less than C or withdrawal. Predictive models were then generated to forecast outcomes using the most significant factors. As many variables can change throughout a course (e.g. points earned), a model was required that could be regularly updated.

Individual models were created for each course. One freshman-level accounting course used as its variables: logins to the LMS and the course homepage, views of the course syllabus, opening and completing of assessments, viewing gradebook comments made by the instructor, opening a lesson, requesting a due date change and selecting a custom calendar option. The naïve Bayes classification method was chosen (see Chapter 9) because of its scalability. It was found that these variables can be efficient predictors of course outcomes as early as the eighth day of the class.

Students were divided into three risk categories: high (below 30% probability of success), moderate (between 30% and 70%) and low (above 70%). The distribution across these groups was fairly uniform at the start of the class; however they tended to coalesce around high and low as it progressed until by the end there were hardly any students in the moderate category. This reflects the increasing accuracy with which outcomes can be predicted as more data is gathered on participation and performance.

A control group was established with half of the 2,300 students categorised as at moderate risk. Attempts were made by instructors to contact these students. However only one-third of phone call attempts resulted in direct student contact. There was some evidence to suggest that students receiving such contact succeeded more often than those in receipt of voicemails or no contact at all.[26]

Another case study in the SoLAR report for the Australian government has some concrete data and significant outcomes: at the University of South Australia 730 students across a range of courses were identified as at risk. Of the 549 who were contacted, 66% passed with an average grade point average (GPA) of 4.29. Fifty-two per cent of at-risk students who were not contacted passed with an average GPA of 3.14.[27] This appears to be a significant finding, implying that intervention strategies with struggling students could be extremely important for institutions: if you are identified as at risk but left alone you are not only considerably more likely to fail but your result is likely to be much worse too. The dearth of such data overall in the literature and rigorous, empirical, replicable studies, however, make it difficult to back up any grand claims for the impact of early alert systems. Nevertheless, investment in student success systems may be justified by institutions on the basis that the implementation costs can be recouped quickly by preventing only a small number of students from dropping out.

## References

1 Essa, A. & Ayad, H., 2012, Improving Student Success Using Predictive Models and Data Visualisations, *Proceedings of ALT-C 2012, Research in Learning Technology*, pp. 58–70.

2 Krumm, A. E. *et al.*, 2012, Increasing Academic Success in Undergraduate Engineering Education using Learning Analytics: A Design-Based Research Project, *Paper presented at the Annual Meeting of the American Educational Research Association*, p. 14.

3 Liu, D. *et al.*, 2015, Validating the Effectiveness of the Moodle Engagement Analytics Plugin to Predict Student Academic Performance, *AMCIS 2015: Proceedings of the 21st Americas Conference on Information Systems*, p. 8.

4 Whitmer, J., 2015, Using Learning Analytics to Assess Innovation and Improve Student Achievement, *Jisc UK Learning Analytics Network Event*, 5 March, p. 16.

5 Barber, R. & Sharkey, M., 2012, Course Correction: Using Analytics to Predict Course Success, *LAK12: Proceedings of the Second International Conference on Learning Analytics and Knowledge*, pp. 259–262.

6 Buerck, J. P. & Mudigonda, S. P., 2014, A Resource-Constrained Approach to Implementing Analytics in an Institution of Higher Education: An Experience Report, *Journal of Learning Analytics*, 1(1), pp. 129–139.

7 Barber & Sharkey, Course Correction: Using Analytics to Predict Course Success, p. 259.

8 Arnold, K., 2010, Signals: Applying Academic Analytics, *EDUCAUSE Review*, 3 March, http://er.educause.edu/articles/2010/3/signals-applying-academic-analytics (accessed 9 October 2016).

9 Arnold, K. E. & Pistilli, M. D., 2012, Course Signals at Purdue: Using Learning Analytics to Increase Student Success, *LAK12: Proceedings of the Second International Learning Analytics and Knowledge Conference*.

10 Essa & Ayad, Improving Student Success using Predictive Models and Data Visualisations, p. 60.

11 Liu *et al.*, Validating the Effectiveness of the Moodle Engagement Analytics Plugin to Predict Student Academic Performance, pp. 7–8.

12 Fisher, J. *et al.*, 2012, Enhancing Distance Education Student Outcomes Utilising Learning Analytics: A Case Study, *ANZAM 2012: Australian and New Zealand Academy of Management Conference*, 29 May.

13 Nelson, K. & Creagh, T., 2013, *Case Study 7. A Good Practice Guide: Safeguarding Student Learning Engagement*, Queensland University of Technology.

14 Dziuban, C., *et al.*, 2012, Analytics that Inform the University: Using Data You Already Have. *Journal of Asynchronous Learning Networks*, 16(3), pp. 21–38.

15 Barber & Sharkey, Course Correction: Using Analytics to Predict Course Success, p. 261.

16 Whitmer, J. *et al.*, 2012, Analytics in Progress: Technology Use, Student Characteristics, and Student Achievement, *EDUCAUSE Review*, 13 August. http://er.educause.edu/articles/2012/8/analytics-in-progress-technology-use-student-chara cteristics-and-student-achievement (accessed 9 October 2016).

17 Morris, L. V. *et al.*, 2005, Tracking Student Behavior, Persistence, and Achievement in Online Courses, *The Internet and Higher Education*, 8, pp. 221–231.

18 Macfadyen, L. P. & Dawson, S., 2010, Mining LMS Data to Develop an 'Early Warning System' for Educators: A Proof of Concept, *Computers and Education*, 54, pp. 588–599.

19 Whitmer, J., 2012, *Logging On to Improve Achievement: Evaluating the Relationship between Use of the Learning Management System, Student Characteristics, and Academic Achievement in a Hybrid Large Enrollment Undergraduate Course*, University of California, Davis.

20 Jayaprakash, S. M. *et al.*, 2014, Early Alert of Academically At-Risk Students: An Open Source Analytics Initiative, *Journal of Learning Analytics*, 1(1), pp. 6–47.

21 Agnihotri, L. & Ott, A., 2014, Building a Student At-Risk Model: An End-to-End Perspective, *Proceedings of the Seventh International Conference on Educational Data Mining*.

22 Jayaprakash *et al.*, Early Alert of Academically At-Risk Students: An Open Source Analytics Initiative, p. 41.

23 Essa & Ayad, Improving Student Success using Predictive Models and Data Visualisations, p. 59.

24 Macfadyen & Dawson, Mining LMS Data to Develop an 'Early Warning System' for Educators: A Proof of Concept, p. 597.

25 Siemens, G. *et al.*, 2013, *Improving the Quality and Productivity of the Higher Education Sector: Policy and Strategy for Systems-Level Deployment of Learning Analytics*, Society for Learning Analytics Research.

26 Smith, V. C. *et al.*, 2012, Predictive Modeling to Forecast Student Outcomes and Drive Effective Interventions in Online Community College Courses, *Journal of Asynchronous Learning Networks*, 16(3), pp. 51–62.

27 Siemens *et al.*, *Improving the Quality and Productivity of the Higher Education Sector: Policy and Strategy for Systems-Level Deployment of Learning Analytics*, p. 20.

# 4    Course Recommendation

Recommender systems are found in a wide range of internet applications. They are designed to help reduce information overload and to guide users into selecting the most suitable options for them. Amazon, for example, provides personalised recommendations for new products, using data about users' previous searches and purchases. After selecting an item, the customer is presented with further suggestions for products that are 'frequently bought together' with the one being considered, thus drawing on the data of other customers as well. Social networking platforms use information about their users to recommend people they might want to connect with, while media providers such as Spotify and Netflix suggest content to their users, based on what they and their friends have already listened to or watched.

Ricci *et al.* list the main reasons why providers deploy recommendation technology:

- To increase the number of items sold.
- To sell more diverse items by, for example, advertising less popular items to the right users.
- To increase user satisfaction with interesting, relevant and accurate recommendations, increasing the likelihood that they will be accepted.
- To increase user fidelity, with the website recognising users and treating them as valuable visitors.
- To better understand what users want, resulting in better provision of products.[1]

These are not all applicable in educational contexts but recommendation is being deployed for a growing range of applications in education. Systems have been developed, for example, to suggest learning resources for students to achieve their specific learning goals – and the sequences in which they should study them.[2] Foremost among the recommendation applications in education, however, are course recommender systems that can suggest which courses students should take and in what sequence. Selecting from the many different options available at some institutions and planning a pathway through them can be a confusing process. In many universities there is the option to choose elective courses from completely different disciplines.[3] This may result in thousands of possibilities from which to select.[4] Often, students decide to switch to another major or qualification, part-way through, adding to their confusion.[5] They may also forget to check the requirements and consequently miss deadlines or take courses simply to graduate, without having any real interest in them.[6]

## Using CourseRank to Choose Future Courses

*CourseRank* was built at Stanford University to help students decide what courses to select. It was designed to incorporate the rules for the selection of courses and to recommend courses that are popular or taken by similar students.[7] It was also clear that the system would be more beneficial if it recommended courses that helped students to graduate.[8]

As well as providing personal recommendations for courses to take, it presents course descriptions, grade distributions and official evaluation results and enables students anonymously to review the courses they have taken and to rank others' comments. Meanwhile faculty are able to add comments on their courses and compare them with others.

The system proved popular with students: within a year of its release almost all undergraduates were using it. In 2009 the service was spun out to other institutions and commercialised and was soon being used by many other US universities.

Students at Stanford made numerous requests for additional functionality. They wanted to be able to select the type of course and to be given recommendations from a particular group (e.g. students in the same discipline with similar grades). The tool's flexible architecture enabled these features to be added with ease in subsequent versions.[9]

The choice of individual courses and the combinations and order in which they are taken have been shown to have a considerable impact on students' chances of success, progression to future courses, completion of their degrees and enrolment on future programmes. Particular combinations of courses may be 'academically hazardous' to some learners, based on their profiles.[10] O'Mahony & Smyth list some of the multiple factors that may influence a student's choice of course:

- their interests, aptitudes and existing knowledge;
- their career goals, depending on whether they want to focus on a single area or keep their options open;
- prerequisite and co-requisite courses, which can affect flexibility in future years;
- the difficulty of the course and other aspects such as whether it involves lab work or a dissertation;
- timetable clashes and whether places are available.[11]

Many students find it difficult to make these choices, particularly if they are the first in their family to study higher education. One US study suggests that students take on average 20% more courses than they need to in order to graduate.[12] Often the choice is made based on what friends or colleagues recommend.[13] Students may also be unaware of the options available to them and consequently make poor decisions.[14] Personalised recommender systems can provide students with options they have not thought of, which may be more aligned to their interests and aptitudes.[15] Advisors, meanwhile, may find it hard to assess a student's future performance on a particular course and may benefit, along with their students, from a system which predicts where learners are most likely to succeed.[16]

## Degree Compass: Linking Course Recommendation to the Early Alert System

At Austin Peay State University in Tenessee 40% of students are non-traditional learners and more than half receive Pell Grants (which indicate a low-income background). Many students therefore find it difficult to navigate through aspects of their degrees, especially the selection of courses. The institution developed the *Degree Compass* system, which uses data from hundreds of thousands of past students' grades to build a predictive model.[17] The software uses grade and enrolment data to predict which courses might best suit a student and in which they are most likely to succeed. The options are then ranked and presented to the student in a web-based interface and via a mobile app. Advisors can also view the personalised recommendations and discuss them with students when advising them on future options.[18]

Degree Compass is linked to the institution's early alert system and provides data to departmental chairs and advisors, helping to target interventions at students who would benefit from additional support. The grade prediction model it incorporates has been found to correctly predict grades to within 0.6 of a letter grade. It also predicts accurately 92% of the time whether students will pass or fail a course. Interestingly, these predictions remain constant across subject, levels and grades. The findings were replicated to a large extent when the software was installed in other institutions such as a rural community college.[19]

There has been a steady improvement in the grades obtained by students since the system was introduced, especially among Pell Grant recipients. Use of the system is now embedded at Austin Peay, partly due to the compelling evidence that students who take the suggested courses achieve significantly better grades. The university is also now tailoring course schedules based on the data gathered through Degree Compass, which also helps it to gauge future demand. Meanwhile, grade predictions are used to guide students to additional tutoring and mentoring opportunities. Finally, the initiative appears to have had a significant impact on institutional funding, which is linked to graduation rates.[20] Degree Compass has now been acquired by D2L.[21]

## Approaches to Recommendation

Recommender systems are based on *content-based filtering* techniques, *collaborative filtering* or a hybrid approach, which draws from both. Content-based filtering systems recommend items to users based on their own characteristics and past choices. Collaborative filtering uses information about others and their choices and can deploy two separate methods:

- *User-based collaborative filtering*, where items are suggested to users based on the ratings provided by their friends or others with similar tastes or profiles.
- *Item-based collaborative filtering*, where items are presented to the user if they are liked by those who have shared similar items in the past with the user. Amazon manifests this in the 'users who bought x also bought y' technique.[22]

Both content-based and collaborative filtering are affected by the 'cold start' problem, meaning that there is initially neither enough data nor a critical mass of users for them to function properly.[23] A related problem is that of 'sparsity',[24] where limited data on a particular option leads to the system not being able to recommend it: if it never appears in suggestion lists users may never find it so the data cannot build up.

*Demographic-based recommender systems* may also have their uses in education. These suggest items to users based on information such as their age or gender, putting those who share similar characteristics into groups of individuals who are assumed to share the same interests. Such systems are limited, though, by having to identify to which groups the user belongs, what the interests are of people within the group and how to collect the demographic data from users.[25] Universities have much of the relevant data already and could use it in course recommendation. Degree Compass at Austin Peay only uses grade data, however, and ignores demographic information. It is possible therefore that the accuracy of the predictions could improve with further integration of such data sources.

Course recommender systems can be more complex than the recommendation algorithms used by platforms such as Amazon and Netflix. One reason for this is the fact that they need to incorporate complicated rules for the sequencing and selection of courses, such as 'you must take two out of five courses'[26] or 'you must take course A before course B'. Moreover, it might not just be the items another user selected and rated that are important, but also, in the case of course recommendation, the grades those users achieved on the courses.[27]

## Conclusion

One problem that has been noted with recommender systems is that they can suffer from *overspecialisation* – they end up recommending items to users which are similar to ones already suggested. So someone who tends to buy historical novels on Amazon might never be recommended a science fiction book. In this case the problem can be addressed by introducing an element of randomness. Another solution to overspecialisation is that, in some situations, items should not be recommended if they show significant similarities to something the user has already tried; diversity may thus be desirable in recommender systems.[28]

In education, such technologies run the risk of being overly deterministic. A student could be channelled into a series of courses for the convenience of the institution or solely because the pathway maximises her chance of success, but this might take her in a different direction from her career objectives. This paternalistic approach[29] might also lead to 'easy' or 'fun' courses being selected by many more students, at the expense of subjects that are more difficult but are desirable for individuals and desirable for society to continue to provide as part of a broad education. A further controversial issue is that the systems could result in students increasingly shunning the courses of unpopular lecturers.

Future possibilities for recommender systems are discussed by Nam and colleagues. These include enabling students to compare how they are likely to perform if they take courses in different sequences. Should they enrol, for example, in a physics lab course at the same time as the lecture-based course or take one of the courses first? Is there a correlation between the semester in which a student enrols in a course and that student's level of success? A shorter gap between semesters might be helpful if a course requires significant recall of what has been learned in a prerequisite course. A further area for investigation is to assess the impact of taking courses from other institutions. It is likely that students entering a university from different community colleges for example will have different requirements for the courses they choose.[30]

The popularity among students at Stanford of CourseRank and the improvements in student grades and graduation rates at Austin Peay – apparently due to the pervasive use of Degree Compass – are noteworthy. Such systems are reported to have had significant impacts on students, improving their chances of graduation and subsequent employment prospects. The analytics are also helping institutions to manage complex course offerings and to understand the types of courses and sequencing that are most beneficial to their learners. If the ethical issues remain under continuous consideration by institutions and are influential in the development and deployment of course recommender systems, it is hoped that students will continue to benefit without becoming slaves to the algorithm.

## References

1 Ricci, F. *et al.*, 2011, Introduction to Recommender Systems Handbook. In: F. Ricci, *et al.*, eds, *Recommender Systems Handbook*, Springer, pp. 1–38.

2 Manouselis, N. *et al.*, 2011, Recommender Systems in Technology Enhanced Learning. In: F. Ricci *et al.*, eds, *Recommender Systems Handbook*, Springer, pp. 387–418.

3  O'Mahoney, M. P. & Smyth, B., 2007, A Recommender System for On-line Course Enrolment: An Initial Study, *RecSys '07: Proceedings of the 2007 ACM Conference on Recommender Systems*, pp. 133–136.

4  Nam, S. *et al.*, 2014, Customized Course Advising: Investigating Engineering Student Success with Incoming Profiles and Patterns of Concurrent Course Enrolment, *LAK14: Proceedings of the Fourth International Conference on Learning Analytics And Knowledge*, ACM, pp. 16–25.

5  Denley, T., 2012, Austin Peay State University: Degree Compass, In: D. G. Oblinger, ed., *Game Changers: Education and Information Technologies*, EDUCAUSE, pp. 263–267.

6  Parameswaran, A. *et al.*, 2011, Recommendation Systems with Complex Constraints: A Course Recommendation Perspective, *ACM Transactions on Information Systems (TOIS)*, 29(4), p. 31.

7  Ibid.

8  Ibid., p. 32.

9  Koutrika, G. *et al.*, 2009, Flexible Recommendations for Course Planning, *Proceedings of the IEEE 29th International Conference on Data Engineering (ICDE)*, pp. 1467–1470.

10 Nam *et al.*, Customized Course Advising: Investigating Engineering Student Success with Incoming Profiles and Patterns of Concurrent Course Enrolment, pp. 16–17.

11 O'Mahoney & Smyth, A Recommender System for On-line Course Enrolment: An Initial Study, pp. 133–134.

12 Office of Information Technology, Austin Peay State University, *Degree Compass – What Is It?* www.apsu.edu/information-technology/degree-compass-what (accessed 1 October 2016).

13 Bendakir, N. & Aïmeur, E., 2006, Using Association Rules for Course Recommendation. In: *Proceedings of the AAAI Workshop on Educational Data Mining* (Vol. 3).

14 O'Mahoney & Smyth, A Recommender System for On-line Course Enrolment: An Initial Study, p. 134.

15 Parameswaran *et al.*, Recommendation Systems with Complex Constraints: A Course Recommendation Perspective, p. 31.

16 Office of Information Technology, Austin Peay State University, *Degree Compass – What Is It?*

17 Denley, T., 2013, *Degree Compass Course Recommendation System*, EDUCAUSE.

18 Denley, 2012, Austin Peay State University: Degree Compass, p. 264

19 Denley, T., 2013, Degree Compass: A Course Recommendation System. *EDUCAUSE Review Online*, http://er.educause.edu/articles/2013/9/degree-compass-a-course-recommendation-system (accessed 9 October 2016).

20 Denley, *Degree Compass Course Recommendation System*, pp. 4–5.

21 Denley, Degree Compass: A Course Recommendation System.

22 Verbert, K. *et al.*, 2011, Dataset-Driven Research for Improving Recommender Systems for Learning, *Proceedings of the First International Conference on Learning Analytics and Knowledge*, ACM, pp. 44–53.

23 Bendakir & Aïmeur, Using Association Rules for Course Recommendation, p. 2.

24 Adomavicius, G. & Tuzhilin, A., 2005, Toward the Next Generation of Recommender Systems: A Survey of the State-of-the-Art and Possible Extensions, *IEEE Transactions on Knowledge and Data Engineering*, 17(6), pp. 734–749.

25 Alsalama, A., 2013, A Hybrid Recommendation System Based on Association Rules. Master's thesis, Western Kentucky University. Masters Theses and Specialist Projects, Paper 1250, http://digitalcommons.wku.edu/theses/1250 (accessed 9 October 2016).
26 Parameswaran *et al.*, Recommendation Systems with Complex Constraints: A Course Recommendation Perspective, p. 31.
27 Koutrika *et al.*, Flexible Recommendations for Course Planning, p. 1467.
28 Adomavicius & Tuzhilin, Toward the Next Generation of Recommender Systems: A Survey of the State-of-the-Art and Possible Extensions, p. 737.
29 Johnson, J. A., 2014, The Ethics of Big Data in Higher Education, *International Review of Information Ethics*, 21, pp. 3–10.
30 Nam *et al.*, Customized Course Advising: Investigating Engineering Student Success with Incoming Profiles and Patterns of Concurrent Course Enrolment, p. 10.

# 5    Adaptive Learning

Adaptive learning systems attempt to provide personalised learning content and activities to meet the individual needs of learners as they progress through their studies. The promise is that they can move education onwards from the 'one-size-fits-all' approach, which attempts to teach students with widely differing levels of skills and abilities the same things at the same time during a course of fixed duration.[1] Traditional learning methods often provide an experience that is either too easy or too hard and can therefore demotivate learners who become bored or frustrated. Online systems can potentially customise aspects of the learning such as its pace and preferred type of media. The content can be targeted at the most appropriate level for the learner, so that it is 'doable but challenging'[2] in a way that human teachers, even with small groups, may not have the capacity to provide for each of their students.[3] Meanwhile, the models can be continuously refined by harvesting the data of the thousands of students who use them.[4]

## Definitions

A confusing mix of terminology and overlapping areas of activity has evolved in this area. Adaptive learning, intelligent tutoring and personalised learning all refer to educational software that is customised in some way for the individual learner. Adaptive learning can be thought of as an *application* of learning analytics. The New Media Consortium's Horizon Report, 2016, groups the two areas together and states that:

> Adaptive learning technologies apply learning analytics through software and online platforms, adjusting to individual students' needs.[5]

*Personalisation* meanwhile can cover a whole range of features and applications, including some of the other applications discussed in this book – early alert (and the interventions it suggests) and course recommendation.

Adaptive learning is an area where developments seem to have been taking place without much input from the learning analytics research community. At the 2016 Learning Analytics and Knowledge Conference in Edinburgh only 4 out of the 89 abstracts of the presentations and pre-conference workshops mention the word 'adaptive'. An additional five abstracts refer to 'personalisation' or variants of the word.[6] There are however growing numbers of researchers and a range of vendors providing adaptive systems and content. Textbooks in particular are becoming increasingly adaptive, learning about users' knowledge and aptitudes as they progress and providing content that is intended to be optimised for their needs. Adaptive learning is rooted in a number of other areas of research, which themselves have a long history, such as artificial intelligence, computer-assisted instruction, intelligent tutoring systems and mastery learning.

The development of the field has been boosted by the Bill and Melinda Gates Foundation, which allocated US$20 million in its Next Generation Courseware Challenge to build more adaptive learning tools than are currently available, with the ultimate aim of improving the academic success of more than a million low-income students in US colleges and universities. It has funded some of the key players in adaptive learning: Acrobatiq, Cerego, CogBooks, Lumen Learning, Rice University OpenStax, Smart Sparrow and Stanford University's Open Learning Initiative.[7] Another initiative from the Gates Foundation, the Adaptive Learning Market Acceleration Program, has provided 14 grants to US institutions to develop their use of adaptive software in collaboration with vendors.[8]

### Rolling out Knewton and CogBooks at Arizona State University

In 2011 Arizona State University began to deploy the Knewton adaptive learning system for its online and blended courses at a cost of $100 per student, which the institution charges the students instead of them having to buy a textbook. Of the first 5,000 students who took a remedial mathematics course, the proportion of those passing jumped from 66 to 75%.

The software measures how long students spend viewing text, video and graphical objects and correlates this with marks in later tests. It then identifies patterns and can recommend appropriate content for students and time its delivery. The MAT110 syllabus has been broken into 52 concepts by Knewton's subject matter experts. Students take mini-tutorials and can take tests when they feel ready to move on. They can only progress if they pass the test. Early trials with Knewton resulted in half of the students finishing at least four weeks early.

An instructor's dashboard shows the progress of each student and clicking through provides details of where individuals might have misunderstandings. Those who have not asked for help but are seemingly stuck on a particular concept can be approached by the instructor to offer them assistance.

The decision to deploy the software was not universally welcomed by the mathematics faculty, who were not consulted when it was purchased and the above statistics have not been replicated in every course in which Knewton has been rolled out. Some students find the number of concepts they need to master overwhelming and can find use of the software isolating. Allowing students to progress at their own pace also meant that some fell so far behind that they could not catch up later. In subsequent courses, though, policies were adapted to ensure this was less likely to happen. Meanwhile senior management at Arizona State is committed to ever greater use of the software. It already enrols 26,000 students annually on adaptive courses and intends to provide an entire degree using the system.[9, 10]

CogBooks is being used as an alternative adaptive learning platform at Arizona State. Funded by the Gates Foundation's Next Generation Courseware initiative, it was piloted in late 2015 in two courses: a blended course on introductory biology (BIO100: 527 students) and an online course on US history (HISTORY110: 25 students). The CogBooks system was populated with content provided by its partner OpenStax. Learning outcomes are created by the instructor and associated with learning content and tests. Default learning paths through the content are defined for a 'typical' student. CogBooks then personalises the learning journey for the students based on their behaviour. The courses took up to three months each to develop by a team of developers, instructional designers and the instructor.

BIO100 required students to complete lessons in CogBooks before coming to the class, where they then worked in small groups to further their understanding of the materials and concepts. Instructor dashboards then enable detailed analysis of learner progress and performance.

In an online survey targeted at students in both courses, 81% of respondents (n = 37) said that they would like to use the system for other courses that they were studying. One student commented:

> Through my years in school, history has always been a tough subject. Historical events were difficult for me to grasp because it was hard for me to imagine something that happened years ago, I never felt that my knowledge was at its full potential when I read page after page of an old textbook. After a while, I would lose concentration and didn't know what I was reading about. The CogBooks software, however, completely changed the way I absorbed the information.

Other questions on navigation, usability and usefulness elicited generally positive responses from the respondents too. In BIO100 the cumulative percentage of A, B and C grades was improved by 3.4% over previous terms, the final grade point average improved by 8% and the dropout rate decreased by 2%.[11]

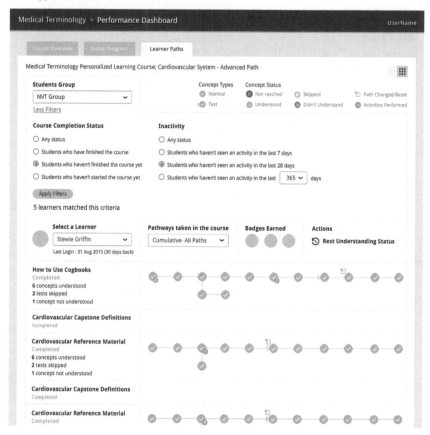

*Figure 5.1* Learner paths report in CogBooks.

## Types of Adaptive Learning System

There is already a diverse range of systems available in this space. Not only do the products reflect different positions on learning theory and on the role of the instructor, but they vary considerably in their purposes, level of sophistication and user interfaces. Some are platforms for individual institutions and instructors to develop and provide their own courses – examples are CogBooks, Knewton, LoudCloud and Smart Sparrow. These are sometimes known as 'open-content' solutions. Content is also provided in certain subject areas by these companies, who are collaborating with publishers. The other main approach is 'closed-content' solutions: self-contained systems with the specific subject material already integrated. These tend to be the preserve of publishers developing products that extend their textbooks – examples are Macmillan, McGraw-Hill, Pearson and Wiley. More recent entrants to this market do not have a print-based legacy and are developing digital content

*Figure 5.2* The instructor dashboard in Acrobatiq.

and educational games and simulations.[12, 13, 14] An example is Acrobatiq, which emerged from Carnegie Mellon's Open Learning Initiative.

Some products contain continuous assessment activities that lead to frequent changes in the content provided to students.[15] These are often rule-based systems, which use a series of if-then statements and are relatively easy to develop content in and to understand.[16] Students may be asked a question. If they answer it correctly they are provided with the next content in the sequence. Otherwise they are given some additional content to build their understanding. The next question may be new but testing the same concept.[17] Many of today's adaptive learning products are provided in areas such as mathematics and science. 'Knewton cannot work when there's no right answer', according to the founder of the company, Jose Ferreira.[18]

Other products develop profiles of the learner to ascertain the best sequencing, duration and frequency of sessions and preferred types of content for the individual. These use algorithms and machine learning to provide greater customisation. The user might, for example, be presented with a mixture of videos and texts; if he performs better in assessments after viewing one type of media, he will be presented with more content in this format subsequently.

Another feature of some systems is attempting to account for memory degradation, identifying the concepts in which the student is weak or lacking confidence and encouraging systematic reviews of the learning in those areas. This may be particularly important in subjects such as language vocabulary learning and medical exam study, where a large amount of detail needs to be memorised. In other 'facilitator-driven' systems, the instructors are provided with dashboards on learning progress and can then decide themselves the most suitable next steps for the learner.[19, 20, 21, 22, 23]

Adaptive learning systems usually contain three main elements, relating to content, the learner and the instruction. The content model structures the topic and includes the learning tasks and outcomes. The sequencing often changes depending on how the learner performs. Models of learners are developed as they proceed, estimating their ability level on each topic and tracking the areas they have already mastered. Aspects such as the best time of the day to study may be incorporated in the model. The instructional model then combines information from the content model and learner model to generate the most appropriate content or activity for the individual.[24]

## Benefits

Reported or proposed benefits of adaptive learning include:

- freeing up instructor time (or 'flipping the classroom'), 'automating the drudgery of teaching basic skills',[25] and enabling them to spend more time helping students;[26]
- deepening student engagement with learning content and hence their persistence and outcomes;[27]
- improving student confidence due to greater awareness of what topics have been mastered;[28]
- providing feedback specific to the task on which the student is working, thus enhancing its effect;[29]
- providing feedback much more quickly than traditional assessment methods;[30]
- customising pathways through the curriculum;[31]
- individualising the pace of learning;[32]
- regulating the cognitive load on the student[33] and maximising knowledge retention;
- reducing costs by increasingly scalability.[34]

Some vendors of the systems and some institutions are making extravagant claims for the effectiveness of their adaptive learning solutions. Some of these are in 'white papers' but make references to peer-reviewed research papers confirming the findings. The statistics quoted may have been cherry picked and should be treated with some scepticism. However, the evidence does seem to be accumulating that the use of adaptive learning can improve grades and retention.

## Integrating Adaptive Learning Systems with other Data and Systems

Adaptive learning packages to date have tended to be self-contained systems, teaching a subject to students without knowledge of their educational background, their engagement with other systems or their attendance on campus. The products will, however, increasingly import data from other systems to further personalise the learning experience for students. Information on their prior qualifications, other courses being studied and further aspects of their learning can be used for greater adaptation. An attendance-monitoring system may, for example, record that a student has missed a lecture that covers some prerequisite knowledge. Knowing this, the adaptive learning system could then offer to summarise the lecture topic to the student before they study the new content.

Most adaptive learning is provided at the course level, but it is possible that the real potential of these technologies will be at the level of the learners themselves, providing a rich picture of their learning and continuous personalised feedback as they progress through their studies.[35] E[2]Coach at the University of Michigan is an interesting example of a system that gathers data from a number of sources including the student information system (SIS) to provide individualised messages to physics students as they learn.[36]

The technical and logistical complexities of linking systems together in such a coordinated approach mean that adaptive learning systems may continue to exist in their own relatively isolated world for some time to come. However, they are increasingly providing analytics in their own right to instructors on the activity and performance of individuals and groups. Meanwhile, as their adoption grows across education, the learning activity data accumulated within these systems is likely to become an important data source for learning analytics, contributing to overall understanding of student engagement and achievement and of use for early alert, course recommendation and curriculum enhancement.

## Conclusion

Despite the long history of intelligent tutoring systems and related educational technologies, the mainstream use of adaptive learning systems is a new phenomenon. They have made greater inroads into corporate settings and in primary and secondary education than in colleges or higher education, perhaps because a more narrow focus of learning content makes it more suitable to be packaged and delivered through these systems.[37] There will be other barriers to their adoption. Some products are unlikely to fit with the pedagogical approaches used at particular institutions. There may also be logistical and cultural issues and objections from some faculty who feel that their role is threatened, or do not have the capacity to integrate the technologies into their existing teaching methods. While findings from pilots of the systems can be encouraging to faculty, the work in retrofitting the technologies to existing courses can be considerable. At the University of Central Florida the move to adaptive learning involved more work than expected. It was found that instructors developing the content had to think at the curricular rather than the course level and incorporate, for example, materials that reinforced a concept that had been taught earlier in the curriculum.[38]

The models can be difficult and time-consuming to author. An automated system cannot recognise when the model is wrong. If this has a negative impact on the student (e.g. they start crying), they are unlikely to be able to adapt in the way that a human teacher can. Students, too, can adapt quickly; reading a helpful message from the system may be encouraging the first time, but the novelty quickly wears off if such feedback is repeated.[39]

A further reservation that has been expressed is that adaptive learning systems tend to treat learning as a solo exercise and, unlike physical textbooks, they cannot be shared with, studied jointly with, or sold on to other students[40] – presumably one of the attractions of the technology for textbook vendors. A student who has studied exclusively in this manner may not be well prepared for a workplace where communication and collaboration skills are valued. Another, not entirely positive, possibility is that students may want to provide data on their performance in adaptive learning systems to future employers. Showing strong and rapid mastery of multiple concepts could be a differentiator between job applicants, putting those who do not provide this information at a disadvantage.[41] Those students may be good at processing highly structured knowledge in the way that most of today's adaptive systems expect and encourage, but how prepared will they be for more chaotic working environments where knowledge and information are distributed across multiple locations, are subject to rapid change and require synthesis and evaluation of their quality? A further possibility is that the jobs that require the highly structured knowledge encapsulated in such systems will increasingly be carried out by machines rather than humans anyway.[42]

It is possible, too, that students will reject the systems, preferring a less monitored and controlled way of learning.[43] However, the textbooks in use by students across the world are already increasingly incorporating adaptive learning methods. It seems likely that, as the systems become ever more sophisticated, the students will become more aware and accepting of the benefits of personalised content and pathways through it. Providing the tools as part of a programme of study involving multiple teaching and learning methods, which prepare them for future employment, should avoid some of the problems noted above. Adaptive learning systems may also increasingly integrate intelligent collaborative learning technologies such as adaptive group formation and peer help, which can match students to others who can help them.[44]

The evolution of textbooks into adaptive formats may mean that the uptake of adaptive learning by students will happen whether institutions are ready for it or not. Meanwhile, those organisations that manage to deploy these technologies successfully with learners and tap into the rich data accumulated on the use of adaptive content by their students, have the potential to make better progress overall with learning analytics for improving student success and enhancing the curriculum.

## References

1 Tyton Partners, 2013, *Learning to Adapt: A Case for Accelerating Adaptive Learning in Higher Education.*

2 Dreambox Learning, 2014, *Intelligent Adaptive Learning: An Essential Element of Twenty-First Century Teaching and Learning.*

3 Oxman, S. & Wong, W., 2014, *Adaptive Learning Systems*, Integrated Education Solutions, p. 6.

4 Upbin, B., 2012, Knewton is Building the World's Smartest Tutor, *Forbes*, 22 February, www.forbes.com/sites/bruceupbin/2012/02/22/knewton-is-building-the-worlds-sma rtest-tutor/ (accessed 9 October 2016).

5 Johnson, L. *et al.*, 2016, *NMC Horizon Report: 2016*, The New Media Consortium.

6 *Proceedings of the Sixth International Conference on Learning Analytics and Knowledge*, http://dl.acm.org/citation.cfm?id=2883851&picked=prox (accessed 1 October 2016).

7 Gates Foundation, 2014, Gates Foundation Announces Finalists for $20 Million in Digital Courseware Investments. Press release, 30 September, www.gatesfounda tion.org/Media-Center/Press-Releases/2014/09/Gates-Foundation-Announces-Fina lists-for-$20-Million-in-Digital-Courseware-Investments (accessed 9 October 2016).

8 Waters, J. K., 2014, The Great Adaptive Learning Experiment, *Campus Technology*, 16 April, https://campustechnology.com/articles/2014/04/16/the-great-adaptive-learnin g-experiment.aspx (accessed 9 October 2016).

9 Kolowich, S., 2013, The New Intelligence, *Inside Higher Education*, 25 January, https://www.insidehighered.com/news/2013/01/25/arizona-st-and-knewtons-grand-experiment-adaptive-learning (accessed 9 October 2016).

10 Oremus, W., 2015, No More Pencils, No More Books, *Slate*, 25 October, slate.com/a rticles/technology/technology/2015/10/adaptive_learning_software_is_replacing_text books_and_upending_american.html (accessed 9 October 2016).

11 Johnson, D., Thompson, J. & Fuchs, S., 2015, *Improved Student Success and Retention with Adaptive Courseware: An Arizona State University Case Study*, Arizona State University; CogBooks.

12 Tyton Partners, *Learning to Adapt: A Case for Accelerating Adaptive Learning in Higher Education*, pp. 7–9.

13 Oxman & Wong, *Adaptive Learning Systems*, p. 7.

14 Brown, J., 2015, *Personalizing Post-Secondary Education: An Overview of Adaptive Learning Solutions for Higher Education*, S+R, p. 7.

15 Tyton Partners, *Learning to Adapt: A Case for Accelerating Adaptive Learning in Higher Education*, p. 10.

16 Oxman & Wong, *Adaptive Learning Systems*, p. 3.

17 Ibid., p. 15.

18 Oremus, No More Pencils, No More Books.

19 Tyton Partners, *Learning to Adapt: A Case for Accelerating Adaptive Learning in Higher Education*, p. 10.

20 Oxman & Wong, *Adaptive Learning Systems*, p. 3.

21  Raths, D., 2015, Tales From the Front Lines of Adaptive Learning, *Campus Technology*, 23 September, https://campustechnology.com/articles/2015/09/23/tales-from-the-front-lines-of-adaptive-learning.aspx (accessed 11 October 2016).

22  McGraw-Hill LearnSmart, 2015, *McGraw-Hill LearnSmart Effectiveness Study: Evaluating the Adaptive Learning Tool's Impact on Pass and Retention Rates and Instructional Efficiencies at Seven US Universities*, p. 1.

23  Thompson, J., 2013, *Types of Adaptive Learning*, CogBooks, p. 10.

24  Oxman & Wong, *Adaptive Learning Systems*, p. 8.

25  Upbin, Knewton is Building the World's Smartest Tutor.

26  Waters, The Great Adaptive Learning Experiment, p. 2.

27  Tyton Partners, *Learning to Adapt: A Case for Accelerating Adaptive Learning in Higher Education*, pp. 4–5.

28  Johnson, C., 2016, Adaptive Learning Platforms: Creating a Path for Success, *EDUCAUSE Review*, 7 March, http://er.educause.edu/articles/2016/3/adaptive-learning-platforms-creating-a-path-for-success (accessed 11 October 2016).

29  Dreambox Learning, *Intelligent Adaptive Learning: An Essential Element of Twenty-First Century Teaching and Learning*, p. 20.

30  Oremus, No More Pencils, No More Books.

31  Tyton Partners, *Learning to Adapt: A Case for Accelerating Adaptive Learning in Higher Education*, p. 4.

32  Dreambox Learning, *Intelligent Adaptive Learning: An Essential Element of Twenty-First Century Teaching and Learning*, p. 3.

33  Ibid.

34  Tyton Partners, *Learning to Adapt: A Case for Accelerating Adaptive Learning in Higher Education*, p. 5.

35  Ibid., p. 7.

36  Huberth, M., Chen, P., Tritz, J. & McKay, T. A., 2015, Computer-Tailored Student Support in Introductory Physics, *PLoS ONE*, 10(9), p. 6.

37  Oxman & Wong, *Adaptive Learning Systems*, pp. 8–9.

38  Raths, Tales From the Front Lines of Adaptive Learning.

39  Baker, R., 2016, Stupid Tutoring Systems, Intelligent Humans, *International Journal of Articial Intelligence in Education*, 26(2), pp. 600–614.

40  Oremus, No More Pencils, No More Books.

41  Kolowich, The New Intelligence.

42  Oremus, No More Pencils, No More Books.

43  Tyton Partners, *Learning to Adapt: A Case for Accelerating Adaptive Learning in Higher Education*, p. 12.

44  Brusilovsky, P. & Peylo, C., 2003, Adaptive and Intelligent Web-based Educational Systems, *International Journal of Artificial Intelligence in Education*, 13, pp. 156–169.

# 6   Curriculum Design

Learning analytics provides unprecedented opportunities to discover whether aspects of the curriculum are functioning as intended. Educators can analyse the places students are visiting online, how much time they spend there, what tools they are using and how frequently they are using them.[1] They can examine whether students are interacting with each other as planned and whether the activities and the content provided are facilitating learning. Analytics based on learners' interactions with the course can then enable evidence-based changes to be made to resources, learning activities and other aspects of the curriculum.[2] Clearly, the more aspects of a course that are situated online, the greater is the potential evidence base.

'Just-in-time pedagogical decisions',[3] which take place while the course is underway, are typically small amendments made by the instructor, such as altering the structure of a discussion. The analytics may also suggest more significant changes to the design of the course that can be made once it is complete and before the next cohort of students begins. Enhancing the curriculum in this way is an area that shows significant promise but is as yet relatively underexploited compared with other applications of learning analytics such as early alert and recommendation.

## Increasing Engagement through Course Redesign at UMBC

In 2009, Tim Hardy at the University of Maryland Baltimore County (UMBC) redesigned his course on the principles of accounting in an attempt to increase student participation. Use of this course in the learning management system (LMS) subsequently became the most active in the whole institution. Hardy had used the 'adaptive release' feature in the Blackboard LMS, which requires students to meet specified conditions in order to access content. For example, before being able to access an assignment on spreadsheets students had to pass a quiz based on a video he had created on the subject.

Because the analytics showed that adaptive release was increasing engagement, Hardy redesigned the entire course to use this feature. This then resulted in students achieving scores in a common final exam that were 20% higher than those who did not take his course. Hardy's students also earned higher grade point average scores in the following course: intermediate accounting.

It is recognised that Hardy has put particular effort into redesigning his course; however, he claims now to be spending less time administering it and sees himself as more of a coach and facilitator rather than a lecturer. Thus, not only have the learning tools and activities been adapted as a result of the analytics, but his teaching practice has too.[4]

Other projects produce interesting findings of this nature, which can be an important early stage in learning analytics. However, they do not necessarily translate these into action as happened at UMBC. In one initiative the differences in online behaviour between successful and low-performing students were examined. It was found that high-performing students accessed the LMS more frequently than low performers but that their sessions were of similar duration. It was suggested that low performers might not be optimising their use of the system, perhaps because of the level of self-discipline and motivation necessary. High performers also spent more time in discussion forums and viewing content pages.[5] As is emphasised elsewhere in this book, there is little point in knowing such information unless something is done to attempt to improve matters as a result – either for current students or future cohorts.

### Analysing Course Effectiveness at the University System of Georgia: Should the Behaviour of Successful Learners be Promoted to Students?

In one of the earliest attempts to analyse the effectiveness of a course using learning analytics, Morris *et al.* examined historic LMS logs from three courses at the University System of Georgia. The data included details of the pages visited, the tools used and activity on the forums. Analyses of the relationship of students' engagement to persistence and achievement were carried out.

The records of 354 students were examined; 284 of these had completed their course whereas 70 had withdrawn. Those who completed were more engaged in the learning activities than those who withdrew. The conclusion was that time on task and frequency of interaction with the LMS have an impact on online learning. Three indicators appeared to be particularly significant: the number of discussion posts viewed, the number of content pages viewed and the time spent viewing forums.

The researchers ask an important question:

> Are our findings on the importance of reading discussions and secondarily on creating discussion and follow-up posts, justification for requiring all students to participate in discussions? Again, our findings

are not conclusive but they do suggest that successful students engage in this type of behaviour with greater frequency and duration than non-successful students. This study also suggests that successful students link their online activities to doing what is important to earn passing grades, that is, repeatedly visiting content pages throughout the course. The data suggest that savvy students likely decided that time spent viewing content pages was more important than creating original posts or follow-up discussion posts, although successful completers did both in relatively high numbers.

As with many other studies, the unsurprising finding emerges that students who are more engaged are more likely to complete their courses. However, the researchers argue that these kinds of studies are essential in order to understand the factors that lead to successful student behaviour. They suggest that this, in turn, can help faculty to enhance their teaching in order to maximise the chance of completion by students. Meanwhile instructional designers can use the findings to develop curricula and activities that are likely to encourage engagement.[6]

Learning analytics can highlight issues that lead to hypotheses or research questions, which in turn may be answered by further data resulting from interventions. To illustrate the type of factors that may be investigated to enhance the curriculum, some possible issues, questions and interventions are provided in Table 6.1.

*Table 6.1* Possible issues, research questions and interventions arising from learning analytics.

| Issue highlighted by the analytics | Possible research question(s) | Possible intervention |
| --- | --- | --- |
| A key piece of learning content is not being accessed by most students. | Is this because the content is too difficult to understand, too difficult to find, sequenced at the wrong time, or the importance of accessing it has not been properly communicated? | Ask the students why they are not accessing it. Content may then need to be made more accessible, sequenced differently or its importance flagged appropriately. |
| Some students are not participating well in collaborative work. | Are less outgoing students disadvantaged by significant requirements for collaborative work? | Enable alternatives to collaborative work or reduce the overall amount of it required in the course. |
| A particular minority group is underperforming in an aspect of the curriculum. | What factors are leading to their underperformance – e.g. linguistic or cultural issues, lack of prerequisite knowledge and skills, financial issues? | Target additional support at the minority group. |

*Table 6.1* (continued)

| Issue highlighted by the analytics | Possible research question(s) | Possible intervention |
|---|---|---|
| Students across several discussion groups are making only minimal contributions to their forums. | Are the discussion group sizes too small to achieve a critical mass? | Merge groups with low participation rates into a larger one. Amend the learning design for the next iteration of the course, with a larger group specified from the start. |
| Views of course content are greater on particular days of the week. | When is the optimum time for releasing key content? | Release key content on a Monday because this is the day that the LMS receives most visits. |
| Students who use e-books in particular ways are more successful. | Does annotation, searching for definitions of unfamiliar words and writing summaries lead to improved learning outcomes? | Provide additional support for students to develop their skills in learning effectively from e-books. |

## The Importance of Theory

At a time when there is more information available than ever, it is tempting to think that the data itself will provide answers. However, the sheer volume of it means that connecting the data with some kind of theory to explain what is happening is essential. Without an underlying theory, moreover, it is difficult to prioritise which of the many separate variables in the data of millions of students should be included in an analysis.[7] Theory that may help instructors and designers to understand the impact of a particular learning design on students, for example, is emerging from the research relating to social network analysis.[8] Meanwhile, educators who are influenced by socio-constructivist approaches may be more likely to provide learning activities that encourage greater degrees of collaboration between learners and to seek validation of their approaches from the data.

Atkisson articulates a danger:

> Faced with access to large collections of data and powerful open source analysis software, researches [sic] will be subject to a variety of temptations to poke about in this data in thoroughly unprincipled ways. While these fishing expeditions may uncover seemingly interesting relationships between constructs, without an interpretive framework grounded in specific theoretical commitments, the data tail may come to wag the theory dog.[9]

At each of the separate stages of designing courses, facilitating learning and adapting the curriculum on the basis of the analytics, theory may lie behind the actions of the educator, whether or not they explicitly recognise it. Ideally, this should lead them to formulate hypotheses about the effectiveness of the curriculum, resulting in questions to test these hypotheses.

**Asking the Right Questions of the Data: Reassessing the Initial Hypothesis after Examining the Data of Students on a MOOC**

The importance of formulating hypotheses or questions when using learning analytics for curriculum enhancement is illustrated by Whitmer and his colleagues, who analysed data from a MOOC with an enrolment of 48,174 learners. They examined interaction data, a readiness quiz, entry and exit surveys and forum posts. One of their research questions was:

*Do early participation activities, such as participation in discussion forums, completion of videos, and submission of assignments, predict final levels of participation and learning outcomes?*

The analytics suggested that the question should be reconsidered:

Disengaged learners, representing the majority of all registrations (62%), never substantially engaged with the course. From an empirical perspective, their low participation level could not be due to MOOC design because they did not access the course enough to be influenced by the content. Increasing the participation of these learners would involve factors and interventions outside the control of MOOC researchers and designers (e.g., time, interest, commitment, access).

In contrast, declining learners (14%) began with high levels of participation but stopped participating by week two. Focussed interventions on this sub-population could be effective because these students demonstrated the potential for higher levels of participation.[10]

## Informing Learning Design with Learning Analytics

A common way of designing a new course is to draw on the educator's past experience in what is often quite an informal process.[11] The focus may be on assembling the content to be absorbed by students, with the assessments designed subsequently and less thought given to how the course is to be taught and what learning activities are to be undertaken. This method of course development provides few ways of discovering whether the course is functioning as planned. Ascertaining whether or not the elements of the course are proving effective and students are learning as intended requires being explicit about aspects of the learning and teaching process in advance. Anticipating the optimum mix of media and activities and articulating these in a consistent and understandable way is not trivial: the learning objectives must be disaggregated into their constituent elements, activities and tools.[12]

Increasingly, such methodologies are being deployed in the development of courses. *Learning design* is the term sometimes used to describe and sequence the elements of a course such as the tools deployed (e.g. forums, wikis), the activities put in place for the students (e.g. attend a webinar, contribute to a forum) and the learning content provided (e.g. course texts, videos). The learning design may specify the role of the instructor throughout the course and may define how groups are formed (e.g. a class of 100 is divided into five groups). Any one of these elements could turn out to be badly designed, resulting in student confusion, lack of participation, negative feedback and subsequent impact on performance, as measured through assessments.

Learning designs can be used as templates and can be reused in other courses or by different instructors.[13, 14] They may be based on educational theory and past experience but the analytics enable the verification of any prior assumptions with real data on student participation.[15] A pedagogical plan based on data regarding student engagement and achievement will be better informed and is likely to be more successful.[16] Arguably then learning design *needs* learning analytics in order to validate itself. However, it also works the other way: learning analytics cannot be used effectively without an understanding of the underlying learning design, including why the particular tools, activities and content were selected and how they were deployed.[17, 18]

## Representing Learning Designs and Learning Analytics

Learning designs can be represented through graphical methods, textual descriptions or formalised languages. The latter can enable formal designs of courses that can be processed automatically, configuring the online learning environment and sequencing the content to students. Given the complexities of these languages, they may not however be easily understood by instructors, who may prefer freer textual descriptions in natural language. Such representations may help to support communication between people about the design of the course but are likely to be less suited to automated processing.

There are advantages and disadvantages of the various types of learning design but we are still a long way from having a *lingua franca* for it.[19] This is compounded by the difficulties for communities formed around particular learning design approaches to sustain themselves after the projects that funded them have come to an end.[20] Meanwhile, LMSs represent learning designs in different ways, complicating matters, particularly where institutions deploy more than one LMS. These factors should give further impetus to the development of a platform-independent data model for learning designs.[21]

Neither do we yet have a common language for describing learning analytics, though standardised representations of the data used for learning analytics and the predictive models are emerging (see Chapter 15). Learning analytics tends to focus on visualisations such as charts and graphs (see Chapter 10). One option is to combine representations for learning design and learning analytics. This would enable course designers to learn from the experience of previous courses.

It would also allow instructors and students to see what is happening during a particular learning activity and to adjust their actions accordingly.[22] Meanwhile the use of learning analytics could help to improve the robustness of learning designs, grounding them in evidence[23] rather than the whims of designers. While there is little sign of this happening yet and there are barriers such as a common language and diverging research communities to be overcome, it is hoped that course designers in the future will be able to combine the methodologies of learning analytics and learning design.

Figure 6.1 presents a model of how learning analytics may interact with learning design to enhance the curriculum. The **learning design** includes

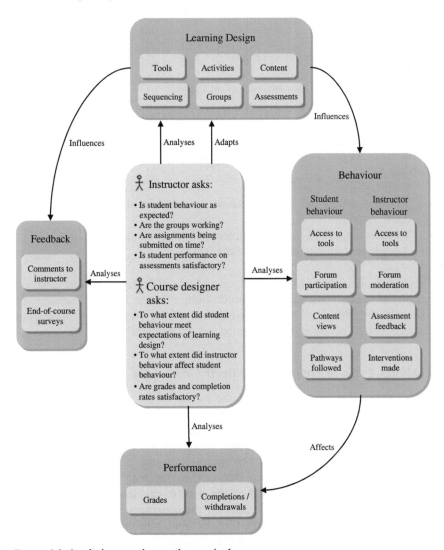

*Figure 6.1* Analytics to enhance the curriculum.

the tools, activities, content, assessments and how they are sequenced, along with the design of the groups. This influences the **behaviour** of students and instructors and how they carry out the specified learning and teaching activities. This in turn is likely to affect the **performance** of the students – whether they complete the course and what grade they obtain. The learning design also influences student **feedback**, for example in the form of comments to the instructor during the course and through end-of-course surveys.

Analytics can be performed on all this data and provided to two key stakeholders, who are able to adapt the curriculum. The **instructor**, who can make adaptations while the course is underway, can then ask questions such as:

- Is student behaviour as expected?
- Are the groups working?
- Are assignments being submitted on time?
- Is student performance in assessments satisfactory?

The **course designer** then has opportunities to adjust aspects of the course for its next iteration and may use the analytics to help answer questions such as:

- To what extent did student behaviour match with expectations of the learning design?
- To what extent did instructor behaviour affect student behaviour?
- Are grades and completion rates satisfactory?

This book is concerned with learning analytics rather than 'teaching analytics' but any enhancements made to the curriculum on the basis of learning analytics clearly require an honest assessment of the effectiveness of teaching practice as well as the activities carried out by learners.

## Analytics Tools to Help Assess Effectiveness of the Curriculum

It is only possible to make sense of the wealth of data available for learning analytics with tools to aggregate and present visualisations effectively. Validation of particular approaches using the analytics may also prove vital in convincing busy educators to introduce new activities or technologies in their teaching. Many institutions wish to increase the use of online learning but struggle to convince academics to change their teaching practices. They may be more inclined to attempt innovations if tools can be provided to demonstrate that there is a beneficial impact on their learners – or themselves.[24, 25] However most reporting tools found in existing LMSs provide data in tabular formats that do not enable teachers to answer the specific questions they might have.[26]

## Developing a Tool to Analyse Student Engagement at Aachen University

Dyckhoff and her colleagues at Aachen University in Germany describe the development of *eLAT*, a learning analytics tool aimed at enabling instructors to reflect on their online teaching methods. A potential scenario requiring such a toolkit is a teacher who provides weekly online exercises in order for her students to prepare for an exam but who does not know if they are proving useful. It would be helpful to know to what extent use of the exercises correlates with success in the exam. The toolkit could assist her by collecting, analysing and providing visualisations of the data.

The system required a clear, simple and easily understandable interface while being flexible enough to enable the exploration of data. It was decided that it should provide step-by-step guidance, helping the formation of research questions, providing appropriate data collection mechanisms and enabling educators to choose from a flexible set of indicators. It should also be possible to integrate it with any LMS.

The tool was developed and included features such as an indicator showing the **top ten resources** accessed. A place in this list might indicate that the resource is useful or is difficult to understand. Further investigation by the teacher could enable improvement of the content if it turns out that difficulty was the issue. Another feature is the **forum usage** indicator. This shows the number of new threads created with corresponding answers to them per day. Thus the levels of communication between students can be assessed and whether there is a problem with the course design if students are not contributing to the forum. A further indicator shows the **adoption rate** – the time taken between uploading learning content and its access by students. This shows not only how quickly students access the content but also whether it has been distributed sufficiently among them. An example may be the requirement to read a document before a class. Low adoption rates might explain a lack of participation in discussions during the class, potentially resulting in a redesign of the course, making it much clearer to future students that it is essential that they read this document in advance.[27]

Kennedy and his colleagues argue that many learning analytics systems have been developed without taking into account the pedagogical design in online environments. The tools do not enable anyone to interpret the data effectively unless they also understand the original learning design of the course.[28] Meanwhile, understanding the effectiveness of learning designs may require course designers to navigate the relevant datasets, categorise the data and develop hypotheses that can be validated with further observations.[29]

**Assessing whether 'Pedagogical Intent' is Reflected in Student Activity**

Corrin *et al.* describe the development of a learning analytics tool, *Loop*, which was funded by the Australian government's Office of Learning and Teaching. This presents data to teachers on the interactions of students. The teacher's 'pedagogical intent' in defining a learning activity is captured and used to define the analytics presented for each learning tool. Loop then uses data from the LMS to assess whether the intent is reflected in the students' interactions and presents this to teachers through dashboards and reports.

Specifically, the tool integrates course structures and schedules in its visualisations to help evaluate the effectiveness of the learning activities. Key learning tasks and events, either isolated (e.g. an exam) or recurring (e.g. a weekly lecture) can be defined so that the tool can use these in representing patterns of activity.[30]

Tools can be envisaged that help to align the learning design with the learning analytics, demonstrating whether learners were able to progress through the course as planned. However, this is not essential: the data could be processed and presented to users without reference to the learning design, leaving it up to users to make their own connections.[31] This is likely, though, to require a higher level of data literacy.

## Faculty Skills in Interpreting the Analytics

It has been argued that teachers need to become increasingly explorative and reflective, adopting the techniques of scientific enquiry, with continual adaptations to their practices informed by data. They should themselves be encouraged to research their own educational practice, rather than leaving this to other professionals. This is particularly important given the range of tools for learning and teaching now at the disposal of instructors, as well as the rapidly evolving requirements of learners. However those who use learning analytics systematically in this way are currently restricted to a small number of early adopters.[32, 33]

In one study, at the University of Missouri–St Louis, Grant found that faculty may have been competent in online teaching but were far less so in their use of learning analytics. They did not know how to extract LMS tracking data to examine student progress or to intervene with those at risk. However, those who met with instructional designers to look at how to improve their courses all adapted their current course rather than waiting until its next presentation. On the basis of the feedback, one instructor completely altered the course with new case studies and simulations.[34]

## Should Learning Analytics Tools Prompt Instructors When Learning Outcomes Are Not Being Met?

The SNAPP tool integrates with an LMS forum to show teachers visualisations of how learners are interacting. In one evaluation of its use, it was reported that the system was largely being used as a reflective tool, especially effective for analysing courses once they were completed. However, teachers were not using it to examine activity while the course was underway. This would have enabled immediate adaptation of the learning design if it was not functioning as expected.

Lockyer & Dawson suggest that additional functionality may be required to prompt instructors when the learning outcomes are not being met. For example, the development of a learning community may be an integral part of the learning design but, if students are not interacting as planned, the teacher needs to know that they should check the visualisations and take action to address the problem.[35]

## Conclusion

Data can be aggregated to assess the effectiveness of different tools and approaches across more than one course, potentially suggesting changes across a programme, faculty or even the whole institution. Learning analytics may provide the data and techniques to support attempts at improving quality and accountability across education.[36] It can help to assess the achievement of objectives in faculty learning and teaching plans.[37] It may also provide information on whether institutional goals, such as greater adoption of e-learning, are being met.

In one study, for example, it was discovered that over 80% of interactions in the institutional LMS involved the discussion forum tool, while quizzes, wikis and blogs showed much lower levels of adoption.[38] Such information may help to understand institutional culture and processes in a way that was not previously articulated. It may also dispel complacency if, for example, it is discovered that new teaching methods and online learning are not used as heavily as was thought by senior management. Meanwhile, data showing increasing trends or patterns of tool usage may help IT departments to plan service provision more efficiently.[39]

Some of the above uses are more in the realm of business intelligence than learning analytics. However, the data could also help to answer fundamental pedagogical questions such as: 'How do we know whether instructional technology improves learning?'[40] Learning analytics is potentially more useful than methods such as course evaluations, student surveys, teacher surveys and user observations because it provides details of immediate student activity in a way that has not been possible before – and also because earlier methods were not designed to capture the interactions between a learner and their device.

Ideally it will be integrated with these other methods to provide a fuller picture.[41, 42] Meanwhile, it is clear that there is a growing necessity for the diverging communities of learning design and learning analytics to come together to develop languages and tools to address the full lifecycle of curriculum development and enhancement.

## References

1  Morris, L. V. *et al.*, 2005, Tracking Student Behavior, Persistence, and Achievement in Online Courses, *The Internet and Higher Education*, 8, pp. 221–231.

2  Lockyer, L. & Dawson, S., 2011, Learning Designs and Learning Analytics, *LAK11: Proceedings of the First International Learning Analytics and Knowledge Conference*, p. 153.

3  Persico, D. & Pozzi, F., 2015, Informing Learning Design with Learning Analytics to Improve Teacher Inquiry, *British Journal of Educational Technology*, 46(2), pp. 230–248.

4  Fritz, J., 2013, *Using Analytics at UMBC: Encouraging Student Responsibility and Identifying Effective Course Designs*, EDUCAUSE Center for Applied Research, pp. 6–7.

5  Dawson, S. *et al.*, 2008, Teaching Smarter: How Mining ICT Data Can Inform and Improve Learning and Teaching Practice. *Hello! Where Are You in the Landscape of Educational Technology? Proceedings Ascilite Melbourne*, p. 227; http://www.ascilite.org.au/conferences/melbourne08/procs/dawson.pdf

6  Morris *et al.*, Tracking Student Behavior, Persistence, and Achievement in Online Courses.

7  Wise, A. F. & Shaffer, D. W., 2015, Why Theory Matters More than Ever in the Age of Big Data, *Journal of Learning Analytics*, 2(2), pp. 5–13.

8  Lockyer & Dawson, Learning Designs and Learning Analytics, p. 155.

9  Atkisson, M. & Wiley, D., 2011, Learning Analytics as Interpretive Practice: Applying Westerman to Educational Intervention, *Proceedings of the First International Conference on Learning Analytics and Knowledge*, p. 119

10  Whitmer, J. *et al.*, 2015, *How Students Engage with a Remedial English Writing MOOC: A Case Study in Learning Analytics with Big Data*, EDUCAUSE Learning Initiative.

11  Lockyer, L. *et al.*, 2013, Informing Pedagogical Action: Aligning Learning Analytics With Learning Design, *American Behavioral Scientist*, 57(10), pp. 1439–1459.

12  Atkinson, S. P., 2015, Using Learning Design to Unleash the Power of Learning Analytics. In: Reiners, B. R. *et al.*, eds, *Globally Connected, Digitally Enabled. Proceedings Ascilite*, pp. 358–364.

13  Lockyer & Dawson, Learning Designs and Learning Analytics, p. 153.

14  Lockyer *et al.*, Informing Pedagogical Action: Aligning Learning Analytics with Learning Design, p. 1443.

15  Lockyer & Dawson, Learning Designs and Learning Analytics, p. 155.

16  Persico & Pozzi, Informing Learning Design with Learning Analytics to Improve Teacher Inquiry, p. 4.

17  Kennedy, G. *et al.*, 2014, Completing the Loop: Returning Learning Analytics to Teachers. In: Hegarty, B., *et al.*, eds, *Rhetoric and Reality: Critical Perspectives on Educational Technology. Proceedings Ascilite*, pp. 436–440.

18 Lockyer *et al.*, Informing Pedagogical Action: Aligning Learning Analytics with Learning Design, p. 1446.

19 Persico & Pozzi, Informing Learning Design with Learning Analytics to Improve Teacher Inquiry, pp. 5–7.

20 Ibid., p. 13.

21 Merceron, A., 2013, Analyzing Users Data Captured in Learning Management Systems, *DAILE13 Workshop on Data Analysis and Interpretation for Learning Environments*, p. 2.

22 Persico & Pozzi, Informing Learning Design with Learning Analytics to Improve Teacher Inquiry, p. 7.

23 Ibid., p. 14.

24 Lockyer & Dawson, Learning Designs and Learning Analytics, p. 155.

25 Dyckhoff, A. L. *et al.*, 2012, Design and Implementation of a Learning Analytics Toolkit for Teachers, *Educational Technology and Society*, 15(3), pp. 58–76.

26 Ibid., p. 60.

27 Ibid.

28 Kennedy *et al.*, Completing the Loop: Returning Learning Analytics to Teachers, pp. 436–437.

29 Dunbar, R. L. *et al.*, Connecting Analytics and Curriculum Design: Process and Outcomes of Building a Tool to Browse Data Relevant to Course Designers, *Journal of Learning Analytics*, 1(3), pp. 223–243.

30 Corrin, L. *et al.*, 2005, Loop: A Learning Analytics Tool to Provide Teachers with Useful Data Visualisations. In: Reiners, B. R. *et al.*, eds, *Globally Connected, Digitally Enabled. Proceedings Ascilite*, pp. CP:57–CP:61.

31 Wise, A. F., 2014, Designing Pedagogical Interventions to Support Student Use of Learning Analytics, *LAK14: Proceedings of the Fourth International Learning Analytics and Knowledge Conference*, p. 2.

32 Persico & Pozzi, Informing Learning Design with Learning Analytics to Improve Teacher Inquiry, pp. 1–2.

33 Ibid., p. 14.

34 Grant, M. R., 2012, University of Missouri–St Louis: Data-Driven Online Course Design and Effective Practices, *Continuing Higher Education Review*, 76, pp. 183–192.

35 Lockyer & Dawson, Learning Designs and Learning Analytics, p. 155.

36 Ibid.

37 Heathcote, E. & Dawson, S., 2005, Data Mining for Evaluation, Benchmarking and Reflective Practice in a LMS. *Proceedings of E-Learn 2005: World Conference on E-Learning in Corporate, Government, Healthcare and Higher Education*, pp. 326–333.

38 Dawson *et al.*, Teaching Smarter: How Mining ICT Data Can Inform and Improve Learning and Teaching Practice, pp. 223–224.

39 Heathcote & Dawson, Data Mining for Evaluation, Benchmarking and Reflective Practice in a LMS.

40 Fritz, *Using Analytics at UMBC: Encouraging Student Responsibility and Identifying Effective Course Designs*, p. 1.

41 Grant, University of Missouri–St Louis: Data-Driven Online Course Design and Effective Practices, p. 190.

42 Rangel, V. S. *et al.*, 2015, Toward a New Approach to the Evaluation of a Digital Curriculum Using Learning Analytics, *Journal of Research on Technology in Education*, 47(2), pp. 89–104.

# 7   Expert Thoughts on Applications

## Adaptive Learning

A theme that emerges from a number of the interviews with experts in learning analytics is that adaptive learning systems and intelligent tutoring will continue to improve and become increasingly important in education. Alan Berg believes that, after tackling retention, these systems should be the next focus for institutions, enabling misconceptions to be spotted much earlier, with machines feeling increasingly like humans. Josh Baron agrees that adaptive learning systems may be the next major development:

> I think we're scratching the surface right now with pretty much all the learning analytics stuff. Academic early alert systems may be where most people are focussed but I think even there ... it's still early days. I would say that adaptive learning systems and cognitive tutoring technology, which I categorise as learning analytics at least, is the one that I think holds the biggest potential for directly impacting on learning, but I think hasn't really left the lab yet too much.
>
> And I think everything from improving learning outcomes to reducing the cost of delivering learning and creating more personalised learning – I think those types of adaptive learning systems hold the potential to do that kind of thing, and that's why I'm really excited about that.

Abelardo Pardo's vision, too, is that we should move beyond visualisation and go

> all the way to true adaptation, true modification of the learning environment ... providing students with recommendations or adaptions that go beyond simple, basic feedback, and focus more on higher level types of constructions, like, for example, learning strategies.

He thinks the systems will increasingly be able to provide students with meaningful suggestions, rather than simply offering new resources or exercises. Mark Milliron, meanwhile, talks about the 'power of the learning moment' and describes how this can lead to greater connections between individuals rather than simply replacing teachers with machines:

There's a moment where you can say, 'here are the right learning resources, here are the right interactivities, here's a set of peers who just wrestled with this, you might want to connect with, here are a set of mentors who are already in the field who have connections on this'. We can bring to that learning moment the right resource at the right time in the right way ... And sometimes that ... means you're going to have to turn the agent off and spend the next hour with this text, dive deep into it and then let's talk about it and let's engage. It does not mean spoonfeeding. The data can point to the fact that you actually need to talk to another person, you need to connect with a peer or a faculty member. That's one of the most exciting parts of this, we can build on the fly communities ... which can be powerful for students.

## Understanding the Learning Process

Several of the interviewees were particularly interested in using data to help understand the learning process. Jeff Grann, for example, has a background in educational psychology and would like to apply techniques such as psychometrics and item-response theory to provide greater insight into the processes and sequences of human learning. Simon Buckingham Shum also sees huge potential in using analytics to understand learning and referred to the work of his colleague Ruth Crick:

> We're very interested in dispositions, habits of mind ... These are the mindsets that students approach their learning with, which may be due to a whole variety of factors like curiosity or aversion to risk and uncertainty. We know that a sense of belonging in a learning community is important. We know that agency and the student's ability to take the initiative, and [having] a sense of how they're developing as a learner – those are important things for integrating a holistic vision of learning. So we need ways of assessing that, and there are ways of doing that both from self-report psychometrics and behavioural measures.

For Bart Rienties, the analysis of emotions, in particular, is the obvious next development:

> It is interesting if you can see I clicked twenty times on a particular website but you don't really know when I'm frustrated, engaged or for some reason I forgot to put my mouse on the keyboard. So the real next step in learning analytics is not just to predict what learners are doing in general but to try and understand what are they experiencing, what are they learning and how we can try to provide personalised environments to react to those critical learning emotions.

## Linking Learning Analytics to Curriculum and Learning Design

Bart is also interested in using analytics to see how learning design influences student success. He has noticed that the reason for student failure is frequently because something is wrong with the learning design. Drawing the connections with pedagogy, he believes, is one of the most promising areas for learning analytics. Similarly, Alyssa Wise wants to see more diagnostic analytics, not simply alerting faculty that intervention is required, but also providing insight into what kind of changes are needed:

> You don't get everything right at the first try. The notion is that learning analytics become tools for (self) monitoring in a useful way, and part of our regular practice – there's this data stream that lets us check how we're doing and make adjustments, as opposed to just trying to find problems.

She also suggests better use of analytics for enhancing the learning design of courses:

> So at the instructor level that means that you want to have some sort of system set up where there's close ties between learning design and learning analytics. So instructors have some sort of framework where they think about what they want to do in the class: they put forward the design, they suggest 'this is what I hope the design will produce in terms of student activity', and then the analytics become a way to check that. And that's that reflective cycle.

Leah Macfadyen has been using data that is already available to analyse areas such as students' enrolment choices, achievement patterns and progress though their degrees. Taking this analysis to mid-level decision makers, such as heads of department, she can say:

> 'Look! Here's a flow chart of how students are travelling through your degree.' You can see the lights coming on, where they're going, 'Wow, look at that – all these people leave after they take that course. What's going on?' And they've never seen data like that. So I think it's not perhaps the Holy Grail area that the purists are aiming at – you know, student-facing, give learners control of their data and feedback on their progress every day – but I think it's the really usable stuff.

# Part III
# Logistics

# 8   Data

**Types of Data used for Learning Analytics**

The data for learning analytics can come from many different sources and can be classified in various ways. One of the primary types is the *demographic data* (type 1 in Figure 8.1) the institution holds about students, such as their date of birth, sex, socio-economic status or ethnicity. Some of this may be 'sensitive' data (type 1a), which in many countries has its own legal definition and needs to be handled especially carefully. Much of it may be irrelevant for learning analytics; however, data such as a student's ethnic group or disability can turn out to be relevant in predicting their academic performance.

A second category is *academic data* (type 2), held for each student about their module choices, assignments and grades obtained to date or partial contributions towards grades. A subset of this is *prior performance data* (type 2a), which may include secondary school results or qualifications obtained elsewhere. This also can be a useful source for predictive analytics, as correlations may exist between how well qualified students are before studying and their likely future success. *Learner-generated content* (type 2b) may consist of the text of essays, group reports, blogs or other artefacts generated by students in the course of their learning. Various techniques such as discourse analytics and sentiment analysis (see Chapter 24) can be carried out on this content.

The types of data described above can be vital for learning analytics but they are recorded and held primarily for other institutional purposes. *Learning activity data* (type 3), by contrast, is often logged by systems as they are used, without any particular anticipated future use. Thus, most activities carried out by students in the LMS, such as logging in, downloading learning content, or posting a comment to a forum, are logged by the system. Data can be extracted from these logs and from other systems, such as records of book borrowing from the library, or systems to monitor students' attendance on campus. These events are captured in what have become known as 'learning activity records': these are key data sources for learning analytics.

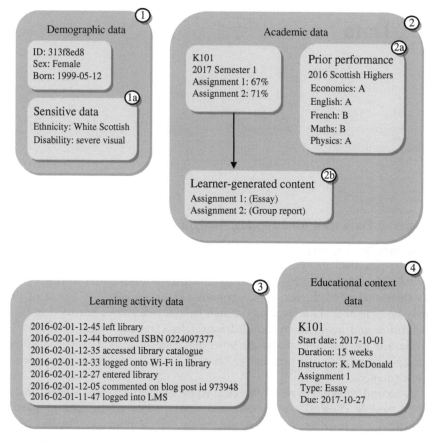

*Figure 8.1* Examples of types of data used for learning analytics.

Data about learners and their learning is not the only information relevant for learning analytics. *Educational context data* (type 4) may be also required. This can include details of the curriculum, the learning design, including content and activities, the assessments, events such as course start and duration and dates of seminars and examinations.[1]

The UK Information Commissioner's Office suggests a method of classifying personal data, based on its origins:

- **Provided data**: consciously given by individuals, for example when filling in an online form.
- **Observed data**: recorded automatically, for example, by cookies, sensors or facial recognition from CCTV pictures.
- **Derived data**: produced from other data, for example calculating customer profitability from the number of items purchased in a store and the number of visits.

- **Inferred data**: produced using analytics to find correlations between datasets in order to categorise or profile people, for example predicting future health outcomes.[2]

Learning analytics generally uses observed, derived or inferred data rather than provided data. This may have implications for privacy if individuals are unaware that their data is being collected and processed (see Chapter 21).

## Data Sources

The learning management system (LMS) and the student information system (SIS) are likely to be the primary systems from which data for learning analytics is extracted in large-scale learning-analytics deployments. Commercial solutions generally target these systems as their main data sources. In my study of leading UK institutions in the field of learning analytics I found that the key sources being used, or being considered for use, were the LMS, the SIS and library systems. Feedback from students in the form of end-of-module surveys and other student questionnaires was also thought to be important.[3] Another UK-based study found that use of lecture capture and media streaming systems was also being considered, along with attendance-monitoring systems and swipe-card access to buildings.[4] Student access to on-campus Wi-Fi is a further potential data source that may indicate their presence on campus or even allow analysis of which parts of the campus they are visiting. Thus, time spent in the student bar when a scheduled lecture is taking place may indicate a lack of engagement. It is possible, however, that the collection of such data is overly intrusive; this is discussed in Chapter 22.

Other potential data sources for learning analytics include:

- E-book platforms, which record learners' interactions with the materials, monitoring frequency of use, the pages they access and even the annotations they make to the text (though there may be ethical and pedagogical implications here too, particularly if such monitoring affects student behaviour).
- Adaptive learning systems that assess student skills, knowledge or understanding of concepts and adapt the content provided to them accordingly.
- Videos, including those captured from traditional lectures, those recorded specifically by lecturers for online teaching and other educational videos. Again, the data can show to what extent students are engaging with the materials. One study has even suggested that the optimum length for video content is six to nine minutes, based on the amount of time most users will watch a clip for before moving on.[5]

- Serious games used for learning, which can build on students' desires for entertainment, promoting high levels of engagement and amassing data that provides insights into the learning experience.[6]

Meanwhile, other low-level or unstructured data created by the learners themselves may help with the analysis of their learning. This could include web logs, clickstreams, keystroke capture data, emails, images and videos.[7]

While the LMS and the SIS are frequently portrayed as the most essential sources, the learning analytics research community has often tended to draw its data from elsewhere. The vast majority of studies analysed in one review of 60 publications used data from adaptive learning systems, intelligent tutoring systems or web-based courses held *outside* the LMS and without reference to demographic or other data held in the SIS.[8] This may reflect the fact that researchers often do not have access to core institutional datasets and have to carry out their research using tools they can configure and analyse directly without input from their information technology departments, which have other priorities. As learning analytics becomes more mainstream in institutions and researchers' expertise is deployed to validate the processes and the predictive models, the gap between research and institutional practice is, however, likely to narrow.

## Incorporating Data from Outside the Institution

A significant problem for learning analytics is that learners may carry out many of their learning activities outside the monitored and recorded confines of the institution's LMS. They are increasingly likely to study content that is freely available on the Web and to interact with other students using social networking tools. Institutions themselves may recommend the use of cloud-based learning tools from which they receive no data on usage by their students. Those who are already in frequent contact with each other using widely adopted, free 'cooler' tools on their smartphones are unlikely to switch willingly to institutionally provided software when required to undertake a collaborative task.[9]

Assuming it is available at all, it remains a challenge to integrate data from external systems and capture the varied activities of learners with the aim of enhancing the analytics.[10] One research project went as far as providing virtual machines to their students, with a range of useful content and software tools for them to use. An attempt was made to capture as much information as possible on what they were accessing, including websites.[11] While this was an interesting exercise for a computer science course, it is unlikely to be scalable across an institution and relies on the consent and ongoing cooperation of students who are happy to set up their computers and phones in specified ways. It fails to address the issue that they are likely to continue to communicate with each other and access the internet using multiple and ever changing applications and devices.

Monitoring everything a student does using technology may be seen as draconian but there are attempts to do so and some students may be willing to trade the loss of privacy with a trusted institution if they perceive there are potential benefits for their learning. Kitto and colleagues at Queensland University of Technology developed a toolkit that transforms data from students' social media accounts into learning activity records in the xAPI format (see Chapter 15) and stores them in a learning record store. Data can be 'scraped' or extracted via the application program interface (API) from YouTube, Facebook, Google+, Google drive, Twitter, StackExchange and WordPress. Ethical objections to this approach are alleviated by transferring all the students' data back to them in an open format.[12]

## Preparing the Data for Use in Learning Analytics

*Transforming* the data is an essential element of learning analytics and can itself involve a wide range of processes. Large datasets generally contain spurious records, which need to be 'cleaned' in order for the analytics to be accurate. One study, for example, found that 2% of the LMS log file records examined were from staff use.[13] An example here might be instructors who log into their LMS course site as students in order to test it out. They attempt the quizzes and get 100% in all of them because they know the answers. This then skews the average scores for the class. An effective cleaning process would remove records of their interactions with the system.

The analytics processes to be performed on the data subsequently may require the removal of 'outliers' that significantly alter the metrics and predictions. Thus an academically struggling student who logs into the LMS a large number of times between 2 a.m. and 4 a.m. every night would increase the figure for the overall number of student logins in the middle of the night. A simplistic analytics process which showed a relationship between logging in at these hours and low levels of academic success could be flawed unless this 'outlying' student's login records were removed, or at least scaled-down in significance. One learning analytics initiative deals with such issues by defining outliers as observations 3+ standard deviations away from the mean and eliminates them from the analysis completely.[14]

Another function of the transformation process may be the aggregation of logs and other data that, in themselves, may not be useful but when combined have more meaning. The Open Academic Analytics Initiative carries out transformation of the LMS log files before the data is stored in a repository, computing for each student the number of LMS course sessions opened, the number of discussion forum threads to which they contribute and the number of assignments and assessments they submit.[15] With the development of formats for the recording and transfer of learning activities, however, it may, at an early stage, make sense simply to dump all learning activity records into the learning record store and leave such processing for later.

## Transforming Learning Analytics Data at California State University, Chico

Whitmer details a number of processes his project deployed to reduce and transform the data at California State University, Chico:

1. **Clean the LMS logs.** First, LMS log file records were filtered to remove any staff use from the analysis. It was also found that one discreet action by a student could result in 20 hits recorded in the logs, so these were consolidated where appropriate. Logs of activities with a dwell time of less than five seconds were then removed as these might represent automated server-level events. Activities with a dwell time of an hour or more were excluded too, as these may have resulted from students starting an activity and then leaving their machines. Use of tools that were rarely used by students were also discounted. By this stage 74% of records had been removed from the log files, a finding that Whitmer says is significant for future studies that consider LMS data for predicting student success. Without such filtering, he says, there is the potential for serious inaccuracies in the analytics.

2. **Clean the 'student characteristics' data.** The academic data showed that six students did not receive a final grade or received a 'withdraw' grade, so these were removed from the analysis.

3. **Join the datasets.** An anonymised identifier was set for each student to join the LMS log files to the characteristics and grade data.

4. **Transform and reduce the data.** For the subsequent regression process, some of the variables needed to be recoded in numerical format, for example male = 0, female = 1. The *generated variables* such as under-represented minority (URM: no = 0, yes = 1) were created at this point from other data fields. The *interaction variables* were also calculated, for example URM and male (no = 0, yes = 1). Next, the *aggregated LMS use variables* were generated for the different use categories of administration, assessment, content and engagement so that the number of logs for activities in each of these areas could be included. Finally, the data was consolidated into one record per student.

5. **Check for missing data.** Several variables were excluded from the analysis because they were missing in more than 10% of cases. For high-school grade point average (GPA), 5.63% of the variables were missing, for example. For this variable, the mean over all the cases was used to impute the missing values.

6. **Carry out final checks.** Some final checks necessary for the statistical analysis were then carried out. The values were inspected to ensure they were sufficiently dispersed and that there were no serious 'outliers'. Data visualisation software was used for this. Variables were also checked to make sure they were independent from each other, as dependent variables would skew the analysis. Any with a correlation of greater than 0.5 would have been removed from the analysis but none were found.[16]

## Conclusion

Institutions need to be able to extract and process data in as 'real-time' a way as possible[17] or they risk providing inaccurate indicators and alienating students and staff. Abelardo Pardo argues, in his interview for this book, that all educational technology products should include, by design, easy access to their data with a few clicks. Until such facilities exist, he believes, it will be difficult to convince academics to engage properly with analytics.

Pedagogical concerns are relevant here too. While it may become increasingly easy to monitor student engagement using attendance monitoring systems or clickstream data from LMSs and other systems, selecting and weighting data and relating this to learners' cognitive development is non-trivial.[18] Ethical and legal concerns are also important in relation to data preparation. If the analytics are intended to be provided anonymously, for example, small groups of students may allow individuals to be identified easily. In one German study, rules were built into the system to avoid such privacy invasions – for example, if there were fewer than five females on a course then data could not be viewed according to gender.[19]

Another issue is that the use of the LMS and other tools often varies considerably between courses and instructors, as well as between individual students. This can make it difficult to incorporate usage of particular features of the software in the analytics. Jayaprakash *et al.* tackled this issue by including a tool in their analysis if it was used by 50% or more of the students at some stage during the course.[20]

Building a predictive model across courses is further confounded by the variety in workload, assessment mechanisms and the practices of individual instructors. If, for example, the frequency of access to course materials by students is seen as an important indicator of engagement, then those students with an instructor who frequently posts materials to the LMS may be rated as more engaged than those with a teacher who rarely uploads content. This can be addressed by substituting frequencies with ratios. Thus the variable for the number of times a page is viewed by the student is replaced by the value of the number of times that student has accessed it, divided by the average number of times students in that course have accessed it.[21]

Even with expertise such as this from data scientists, the possibility remains that 'false' data will be impossible to eradicate completely. McKay suggests that data is 'culturally powerful' and that numbers in tables tend to be taken as the truth. He outlines three issues around data to be aware of when carrying out learning analytics:

- Data can be invalid: it can be corrupted if the processes of production and handling are carried out incorrectly.
- Data can be incomplete: student record systems frequently contain missing data fields.

- Data frequently fails to represent what it is supposed to represent – for example grades do not represent actual performance in a class; they represent the assessment of student performance by a particular instructor.

McKay argues that measurements are always uncertain and that ambiguity in the data will be there to a varying extent, whether we are aware of it or not. In the same way, the analysis of data always presents a variety of answers and some are more likely to be correct than others. Paying too much attention to positive or interesting results can lead to overestimation of their significance. Particularly exciting or surprising results, he suggests, are likely to be false. He recommends an approach of 'aggressive scepticism' when carrying out analytics.[22]

## References

1 Dyckhoff, A. L. *et al.*, 2012, Design and Implementation of a Learning Analytics Toolkit for Teachers, *Educational Technology and Society*, 15(3), pp. 58–76.
2 Information Commissioner's Office, 2010, *Personal Information Online Code of Practice*.
3 Sclater, N., 2014, *Learning Analytics: The Current State of Play in UK Higher and Further Education*, Jisc.
4 Newland, B. *et al.*, 2015, *Learning Analytics in UK: A HeLF Survey Report*, Heads of e-Learning Forum.
5 Guo, P., 2013, Optimal Video Length for Student Engagement, *edX Blog*, 13 November, http://blog.edx.org/optimal-video-length-student-engagement (accessed 11 October 2016).
6 Baalsrud Hauge, J. *et al.*, 2015, Learning Analytics Architecture to Scaffold Learning Experience through Technology-Based Methods, *International Journal of Serious Games*, 2(1), pp. 29–44.
7 Tabaa, Y. & Medouri, A., 2013, LASyM: A Learning Analytics System for MOOCs, *International Journal of Advanced Computer Science and Applications*, 4(5), pp. 113–119.
8 Chatti, M. A. *et al.*, 2012, A Reference Model for Learning Analytics, *International Journal of Technology Enhanced Learning*, 4(5/6), pp. 318–331.
9 Pardo, A. & Kloos, C. D., 2011, Stepping Out of the Box: Towards Analytics Outside the Learning Management System, *LAK11: Proceedings of the First International Conference on Learning Analytics and Knowledge*, pp. 163–167.
10 Chatti M. A. *et al.*, A Reference Model for Learning Analytics.
11 Pardo & Kloos, Stepping Out of the Box: Towards Analytics Outside the Learning Management System.
12 Kitto, K. *et al.*, 2015, Learning Analytics beyond the LMS: The Connected Learning Analytics Toolkit, *LAK15: Proceedings of the Fifth International Conference on Learning Analytics and Knowledge*.
13 Whitmer, J., 2012, *Logging On to Improve Achievement: Evaluating the Relationship between Use of the Learning Management System, Student Characteristics, and Academic Achievement in a Hybrid Large Enrollment Undergraduate Course*, University of California, Davis, p. 80.
14 Jayaprakash, S. M. *et al.*, 2014, Early Alert of Academically At-Risk Students: An Open Source Analytics Initiative, *Journal of Learning Analytics*, 1(1), pp. 6–47.

15 Ibid.
16 Whitmer, *Logging On to Improve Achievement*.
17 Arnold, K., 2010, Signals: Applying Academic Analytics, *EDUCAUSE Review*, 3 March, http://er.educause.edu/articles/2010/3/signals-applying-academic-ana lytics (accessed 11 October 2016).
18 Greller, W. & Drachsler, H., 2012, Translating Learning into Numbers: A Generic Framework for Learning, *Educational Technology and Society*, 15(3), pp. 42–57.
19 Dyckhoff *et al.*, Design and Implementation of a Learning Analytics Toolkit for Teachers.
20 Jayaprakash, Early Alert of Academically At-Risk Students.
21 Ibid.
22 McKay, T., 2015, An Introduction to Modern Learning Analytics, *Practical Learning Analytics* (MOOC), Coursera.

# 9   Metrics and Predictive Modelling

The numerous emerging applications of learning analytics aim to improve various aspects of educational provision. For many people and institutions, though, learning analytics is synonymous with *predictive analytics*, in particular with determining how students are likely to perform academically and whether they are at risk of failure or dropping out. These predictions can then be used to determine which students may benefit from an intervention, either automated or human mediated.

Predictions of student success depend on *metrics* derived from the data (also often referred to as *indicators*). The development of relevant and accurate metrics may require knowledge of the curriculum, pedagogy and assessment requirements, as well as the input of a data scientist who deploys statistical methods and can develop and 'train' predictive models. The models should improve as more data accumulates over time, enabling ever better predictions, but this is not an exact science: selecting the data in the first place requires human judgement, as does the development of metrics from that data. Nevertheless, statistical methods can be used to help identify the most relevant metrics for predicting student success and to build these into the models.

This chapter shows how key metrics are being derived from the data by researchers and outlines three statistical methods commonly used in learning analytics: *linear regression, logistic regression* and *naïve Bayes*.

## Developing Metrics from the Data

Metrics can measure attributes of learners themselves or aspects of the learning process. They may be computed using demographic data from the SIS or drawn from the records of learning activity in systems such as the LMS or attendance monitoring systems. Simple metrics might include the number of times students have logged into the LMS or the number of forum postings they have made. In one institution, the University of Derby, 29 metrics were developed for monitoring student engagement. These included attendance at, and interaction in, tutorials and seminars, grade profiles, performance in formative assessments, access to resources in the LMS, entry qualifications and background, outside commitments such as childcare, age group and whether the student was part time or full time.[1]

*Composite* metrics are derived from two or more variables. One example might be 'use of library', which combines figures for the number of visits a student has made to the library, the number of books the student has withdrawn and the number of online journal articles the student has accessed. Each of these may be weighted differently in the composite metric so, for example, withdrawing a book might be regarded as more significant than simply visiting the library. The weighting given may depend on the institution, the subject area and the individual course: thus library visits and book borrowing may be less relevant for computer science students than access to online journals. Meanwhile, in a course where use of the forum is regarded as essential, a metric that measures forum usage is likely to have more relevance for predicting student attainment than in one where online discussion is optional.

A composite metric that combines several metrics is likely to be created in order to decide when to intervene in some way with students. Often this simply indicates whether a student is either academically 'at risk' or 'not at risk'. In this case all the relevant data known about a particular student, including for example 'entry qualifications', 'LMS engagement' and 'use of library' may ultimately boil down to a simple binary indicator that drives the intervention.

## Developing Composite Metrics to Measure Persistence and Interaction in a MOOC

Tabaa & Medouri developed a system for analysing the big data accumulated from massive open online courses (MOOCs) to identify learners who are likely to drop out. They identified two factors that they considered important in measuring this: *persistence* and *interaction*.

The first metric, persistence, is defined as the ability of learners to maintain their concentration over time. It is calculated by measuring the proportion of materials such as slides and lecture videos that a learner has downloaded. While the researchers do not mention including how long users spend watching each video, this has been measured by others and would clearly be a way of further refining the measurement of student persistence.

Interaction is calculated based on the number of assessments and surveys that learners submit. There is an assumption that the more assessments and surveys completed, the more likely a user is to continue to the end of the course. It is also assumed that submitting *correct* assessments further encourages learners to continue.

Figures for persistence and interaction are multiplied together into a further composite binary metric they call *engagement degree*, which suggests whether a learner is 'at risk' of dropping out of the MOOC.

Unfortunately, Tabaa & Medouri offer no evaluation of how effective this metric is in predicting completion or dropout but they do suggest that the indicator could be used to help optimise learning through MOOCs and reduce the number of learners failing to complete courses.[2]

The relevance of individual metrics is clearly dependent on the educational context and varies to some extent across nations and institutions. At Purdue University the metrics are derived from data on performance, effort, prior academic history and student characteristics.[3] At New York Institute of Technology, key risk factors include grades, the major subject, students' certainty in their choice of major subject and financial data such as parental contribution to fees.[4]

## Linear Regression

When the appropriate metrics have been calculated, they form the basis for models that enable predictions to be made about student performance. One of the most commonly used methods for predictive analytics is *linear regression*. The most basic type of this, *simple regression*, shows the relationship between two variables, $x$ and $y$, where $x$, the *criterion variable*, is a value for something already known and $y$, the *predictor variable*, is a predicted value.

To illustrate this, a typical scenario in learning analytics examines whether there is a correlation between something measurable known about students and their subsequent academic success. Is there a relationship for example between the number of times a learner accesses the LMS and the result he later obtains for the course? A predictive model can be developed to show the result he is likely to obtain based on his LMS accesses. Historical data about other students is first used to 'train' the model. In Table 9.1 the total number of accesses to the course site on the LMS is shown for eight students, along with the results they obtained for the course.

This data is then plotted on the scatter chart in Figure 9.1. Each point shown represents an individual student's total number of LMS visits and the student's course result. Linear regression involves drawing a line that shows the best fit between these points, known as the *regression line*. This shows that there does indeed appear to be some relationship between these two variables.

While predictions can be made about what results students are likely to obtain based on their LMS accesses, there is, of course, a margin of error. The *error of*

*Table 9.1* Total LMS accesses for eight students and the results they obtained subsequently.

| Student | LMS accesses (x) | Result (%) (y) |
|---------|------------------|----------------|
| 1 | 27 | 70 |
| 2 | 70 | 62 |
| 3 | 36 | 51 |
| 4 | 85 | 75 |
| 5 | 17 | 53 |
| 6 | 55 | 65 |
| 7 | 12 | 48 |
| 8 | 59 | 67 |

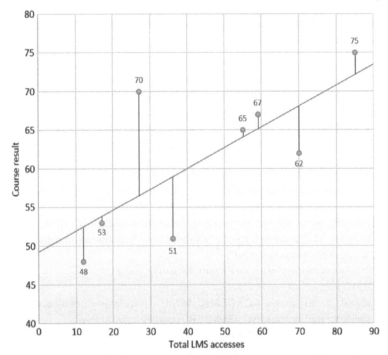

*Figure 9.1* Total LMS accesses and course results with regression line and errors of prediction.

*prediction*, as it is known, for each student is shown by the vertical lines between their point and the regression line. Student 5, for example, who accesses the LMS 17 times, is predicted to obtain a result of 54% but actually manages 53%, a 1% error of prediction. Meanwhile student 1 accesses the LMS only 27 times but achieves a result of 70%, 13% more than the predicted score. The angle of the regression line is calculated to minimise the errors of prediction over the whole dataset.

The *correlation* between the two variables over the whole dataset is computed as 0.72, quite a high value. Sometimes it is possible to improve the predictions by incorporating further indicators. Thus if we know the results a student obtained at school, prior to joining university, we may be able to refine the model. When we use two or more criterion variables this is known as *multiple regression* rather than simple regression.

## Logistic Regression

If the aim is to calculate the probability of a binary value, e.g. determining if the student is academically at risk or not at risk, then *logistic* rather than linear regression can be applied. As with linear regression, logistic regression can be computed either using one variable (simple logistic regression) or several (multiple logistic regression).

## Developing a Predictive Model for Academic Risk at Marist College

Jayaprakash and his colleagues at Marist College deployed logistic regression to calculate whether students were either academically 'in good standing' or 'at risk'. They compared the resulting predictions with those produced from three other methods and found that logistic regression appeared to be the best, more accurately predicting whether a student was at risk than the others.[5]

The predictive model itself is encoded in an XML-based language known as the Predictive Model Markup Language (PMML). A relatively human-readable, edited excerpt from the code[6] is included below in order to show what a predictive model looks like:

```
<GeneralRegressionModel targetVariableName="ACADEMIC_RISK"
modelType="multinomialLogistic" modelName="multinomialLogistic"
functionName="classification">
  <Extension name="numberParameters" value="21"/>
  <MiningSchema>
    <MiningField name="ACADEMIC_RISK" usageType="predicted"/>
    <MiningField name="RC_GENDER" usageType="active"
      importance="0.00621066"/>
    <MiningField name="RC_FTPT" usageType="active" importance=
      "0.00221888"/>
    <MiningField name="RC_CLASS" usageType="active" importance="0"/>
    <MiningField name="ACADEMIC_STANDING" usageType="active"
      importance="0.236203"/>
    <MiningField name="ENROLLMENT" usageType="active" importance=
      "0.00420522"/>
    <MiningField name="SAT_VERBAL_SCORE" usageType="active"
      importance="0"/>
    <MiningField name="SAT_MATH_SCORE" usageType="active"
      importance="0"/>
    <MiningField name="APTITUDE_SCORE" usageType="active"
      importance="0.0127897"/>
    <MiningField name="AGE" usageType="active" importance=
      "0.00380369"/>
    <MiningField name="CUM_GPA" usageType="active" importance=
      "0.392901"/>
    <MiningField name="RMN_SCORE_PARTIAL" usageType="active"
      importance="0.311152"/>
    <MiningField name="R_CONTENT_READ" usageType="active"
      importance="0.0120979"/>
    <MiningField name="R_SESSIONS" usageType="active" importance=
      "0.018418"/>
  </MiningSchema>
```

This is the key part of the model that clearly shows the relative importance of the different metrics in predicting the 'academic risk' variable. It can be seen that the two most significant metrics here are CUM_GPA – the cumulative grade point average achieved by the student in high school – and RMN_SCORE_PARTIAL, which is a measure for the proportion of the final marks the student has achieved to date. Also of considerable importance is ACADEMIC_STANDING, the student's current academic standing. Meanwhile some other metrics are found to be relatively unimportant – or even completely irrelevant – such as SAT_MATH_SCORE.

## Naïve Bayes

Another statistical method used for predicting student performance in learning analytics is *naïve Bayes*, based on the theorem of Thomas Bayes, the eighteenth-century English statistician.[7]

In Figure 9.2, the example of LMS accesses plotted against subsequent performance for the course now shows 30 students. Those students with 30 LMS accesses or fewer are considered to be academically at risk – there is a high chance of them obtaining less than 50% for their course. They are represented by the darker points on the chart. In Figure 9.3 a further student's data is added, but it is not immediately clear if this student is at risk or not. Drawing a circle around the point shows that there are more at-risk students close to this student than students not at risk. Naïve Bayes therefore classifies the student as at risk.

The 'naïve' part of naïve Bayes is that the method assumes that there is no dependence between the variables. As with regression, naïve Bayes can use multiple criterion variables, so predictions may improve as more metrics are included. One study showed that standardised test (SAT) scores are mildly predictive of student success. Adding LMS logins to the analysis however dramatically improved the predictions – by a factor of three. The data also suggested that students who entered with low SAT scores could

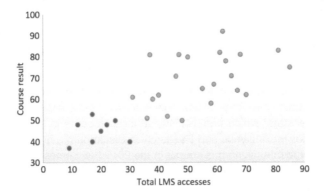

*Figure 9.2* Total LMS accesses and course results for 30 students.

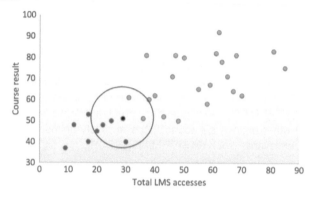

*Figure 9.3* A new student is added and classified as at risk.

achieve better results through greater effort, measured by the number of logins.[8]

Naïve Bayes is known to be more effective at classifying items as described above than in providing fine-grained predictions.[9] It is, however, considered to be particularly useful when the dimensions of the inputs vary considerably.[10]

The charts shown above have been included here to explain how the regression and naïve Bayes statistical methods can be used for classification and prediction. Such visualisations may be useful for statisticians and researchers but the mathematical formulae behind these methods are incorporated within the predictive analytics software deployed: end users may never see this type of chart. Alerts and lists of at-risk students may be more useful, however there is a growing range of visualisations aimed at faculty and students too, as discussed in Chapter 10.

As mentioned above, Jayaprakash and his colleagues discovered that the three most significant metrics for predicting student success were marks on the course so far, grade point average and current academic standing. Researchers in other institutions have identified partial contributions to the final grade of the course to be key. The relative importance of the different metrics may vary considerably depending on the institutional context and the learning design of the course.

### Fine-Grained Analysis of Student and Activity Data at California State University, Chico

John Whitmer analysed an 'Introduction to Comparative Religion' course at California State University, Chico. This is a mid-sized campus in the northwest of the state, which had 14,640 full-time students in 2010. Whitmer, now Director for Analytics and Research at Blackboard, analysed the data of the 73 students taking this course in the 2010 Fall Semester. The course had recently been redesigned to integrate much deeper use of learning technology.

Whitmer believed that existing learning analytics initiatives tended to ignore most of the data in the LMS and there was minimal justification for why some variables were included and not others. He wanted to find answers to the following questions:

- Is the frequency of use of the LMS related to academic achievement?
- How relevant in this are the pedagogical functions of the LMS – for example, do tools that promote engagement such as forums have more impact than administrative tools such as the calendar?
- Is LMS use a better predictor of success than demographic and other personal data?
- Are students deemed to be academically at risk (due, for example, to ethnicity or socio-economic group) impacted by LMS use differently from those considered not to be at risk?

Whitmer notes other studies, such as those by Arnold[11] and Macfadyen & Dawson,[12] where alerts were triggered if a student had a low level of LMS use, but says that the pedagogical features deployed are largely ignored by these researchers. He groups LMS use measures into broader categories – for instance, posting to a discussion becomes an *engagement* activity. He then looks for examples of whether students who are more engaged in this way are more successful academically.

Whitmer also looked at nine student characteristic variables:

- gender;
- whether the student's racial/ethnic group is under-represented in higher education;
- income status (based on whether the student qualifies for federal financial assistance);
- high-school grade-point average;
- first in family to attend college;
- university college in which the students have their major;
- enrolment status – for example, first year, continuing student, transfer from another university;
- whether the student is both from an under-represented racial/ethnic group *and* has low income;
- whether the student is both from an under-represented racial/ethnic group *and* is male.

Other variables that measure student motivation or learning styles for example could increase the accuracy of the predictions. Meanwhile, the *quality* of student interactions such as a thoughtful posting to a forum is not analysed but could further refine the model. He points out that earlier studies consistently found that combinations of student characteristics correlated much better with student success than single demographic variables. In other words, if the student's ethnicity/race, income level and gender are used, the predictions should be considerably more accurate than simply using one of these variables. The researchers found that variables relating to the student's current studies, such as financial aid status and current grade point average, are stronger in predicting success than the student's historical data.

*Table 9.2* Predictive value of demographic/educational variables.[13]

| Variable | % Var. |
| --- | --- |
| HS GPA | 9 |
| URM and Pell-eligibility interaction | 7 |
| Under-represented minority | 4 |
| Enrolment status | 3 |
| URM and gender interaction | 2 |
| Pell eligible | 2 |
| First in family to attend college | 1 |
| *Mean value all significant variables* | 4 |

**Not statistically significant**

Gender

Major-college

Whitmer gathered data from the LMS and the SIS and transferred it to a data warehouse, going through various processes to transform and clean it, as discussed in Chapter 8. Seven of the nine student characteristic variables were found to be statistically significant. The LMS variable correlations however were more significant. In other words LMS use is a better predictor of student success than the demographic and enrolment data traditionally used to identify at-risk students. It was also found that use of individual tools varied widely between students but that there was less dispersed use within the categories that had been defined – administration, assessment, content and engagement. Whitmer recommends, therefore, that predictive analytics should not be performed at the level of individual tools.

From Table 9.3 it can be seen that Total Hits are the strongest predictor of student success, with Assessment Activity Hits coming a close second. In his conclusions, Whitmer suggests that using total LMS hits would be an excellent starting point for predictive modelling and early warning systems.

He was surprised that Engagement Activity Hits came below LMS Content Activity Hits but suggested that this was because much of the content was only available through the LMS rather than through lectures, so it was essential to use this feature. Administrative Activity Hits have the lowest correlation coefficient, which, he points out, is not surprising as viewing your calendar, for example, is likely to have less impact on achievement than submitting an assessment.

*Table 9.3* Correlation results of LMS use with course grade.

| LMS Use Variables (ordered by r values) | r | % Variance | Sign. |
|---|---|---|---|
| Total hits | 0.48 | 23 | 0.000 |
| Assessment activity hits | 0.47 | 21 | 0.000 |
| LMS content activity hits | 0.41 | 17 | 0.000 |
| Engagement activity hits | 0.40 | 16 | 0.000 |
| Administrative activity hits | 0.35 | 12 | 0.000 |
| *Mean value all significant variables* | | *18* | |

A multivariate regression was carried out using all the above variables except Total Hits. It was found that these explained 25% of the variation in final grade. Including all the student characteristic variables in the analysis added another 10% to the predictive relationship with course grade.

Whitmer considers that this work is relevant for those responsible for implementing technology in universities because it analyses an assumption behind their work: that increased use of technology in learning enhances academic achievement. Overall he made the expected finding that use of the LMS is related to student achievement. What his research does do though is to *quantify* the difference the various types of LMS usage can make and therefore enable instructors to monitor the efforts on their students and have at-risk students flagged to them. He found that LMS variables were more than four times as strongly related to achievement as demographic ones. This suggests that what students do on a course is more important than their background or previous results.[14]

## Conclusion

The term 'predictive analytics' has been questioned by Tim McKay, who notes that you can 'only predict the future if nothing in the system changes. But changing the system to improve outcomes is the whole goal of learning analytics. When we study the past, we do so not to predict the future, but to change it.'[15] The predictive models may thus be inherently unstable. As soon as interventions are taken with students on the basis of the predictions, these may alter student behaviour and performance. Refining a model based on the latest data will need to take into account the impact of the interventions as well.

The accuracy of the models has been tested in various studies, such as at the New York Institute of Technology, where recall of their model was found to be 74%. Although many institutions have developed their own specific models rather than adopting those developed elsewhere, a key finding of the Open Academic Analytics Initiative led by Marist College is that the predictive models developed at one institution can be transferred to very different institutions while retaining most of their predictive abilities.[16] The development of transferable models and their continual refinement at individual institutions and for specific courses, will be key to the uptake of predictive analytics in education.

## References

1  Sclater, N., 2014, *Learning Analytics: The Current State of Play in UK Higher and Further Education*, Jisc, p. 23.
2  Tabaa, Y. & Medouri, A., 2013, LASyM: A Learning Analytics System for MOOCs, *International Journal of Advanced Computer Science and Applications*, 4(5), pp. 113–119.
3  Arnold, K. E. & Pistilli, M. D., 2012, Course Signals at Purdue: Using Learning Analytics to Increase Student Success, *LAK12: Proceedings of the Second International Learning Analytics and Knowledge Conference*, pp. 267–268.
4  Agnihotri, L. & Ott, A., 2014, Building a Student At-Risk Model: An End-to-End Perspective, *Proceedings of the Seventh International Conference on Educational Data Mining*.
5  Jayaprakash, S. M. *et al.*, 2014, Early Alert of Academically At-Risk Students: An Open Source Analytics Initiative, *Journal of Learning Analytics*, 1(1), pp. 6–47.
6  See   https://confluence.sakaiproject.org/download/attachments/75671025/Marist_OAAI_Logistic_PMML.xml?version=1&modificationDate=1396470152000&api=v2 (accessed 1 October 2016).
7  Bellhouse, D. R., 2004, The Reverend Thomas Bayes, FRS: A Biography to Celebrate the Tercentenary of His Birth, *Statistical Science*, 19(1), pp. 3–43.
8  Dawson, S. & Macfadyen, L. P., 2010, Mining LMS Data to Develop an 'Early Warning System' for Educators: A Proof of Concept, *Computers and Education*, 54(2), pp. 588–599.
9  Skicit Learn: http://scikit-learn.org/stable/modules/naive_bayes.html (accessed 1 October 2016).
10  Dell, 2015, Naive Bayes Classifier, *Statistics – Textbook*, 5 August, http://documents.software.dell.com/Statistics/Textbook/naive-bayes-classifier (accessed 1 October 2016).
11  Arnold, K., 2010, Signals: Applying Academic Analytics, *EDUCAUSE Review*, 3 March,   http://er.educause.edu/articles/2010/3/signals-applying-academic-analytics (accessed 11 October 2016).
12  Macfadyen, L. P. & Dawson, S., 2012, Numbers are Not Enough: Why E-Learning Analytics Failed to Inform an Institutional Strategic Plan, *Educational Technology and Society*, 15(3), pp. 149–163.
13  Whitmer, J., 2015, Using Learning Analytics to Assess Innovation and Improve Student Achievement, *Jisc UK Learning Analytics Network Event*, 5 March, p. 16.
14  Whitmer, J., 2012, *Logging On to Improve Achievement: Evaluating the Relationship between Use of the Learning Management System, Student Characteristics, and Academic Achievement in a Hybrid Large Enrollment Undergraduate Course*, University of California, Davis, p. 90.
15  McKay, T., 2015, An Introduction to Modern Learning Analytics, *Practical Learning Analytics MOOC*, Coursera/University of Michigan.
16  Jayaprakash *et al.*, Early Alert of Academically At-Risk Students: An Open Source Analytics Initiative.

# 10  Visualisation

It is difficult to extract meaning from raw data and metrics without being able to visualise them in the form of tables, graphs and other graphical representations. If presented cleverly, visualisations can grab our attention[1] and unlock the information, making it compelling and accessible[2] and providing the motivation for interventions and changes to behaviour.

There are many aspects of a learning experience that are invisible to students and instructors. In other aspects of our lives we use indicators such as weather forecasts and the battery level of a mobile phone to guide us and prompt us to take early interventions.[3] Visualisations of aspects of the learning process can show trends over time and allow comparisons between individuals or between an individual and a group. A quick visual overview can enable the identification of outliers, typically students who are at risk of dropping out or who need additional assistance in an aspect of their learning. Visualisations are also available that highlight a part of the online course content, which students have spent an unusually long time accessing, suggesting that they may be finding the topic difficult or that the materials could be improved.

## Dashboards

The provision of a list of students in a tabular format can give an overview of the learners an instructor is responsible for, with visual indicators that immediately draw attention to those students who may need assistance. Figure 10.1 shows a tutor dashboard, enabling alphabetical browsing, viewing by group or searching for an individual student, highlighting those predicted to be at risk of failure or attrition. The traffic signals pioneered by Course Signals at Purdue to show risk have been widely adopted in other systems.[4] In the dashboard in Figure 10.1 there are four levels of engagement: high, good, satisfactory and low, represented by 'traffic lights'. They are calculated from multiple sources, including the LMS, library data and access to buildings. Many systems provide similar ways for tutors or instructors to visualise this risk.

Some dashboards break down the indicators into further categories. Figure 10.2 provides details for the *time spent on the course*, together with an assessment of *academic risk*, calculated on the grades achieved to date, *social risk*, based on

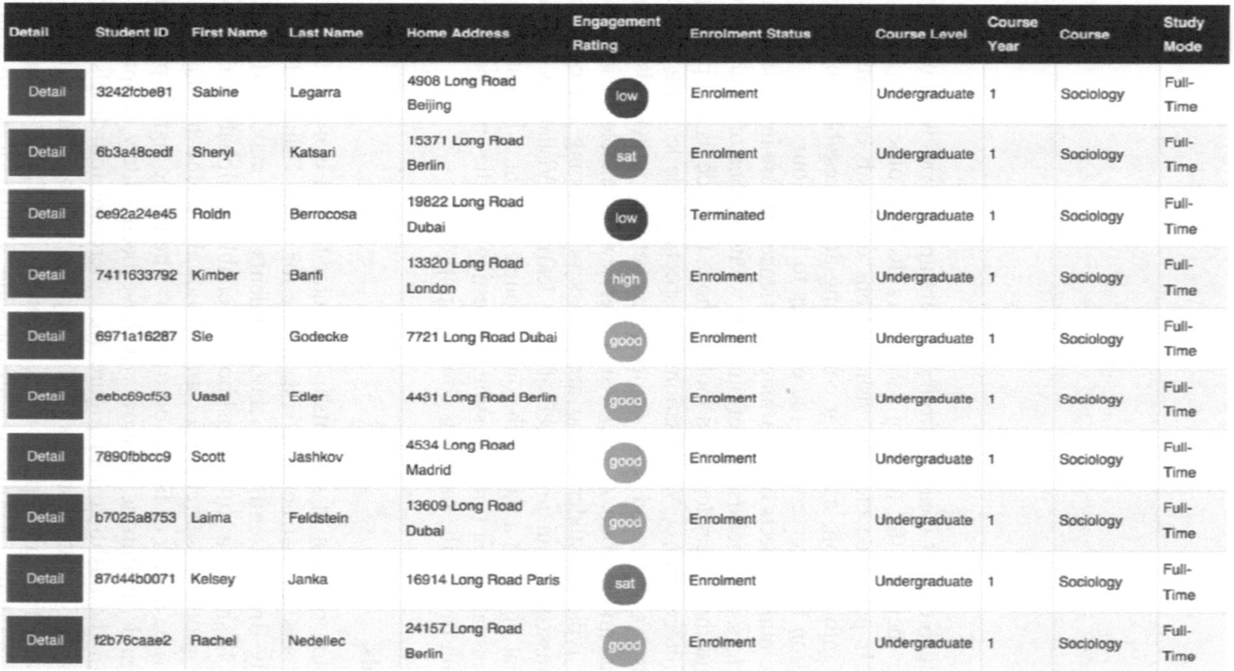

| Detail | Student ID | First Name | Last Name | Home Address | Engagement Rating | Enrolment Status | Course Level | Course Year | Course | Study Mode |
|---|---|---|---|---|---|---|---|---|---|---|
| Detail | 3242fcbe81 | Sabine | Legarra | 4908 Long Road Beijing | low | Enrolment | Undergraduate | 1 | Sociology | Full-Time |
| Detail | 6b3a48cedf | Sheryl | Katsari | 15371 Long Road Berlin | sat | Enrolment | Undergraduate | 1 | Sociology | Full-Time |
| Detail | ce92a24e45 | Roldn | Berrocosa | 19822 Long Road Dubai | low | Terminated | Undergraduate | 1 | Sociology | Full-Time |
| Detail | 7411633792 | Kimber | Banfi | 13320 Long Road London | high | Enrolment | Undergraduate | 1 | Sociology | Full-Time |
| Detail | 6971a16287 | Sie | Godecke | 7721 Long Road Dubai | good | Enrolment | Undergraduate | 1 | Sociology | Full-Time |
| Detail | eebc69cf53 | Uasal | Edler | 4431 Long Road Berlin | good | Enrolment | Undergraduate | 1 | Sociology | Full-Time |
| Detail | 7890fbbcc9 | Scott | Jashkov | 4534 Long Road Madrid | good | Enrolment | Undergraduate | 1 | Sociology | Full-Time |
| Detail | b7025a8f753 | Laima | Feldstein | 13609 Long Road Dubai | good | Enrolment | Undergraduate | 1 | Sociology | Full-Time |
| Detail | 87d44b0071 | Kelsey | Janka | 16914 Long Road Paris | sat | Enrolment | Undergraduate | 1 | Sociology | Full-Time |
| Detail | f2b76caae2 | Rachel | Nedellec | 24157 Long Road Berlin | good | Enrolment | Undergraduate | 1 | Sociology | Full-Time |

*Figure 10.1* A tutor view from DTP Solutionpath.
Image courtesy of Solutionpath Ltd

## Risk Metrics ⍰

| Surname | Given Name | Time spent in course (HH:MM) | Academic risk | Social risk | Total risk ▸ |
|---|---|---|---|---|---|
| Bailey | Anna | - | - | - | High 100% |
| Kim | Jonathan | 00:47 | High 30.2% | High 27.9% | High 58.1% |
| Duncan | Bryan | 06:38 | Medium 12.9% | High 26.8% | High 39.8% |
| Stevenson | Charlie | 04:51 | High 17.2% | Low 0.6% | Low 17.8% |
| Snyder | Theresa | 08:41 | Low 9% | Low 4.2% | Low 13.2% |
| Singh | Beth | 09:03 | Low 8.4% | Low 3.8% | Low 12.2% |
| Guzman | Marvin | 17:16 | Low 0.9% | Low 0.7% | Low 1.6% |
| Payne | Shawn | 18:00 | Low 0.6% | Low 0% | Low 0.7% |
| Figueroa | Jeanne | 18:12 | Low 0.6% | Low 0% | Low 0.6% |
| Pearson | Debbie | 24:33 | Low 0% | Low 0% | Low 0% |

Show 10 ⥮

Close table

*Figure 10.2* Risk metrics – X-Ray Analytics.
Image is the property of Blackboard and has been used with the permission of Blackboard

connections with other learners in the discussion forum, and *total risk*, a composite of the three metrics. This can help tutors to understand whether effort, academic or social factors are causes for concern. However, there is a continual trade-off in visualisations between the display of aggregated and granular data.[5] One design principle embodied in many systems is to provide an overview at first and enable drilling down to lower-level data by clicking.

Dashboards may explicitly flag high-risk students, showing at a glance what their problem might be. In Figure 10.3 it can be seen instantly that eight out of 40 students are deemed to be high risk, two of these with 0% likelihood of passing.

The circle visualisation at the top of the dashboard gives an immediate feel for the proportion of students at each colour-coded level of engagement. Thus, high levels of red indicate to the tutor that the cohort is struggling. Ballard points out two possible drawbacks of using colours in this way: that colours can be emotive and that accessibility can be an issue.[6] Red, of course, strongly equates to danger, potentially negatively affecting an instructor's view of the student. Meanwhile green may give a false sense of security, meaning their attention is always drawn to those in the red category, at the expense of others who may need assistance. Colour blindness can of course be addressed by including the words in the visual representation, as has been done in the more detailed breakdown beside the circle in Figure 10.3.

## Other Cohort Overview Visualisations

Dashboards and traffic lights may be effective in alerting instructors to at-risk students. Other techniques may prove more effective at providing overviews of a class or range of students. One of these is the scatterplot (see Figure 10.4) which, especially in a large cohort, may help to identify 'outliers'. The dots represent individual students and provide an immediate overview of the cohort's scores to date and LMS accesses. Student 1, in this example, appears to be at risk, while student 2 seems to be working hard but not reaping the benefits, so may also need assistance. In some systems clicking on a dot will bring up further details on an individual student, helping the instructor to decide what kind of intervention is required.

Courses where there is an expectation on students to interact in discussion forums may also benefit from social network analysis visualisations, enabling the identification of socially isolated or less engaged learners. In Figure 10.5 the lines represent interactions between learners. The level of connectedness between individuals is represented by the thickness of the lines: Jonathan and Debbie here have a higher level of interaction than any of the other participants. Users highlighted in red, such as Jerome and John, are disconnected from the others. Seeing this might prompt the instructor to suggest that they engage more in the forums. An automated process for this, where a student is prompted electronically, can also be envisaged.

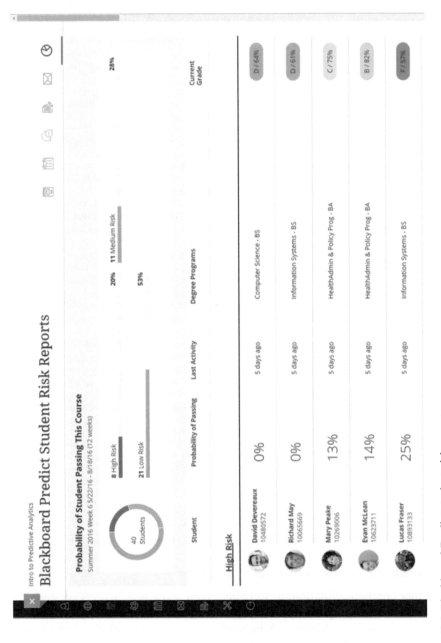

*Figure 10.3* Blackboard Predict student risk reports.
Image is the property of Blackboard and has been used with the permission of Blackboard

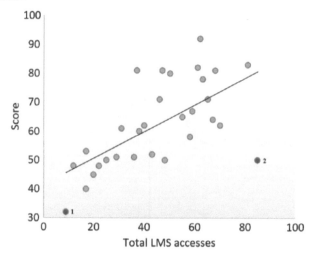

*Figure 10.4* Scatterplot, showing the correlation between LMS accesses and score achieved.

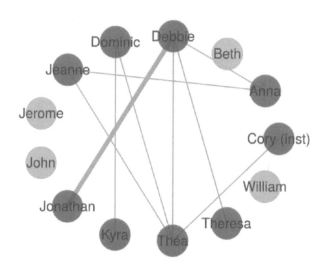

*Figure 10.5* Interaction analysis – X-Ray Learning Analytics.
Image is the property of Blackboard and has been used with the permission of Blackboard

## Representing Trends and Changes over Time

Another common visualisation technique is to show how aspects of student performance or engagement have changed over time. In Figure 10.6, a student's engagement score is shown week by week, in comparison with the class mean. From the graph it appears that this student's engagement is a serious cause for concern. The expertise of a tutor may help to ascertain if this is actually the case.

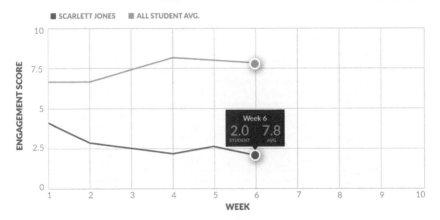

*Figure 10.6* Student engagement over time compared with the cohort average – Civitas Learning.
Source: Civitas Learning, Inc

A student's workload is not necessarily evenly distributed during a term or semester and does not have to correspond to that of her peers. She might be concentrating on one course at the expense of another but be perfectly capable of catching up later. In Figure 10.7, a student's cumulative engagement score on a course is shown in comparison with the group, demonstrating that overall she has engaged less than the mean; however, most recently she has been catching up with the rest of the group in overall engagement. In addition the traffic signal shows that the individual's current rating is high and that it has gone up since the previous week – a simple visual means of showing that the situation is improving. Meanwhile, the vertical lines on the graph show when a student was subject to different interventions. These lines can be clicked to show details of the interventions that took place.

Plots of activity in various dimensions can show which areas might require more effort from the student. In Figure 10.8, the student is shown three different projections of their final grade for a. if they get maximum scores, b. if they stay at the same pace and c. if they do nothing.

Instructors may be interested primarily in student engagement with their course but other staff (and the students themselves) may wish to visualise activity across a range of courses. Figure 10.9 shows a student's weekly performance and grades across four courses. Three metrics are shown: days attended, posts and assessments. Again, colour is used to highlight areas of concern. At a glance, an instructor can see whether there are issues in other courses – or across them all.

The various overviews available help to overcome the 'blind driving' experienced by students and instructors[7] where learning takes place in relative ignorance of how students are progressing in comparison with others and with what might be expected of them. However, while many of the graphics are visually appealing,

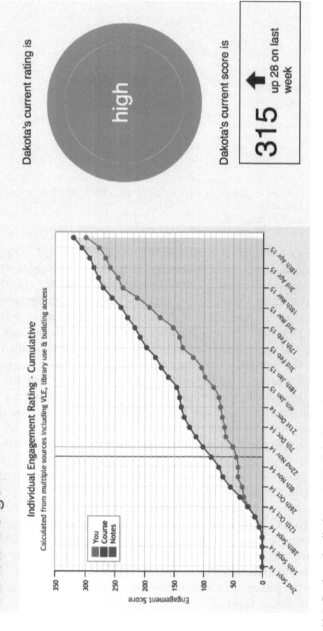

*Figure 10.7* Student detail view – DTP Solutionpath.
Image courtesy of Solutionpath Ltd

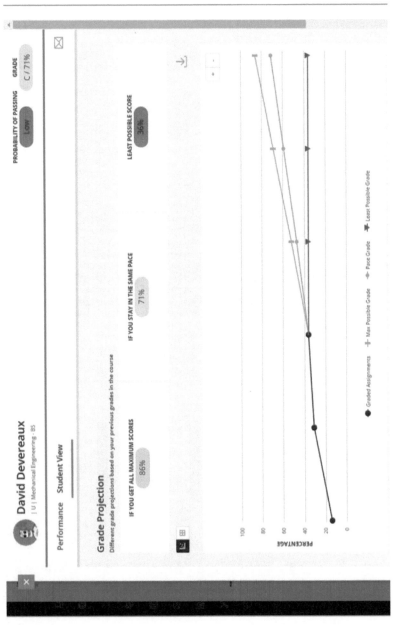

*Figure 10.8* Student's activity compared to others – Blackboard Learn.
Image is the property of Blackboard and has been used with the permission of Blackboard

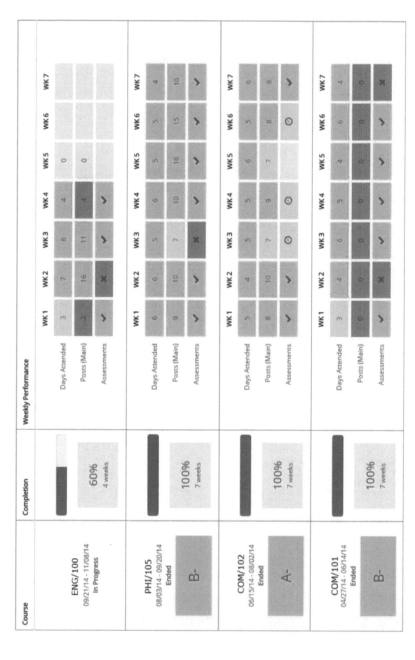

*Figure 10.9* Instructor's view of student performance history – Blackboard Blue Canary. Image is the property of Blackboard and has been used with the permission of Blackboard

it is important not to be taken in by the 'wow' factor and to have goals in mind when examining the information and actions that can be taken subsequently.[8]

Ritsos & Roberts report that most learning analytics tools focus on dashboards, resulting in environments that enable little interaction and consist of traditional representations such as bar charts, line graphs and scatterplots. They believe that better visualisation could transform learning analytics, providing insights into how learning could be improved and prompting more informed interventions.[9] Effective visual representations can enable a more intuitive interpretation of data, sometimes bringing to the fore aspects that would otherwise be hidden.[10]

Ballard provides a number of guidelines for building visualisations for predictive analytics in particular:

- visualisations should be simple to interpret;
- adapt content to the user;
- indicate how prediction is built up;
- bridge the gap between predictive and historic data;
- enable users to respond and take action;
- allow users to monitor the effectiveness of their actions.[11]

### Designing Visualisations for Medical Students at the University of Wollongong

Olmos & Corrin discuss how visualisations were developed for medical students to assess their interactions with patients. The students are required to keep records of their clinical experiences throughout their studies. They enter details of each consultation with a patient in a web-based clinical log and are encouraged to reflect on their learning needs related to each experience. The software enables them to check that they are meeting assessment requirements, while use of the log itself is assessed formally.

Challenges of designing the visualisations included:

- being able to show important contextual information without crowding out critical details;
- showing multiple levels of abstraction in the dataset – for example patient, student, town or region – 'Should data be somehow aggregated and summarised per town or region, or should the raw data be displayed with some grouping?';
- reliability of students in logging each interaction, particularly as they are not permitted to log any identifiable information on patients, thus potentially leading to confusion between patients.

Despite the concerns about reliability, the researchers note that perfect datasets are rarely available and visualising the data that exists can highlight its inadequacies, thus leading to the better collection of data in the future.

They also suggest that is it important to understand both the questions to be answered by the visualisations and the data available. Starting with the questions is necessary in order not to be limited by the available data. That can then prompt the collection of appropriate data. Conversely, focussing on the data may provide answers to questions that are irrelevant.

Another issue is an economic one: whether to provide a standard type of chart, which may not be ideal, or to develop a more expensive but better visualisation. They suggest that standard chart types can be used in most situations, sometimes 'stretching' them to suit the required purpose without the need for programming.[12]

## Conclusion

While analytics functionality in most LMSs has only been present for a few years, some commentators have pointed out that this tends to focus on visualising student performance in dashboards, *after the event*, rather than looking at the learning process itself.[13] Dragan Gašević suggests that part of the problem is that logging systems have been set up to capture clickstream data in order to test the software and are not built to capture meaningful learning events.[14] Meanwhile the visualisations may give indications of student engagement but do not necessarily provide an accurate view of the learner's understanding.[15]

There are many learning resources available to learners and much information is directed to them, their faculty and other stakeholders by the institution. Learning analytics tools, dashboards and apps, if not introduced carefully, may simply add to the information overload.[16] Greller & Drachsler express concern, too, about the possibility of users being deluded by enticing visualisations, potentially influencing instructors regarding their pedagogical assessment of a student's performance and hence their grading.[17] This is, of course, assuming that assessment processes do not start taking into account learning analytics data. Jisc's Code of Practice suggests that learning analytics 'is distinct from assessment and should be used for formative rather than summative purposes'.[18] However if participation in a forum, for example, is an assessment requirement, then a visualisation showing engagement levels of individual students in online discussions may serve for learning analytics purposes and also provide a mechanism for grading.

Another important issue is that, despite the allure of visualisations, a level of data literacy is required to interpret them and this cannot be assumed in students, staff or faculty.[19] In Chapter 23 Leah Macfadyen discusses her experiences of working with faculty on learning analytics in the Faculty of Arts at the University of British Columbia. Despite putting considerable effort into creating visual reports, she finds that many faculty members do not have the data skills to interpret them.[20]

Interpreting visualisations also requires knowing the pedagogical context, the learning design and the goals of the teacher.[21] Thus, there may be little point in analysing student interactions with each other if there are no learning activities built into the course to engage in that way, or the instructor sets no expectation that learners should use the forum.

In summary, there is a growing range of useful visualisations available. They can highlight issues in ways that are otherwise difficult or impossible and are potentially transformative in educators' and students' understanding. No doubt many new types of graphical representation will emerge: one possibility is using animations to show how engagement changes over time. Learning analytics has much to learn, too, from the field of information visualisation and there is potential to bring the two fields closer together.[22] It the meantime there are dangers that visualisations entice users, that they are based on inadequate data and that users do not have the levels of data literacy required to interpret them properly. However, the greater adoption of learning analytics and continual innovation by researchers and vendors, is set to result in an increasingly rich and meaningful set of visualisations, which will help understand and drive changes to processes and practices at all levels of education.

## References

1 Duval, E., 2011, Attention Please! Learning Analytics for Visualization and Recommendation, *LAK11: Proceedings of the First International Conference on Learning Analytics and Knowledge*, ACM.

2 Brown, M., 2012, *Learning Analytics: Moving from Concept to Practice*, EDU-CAUSE Learning Initiative.

3 Pardo, A. & Dawson, S., 2016, Learning Analytics: How Can Data be Used to Improve Learning Practice? In: Reimann, P. *et al.*, eds, *Measuring and Visualizing Learning in the Information-Rich Classroom*, Routledge, pp. 41–55.

4 Arnold, K. E. & Pistilli, M. D., 2012, Course Signals at Purdue: Using Learning Analytics to Increase Student Success, *LAK12: Proceedings of the Second International Learning Analytics and Knowledge Conference*, ACM.

5 Ballard, C., 2013, July 9, *Data Visualisation with Predictive Learning Analytics*, p. 13, www.slideshare.net/ChrisBallard/data-visualisation-with-predictive-learning-analytics (accessed 1 October 2016).

6 Ibid.

7 Duval, Attention Please! Learning Analytics for Visualization and Recommendation, p. 13.

8 Ibid., p. 11.

9 Ritsos, P. D. & Roberts, J. C., 2014, Towards More Visual Analytics in Learning Analytics, *EuroVis Workshop on Visual Analytics*, Eurographics: European Association for Computer Graphics, p. 4.

10 Papamitsiou, Z. & Economides, A. A., 2015, Temporal Learning Analytics Visualizations for Increasing Awareness during Assessment, *RUSC Universities and Knowledge Society Journal*, 12(3), pp. 129–147.

11 Ballard, *Data Visualisation with Predictive Learning Analytics*, p. 17.

12 Olmos, M. M. & Corrin, L., 2012, Learning Analytics: A Case Study of the Process of Design of Visualizations, *Journal of Asynchronous Learning Networks*, 16(3), pp. 39–49.

13 Ritsos & Roberts, Towards more Visual Analytics in Learning Analytics, p. 1.

14 Gašević, D., 2016, February 9, Future of Learning Analytics (N. Sclater, interviewer).

15 Pardo & Dawson, Learning Analytics: How Can Data be Used to Improve Learning Practice? p. 46.

16 Duval, Attention Please! Learning Analytics for Visualization and Recommendation, p. 1.

17 Greller, W. & Drachsler, H., 2012, Translating Learning into Numbers: A Generic Framework for Learning, *Educational Technology and Society*, 15(3), pp. 42–57.

18 Sclater, N. & Bailey, P., 2015, *Code of Practice for Learning Analytics*, Jisc.

19 Lockyer, L. *et al.*, 2013, Informing Pedagogical Action: Aligning Learning Analytics with Learning Design, *American Behavioral Scientist*, 57(10), pp. 1439–1459.

20 Macfadyen, L., 2016, February 10, Future of Learning Analytics (N. Sclater, interviewer).

21 Lockyer *et al.*, Informing Pedagogical Action: Aligning Learning Analytics with Learning Design.

22 Dawson, S., 2016, February 11, Future of Learning Analytics (N. Sclater, interviewer).

# 11  Intervention

Intervention in educational processes on the basis of analytics can take numerous forms. It can be at a high level, altering the structure of a degree by, for example, removing an unpopular or outdated course. It could result in changes to the curriculum, either during the course or after it is complete, as discussed in Chapter 6. Providing automated visualisations of students' progress to them directly through dashboards and apps is also, arguably, a form of intervention (see Chapter 12). Then there are interventions taken by educators with students. These categories are not mutually exclusive but this chapter is largely concerned with the logistics of human-mediated interventions taken directly with learners while courses are under way.

There is relatively little coverage in the literature regarding how educators can take effective interventions with learners while they are studying on the basis of learning analytics.[1] Yet this is a vital part of the process, which uses what has become known as 'actionable intelligence', to prompt actions that are intended to have a beneficial impact on learners.[2]

## Feedback

Unlike learning analytics interventions, the role of feedback in the learning process and how it can benefit learners, is already widely researched. Feedback enables students to see how far they are from what is expected of them, or from what they expect of themselves. Positive feedback on performance can reinforce existing behaviours whereas negative feedback may encourage students to do something differently. Feedback can also be categorised as *motivational* or *informative*. Motivational feedback may involve comments such as 'well done'. Informative feedback, however, gives learners more information on their progress and how it compares to where they were previously or to others in the class.[3]

Nicol & McFarlane-Dick suggest that good feedback practice:

- helps clarify what good performance is (goals, criteria, expected standards);
- facilitates the development of self-assessment (reflection) in learning;

- delivers high-quality information to students about their learning;
- encourages teacher and peer dialogue around learning;
- encourages positive motivational beliefs and self-esteem;
- provides opportunities to close the gap between current and desired performance;
- provides information to teachers that can be used to help shape the teaching.[4]

Interventions that provide feedback to students can be targeted at an individual student, a group of students or a whole class.[5] They can be automated (e.g. an email, a text message or a traffic light on the student's home page) or human mediated (e.g. an email, text message or phone call from a tutor, perhaps to arrange a face-to-face meeting).

Providing feedback to students is, of course, a key part of education and is nothing new. Traditionally, intervening might rely on the teacher noticing some unexpected or adverse aspect of learning behaviour. This is facilitated in the face-to-face environment by visual clues.[6] With greater class sizes and more online learning such signs are difficult to pick up. Learning analytics can, however, help tutors to know *when* to intervene. In addition the systems may provide guidance or suggested individualised text for messages to send to students. Thus the process may be automated to some extent but can enable an educator, who may know the individual learner's circumstances, to customise the intervention.

## Triggers

Triggers for an intervention are likely to be based on the metrics, which may, for example, identify a student who has just become at risk. In one institution, the University of New England, the triggers in some courses were:

- No access to the LMS and learning materials for more than seven days in the first two weeks of the trimester.
- With early assessment tasks reminders had to be sent prior to the due date and either poor results were obtained or the task was not completed.
- With major assessment tasks there was limited or no access of assessment information for over seven days prior to the due date.[7]

The literature on the different types of triggers deployed at institutions to date is limited. Triggers may vary considerably across institutions and will be dependent on their overall approach to learning analytics, as well as the learning design of individual courses. Non-submission of an early assessment may be a valid trigger for intervention but only, of course, if such an assessment is in place in the first place.

**Providing Analytics to Tutors at the Open University**

At the Open University in the UK, a pilot study to put predictive analytics in the hands of tutors took place with around 100 students. Five tutors were provided with weekly reports. Combining this information with their knowledge of the student, they took the decision whether to intervene. The study found that

> while predictive analytics often confirmed tutor predictions, it was regarded by tutors as a crude measure compared with the details of experiential knowledge.

Concerns were raised that either telling students that they were predicted not to complete or providing overbearing support could have adverse effects and would be against the ethos of the institution. The approach, then, was for a tutor to send an email asking how the student was getting on. If the message was ignored, they would use other channels such as text messages. However, they felt that any more than three attempts at contacting the student could be perceived as bullying; in this event they would refer the matter to the student support team.

Tutors felt that using the reports did not add significantly to their workload. Where contact was successfully established with the students it was often reported to be positive or productive. The predictions helped the tutors to decide *when* to intervene, particularly when there were sudden or unexpected changes in student behaviour, which they might not otherwise have spotted. There was also evidence that the weekly provision of the reports resulted in tutors systematically examining each student's progress in a way that they had not done before.[8]

## Types of Intervention

A wide range of interventions with students is available and may include:

- reminders sent to students about the suggested progression through the task;[9]
- questions to promote deeper investigation of the content;[10]
- invitations to take additional exercises or practice tests;[11]
- attempts to stimulate more equal contributions from participants in a discussion forum;[12]
- simple indicators such as red/yellow/green traffic signals, giving students an instant feel for how they are progressing;
- prompts to visit further online support resources;
- invitations to get in touch with a tutor to discuss progress;
- supportive messages sent when good progress is being made;[13]
- arranging of special sessions to help students struggling with a particular topic.[14]

Van Leeven and colleagues coded a sample of 96 interventions that had been made using a chat tool with students in groups that had problems with participation or discussion. They found that the messages concerned task content, planning or task strategies, the mood of the group, the collaborative process, strategies for collaborating or consequences of the way students were collaborating. Some messages were designed to enhance the mood of the group or to motivate students. Some were answers to a specific student's question.[15]

Interventions can be targeted at one or multiple students asynchronously through email, text messages, video/audio messages, forums, indicators or messages posted on an LMS home page. Logistically more difficult, as they require the simultaneous presence of instructor and student(s), synchronous interventions can be deployed using chat tools, video/audio conferencing, phone calls and face-to-face meetings. One of the asynchronous methods may be used to schedule a synchronous event; a tutor might, for example, send a text message to a student to arrange a visit to her office.

## Interventions with Signals at Purdue University

At Purdue University, instructors can decide to intervene by posting a red, yellow or green traffic signal on a student's home page, sending them an email or text, referring them to an academic advisor or resource centre or scheduling a face-to-face meeting with them.

A green traffic light can be reinforced by the instructor with a positive message. Yellow or red is regarded as negative feedback and can be sent with a warning message. The instructors were, however, concerned that the lights were not always being set appropriately or understandably. Students could be given a 'false sense of security' by seeing a green light. Meanwhile it was not clear what a yellow light meant: it could signify unsatisfactory scores for exams, quizzes or homework.

Students were sometimes confused, too, by the multiplicity of interventions deployed by different instructors, implying that consistency of approach across the institution may be important. Learners also found information such as 'the next assignment is in two weeks' distracting.[16]

A mentoring programme at the Michigan Science Technology and Engineering Academy presents traffic signals to mentors only and not to the students. They are designed to prompt the mentor to take different types of action: 'encourage' the student to keep doing well (green), 'explore' student progress in greater detail (yellow) or 'engage' them to assess possible academic difficulties (red). Triggers for each action are based on student grades and measures of their week-to-week 'effort' levels.[17, 18]

Another interesting approach was tried at Marist College. Students deemed to be at risk were subjected to one of two intervention strategies available.

One of these involved sending a message stating that they were at risk of not completing the course and providing guidance in how they could better their chances of success. The other group was advised to visit a special online support environment containing resources for study skills, time management, stress reduction and content in algebra, statistics, writing and researching. Mentoring opportunities were also available on this site from peers and support staff.[19]

## Intervention with Physics Students at the University of Michigan

At the University of Michigan, a project was initiated to discover which interventions would help physics students to perform better than was expected. Structured interviews with students helped to discover the reasons for better than expected or worse than expected performance. The interviews revealed some important predictors of success that were not visible in other data. In particular, it was found that students' responses to their performance in the first exam was an important factor in their ultimate performance. Those who changed their behaviour after the exam were likely to improve their outcomes. Prompt attention to setbacks was also found to be vital. This feedback from students was combined with the experience of physics faculty members and students who had successfully completed the course, providing advice on what to do with each student.

On the basis of this intelligence, the $E^2$Coach system was deployed to customise content provided for each student in areas such as study habits and to tailor formative assessments, feedback on progress and encouragement. At key points in the course students receive details of their current status, how their work compares to others and predictions of their final grades. Advice is also provided to each learner from a former student who has a similar background, goals and concerns. Students are told how much better they might do if they address certain issues.

This is one of the few examples of an automated system that directs interventions at students at all levels of ability and performance, ranging from those at risk of failure or drop out to the most successful.[20]

## Timing and Frequency

The timing and frequency of interventions is likely to have a significant impact on their effectiveness. Much more research is required to determine the optimum levels for these, which will vary depending on factors such as the type of institution, subject discipline, level of study and the backgrounds and preferences of individual students. At Purdue there was no clear consensus around timing and frequency for messages sent to students among the faculty surveyed in one study. Some were concerned not to overdo the sending of messages and two students did indeed report being demoralised by overly frequent messages. Excessive positive feedback may bore students and result in them ignoring the messages, whereas continual negative feedback could reduce the motivation to learn. Many students using Signals felt that too many similar messages were sent to them by email, text and on their LMS home page.

The dangers of feedback being too early were also highlighted at Purdue. One instructor said that they did not want students to become overconfident by providing early positive feedback; another found that many students were anxious by being given red lights after the first test. Meanwhile, some believed that their traffic lights were not updated frequently enough and did not reflect their current status.[21]

Other institutions also give control to faculty as to whether or not to intervene with students. At Marist College, instructors are sent details of students at risk at three points during the semester (25%, 50% and 75% of the way through it) and can then decide whether to send messages to them.[22] At Nottingham Trent University, tutors are alerted by email when students have had no engagement for two weeks. The emails suggest to the tutors that they may already know the learners' circumstances but they might wish to contact them. Mike Day, former Director of Information Systems, adds:

> we are interested in finding ways that we can use the technology to improve the dialogue. For example, we might develop the system to generate more personalised emails to tutors, for example, where engagement drops from good to partial, where students don't use the library by a particular cut-off date, or for students with a history of late submission. Although it would be necessary to avoid 'spamming' tutors with too many alerts.[23]

## Wording

Perfecting the messages sent to students is taken very seriously at some institutions. The effects on individuals of particular wording could range from motivational to deeply upsetting. At Purdue more than 1,500 students were surveyed anonymously across five semesters to gather feedback on their use of Signals. Most of them considered that even though the messages and warnings sent to them by the system were automated, they were nevertheless a kind of personal communication with their instructor, which reduced their feelings of 'being just a number'. Because messages are perceived by students as personalised communication with instructors, it is important to take care as to how they are formatted. One instructor at Purdue failed to fill in the gaps in a templated message with the result that an email was sent saying:

> please continue to work and if you have any questions, I am in my office, [office location], each day from [h:mm]AM to [h:mm]AM.[24]

The interventions at Marist involve standardised text, which becomes more serious in tone with every message. Messages such as the following were available for instructors to send out:

> I am reaching out to offer some assistance and to encourage you to consider taking steps to improve your performance. Doing so early in the semester will increase the likelihood of you successfully completing the class and avoid negatively impacting your academic standing.

and

> Based on your performance on recent graded assignments and exams, as well as other factors that tend to predict academic success, I am becoming worried about your ability to complete this class successfully.[25]

## Adoption

The vital importance of faculty changing their working practices to view the analytics and take interventions accordingly is highlighted in a number of studies. Lonn *et al.* report that:

> Faculty members may be too burdened with teaching, research and service to effectively interpret the complex data that is available from the Learning Management System without significant training efforts that have proven difficult at a large research institution like Michigan.[26]

At Michigan it was noticed that after initial viewings of the visualisations, few mentors used them again on a regular basis. One reason given for this was that they had not found ways to integrate the tools into their working practices.[27] Whale *et al.* also note the issue of additional workload at their institution, the University of New England, pointing out that teaching staff were spending significantly more time supporting students than previously. However, they suggest that if the extra effort can be proven to have been successful then institutions will have incentives to provide further support to instructors.[28]

## Evaluating the Interventions

While learning analytics is arguably a fruitless exercise without accompanying interventions, carrying out interventions without ever attempting to understand their effectiveness makes little sense either. In this section, three separate case studies are presented to show how different institutions evaluated their interventions.

## Evaluating the Success of Signals at Purdue

Various evaluations of Signals have been carried out at Purdue University, examining the data and interviewing students, instructors and administrators. One of these examined the impact of the project on final grades and behaviour, which was measured through interactions with the LMS and students' help-seeking behaviour. It was found that in courses that deployed Signals there were consistently higher levels of Cs and Ds obtained by students than Es and Fs. Students who received automated interventions also sought help earlier and more frequently. In another pilot, while withdrawal rates from the course remained static, there was a 14% increase in students withdrawing early enough for their grade point average (GPA) scores to be unaffected.

It also seemed that when students became aware of their risk level, they tended to alter their behaviour, with a consequent positive impact on their performance. For example in one course of 220 students, there were 45 high-risk students. By the end of the course only 10.6% of these were still in the high-risk group. Meanwhile, 69% of those in the moderate group had risen to the low-risk group. Students in pilot groups sought help earlier and more frequently than those not taking part. Even after the interventions stopped, these students were seeking help 30% more often than those in the control group.

In order to establish whether there was a relationship between interventions through Signals and student success, 522 messages sent to students via Signals were analysed anonymously in conjunction with results data. Key findings included:

- No relationship was established between student success and the *frequency* of feedback.
- Instructional feedback appeared to be more effective than motivational feedback.
- Explicit feedback that compared students to their peers seemed to be more effective than comparing them to standards.
- Succinct messages appeared to have a more positive impact than longer ones.
- Retention levels increased significantly among those taking one or more courses that deployed Signals. The suggestion was therefore that the earlier a student took a Signals course the more likely they were not to drop out.
- Those studying two or more courses that used Signals were even more likely to be retained.
- Lesser-prepared students taking Signals-based courses did better than better-prepared students on courses that did not use Signals.

Mike Caulfield disputes some of Purdue's claims of the improved retention of students using Signals and in particular that those taking two or more Signals courses were 21% more likely to be retained. He suggests that there is a selection bias: those taking two classes, whether Signals-based or not, are already more likely to be retained than those only taking one. Conversely, those who drop out are taking fewer Signals courses because they are not taking any classes at all. So students are taking more Signals courses because they are continuing: they are not continuing because they are taking more Signals courses. Purdue does not appear to have responded in detail to these claims and their subsequent exposure in the media. They relate to claims of improved retention – the improvement in grades does not appear to be questioned currently. However Caulfield points out that it is retention that has more significant financial implications for institutions rather than improved grades.

A key benefit of Signals noted by one administrator at Purdue in another study was that those who used Signals tended to use subject help desks and additional tutoring sessions more frequently. They also reported that the system appeared to improve communication between students and faculty. Instructors meanwhile agreed that students tended to show improvements in engagement after using Signals and were thinking about their assignments earlier. They did express reservations about the number of emails from concerned students and were worried that learners would become dependent on the system rather than develop skills in independent learning.[29, 30, 31, 32, 33, 34]

## Evaluating the Effectiveness of Different Types of Intervention at Marist College

At Marist College, New York, two cohorts of 1,739 and 696 students were divided into three groups: students who were sent a message, those who were directed to an online support environment and a control group that received no interventions. No differences were found between the two treatment groups overall. However, in one course there was a 6% improvement in final grade for those subjected to an intervention over the control group.

It was also discovered that withdrawal rates were larger in the intervention group than among control subjects: 25.6% of interventions students withdrew in contrast with only 14.1% of control students. However, the results vary considerably between semesters and the authors refer to research at Purdue that showed similar inconsistencies. What differences there are may be explained by students preferring to withdraw early rather than running the risk of failing later. It is possible that the model will falsely identify students as at risk who might not have failed but are prompted to withdraw by being told they are at risk. The authors argue that this is a reason to strive to develop more accurate predictive models rather than not to present students with findings that have a small chance of being wrong.

Some students were found who appear to be 'immune' to interventions. Few students who failed to respond to the first intervention improved after the second or third.[35]

**Assessing Student Perceptions of the Impact of Interventions at the University of New England**

At the University of New England, in Australia, an online survey was directed at students in order to discover how satisfied they were with the interventions and to ascertain the impact of the interventions on their learning experience. Students rated these very highly. They liked the initial prompts, suggesting that they encouraged them to engage with the content. They also felt that the prompts had helped them to prepare for assessments.

A further survey was sent to all students, including those not involved in the interventions. One of the questions was about the students' overall learning experience and asked them to rate it on a scale of 1 to 5. There was a significant difference between the two groups: means of 4.0 for those who had not experienced interventions and 4.3 for those who had.[36]

## Conclusion

This chapter has examined some of the emerging practice in the, as yet, relatively undocumented area of interventions taken directly by educators with students on the basis of learning analytics. Chapter 6 discussed the argument that learning design and learning analytics should be conceived of together: that taking course development seriously will increasingly involve using analytics to measure its effectiveness and that carrying out analytics without understanding the underlying motivations and mechanisms of the course is inadvisable. Intervening with learners also requires knowledge of the intentions of the course designer: interventions can be put in place when the analytics show that an aspect of the learning design is not happening as planned.

Some interventions, prompted by the analytics, can clearly be planned for and built into processes well in advance, for example if a student has not logged into the LMS for two weeks an email can be sent to a tutor suggesting that they contact the student. Such actions may be part of an intervention strategy at institutional, faculty or course level. Other interventions will inevitably be put in place 'on the fly' by instructors who become aware that something is not going as planned during the course – for example, the analytics flag that a subgroup of students appears to be struggling with a particular topic so the instructor posts additional explanatory content. Interventions such as these, based on learner behaviour, are integral to teaching; what is new is the additional insight provided to teachers by analytics. The type of intervention with perhaps the most potential for enhancing learning behaviour, though, is the subject of the next chapter: putting apps and dashboards into the hands of the students themselves.

# References

1 Greller, W. *et al.*, 2014, Learning Analytics: From Theory to Practice – Data Support for Learning and Teaching, *Computer Assisted Assessment. Research into E-Assessment, Proceedings of CAA 2014*, pp. 79–87.

2 Clow, D., 2012, The Learning Analytics Cycle: Closing the Loop Effectively, *LAK12: 2nd International Conference on Learning Analytics and Knowledge*, p. 135.

3 Tanes, Z. *et al.*, 2011, Using Signals for Appropriate Feedback: Perceptions and Practices, *Computers and Education*, 57, pp. 2414–2422 (p. 2416).

4 Nicol, D. J. & Macfarlane-Dick, D., 2006, Formative Assessment and Self-Regulated Learning: A Model and Seven Principles of Good Feedback Practice, *Studies in Higher Education*, 31(2), pp. 199–218.

5 van Leeuwen, A. *et al.*, 2014, Supporting Teachers in Guiding Collaborating Students: Effects of Learning Analytics in CSCL, *Computers and Education*, 79, pp. 28–39.

6 Lockyer, L. *et al.*, 2013, Informing Pedagogical Action: Aligning Learning Analytics with Learning Design, *American Behavioral Scientist*, 57(10), pp. 1439–1459.

7 Whale, S. *et al.*, 2013, Implementing Timely Interventions to Improve Students' Learning Experience, *Electric Dreams: 30th Ascilite Conference*, 1–4 December, pp. 908–912.

8 Rienties, B. *et al.*, 2016, Analytics4Action Evaluation Framework: A Review of Evidence-Based Learning Analytics Interventions at the Open University UK, *Journal of Interactive Media in Education*, 2016(1), p. 12.

9 Lockyer *et al.*, Informing Pedagogical Action: Aligning Learning Analytics With Learning Design, p. 1454.

10 Ibid.

11 Jayaprakash, S. M. *et al.*, 2014, Early Alert of Academically At-Risk Students: An Open Source Analytics Initiative, *Journal of Learning Analytics*, 1(1), pp. 6–47.

12 Lockyer *et al.*, Informing Pedagogical Action: Aligning Learning Analytics With Learning Design, p. 1454.

13 Rienties *et al.*, Analytics4Action Evaluation Framework: A Review of Evidence-Based Learning Analytics Interventions at the Open University UK, p. 6.

14 Ibid.

15 van Leeuwen *et al.*, Supporting Teachers in Guiding Collaborating Students: Effects of Learning Analytics in CSCL.

16 Tanes *et al.*, Using Signals for Appropriate Feedback: Perceptions and Practices.

17 Krumm, A. E. *et al.*, 2012, Increasing Academic Success in Undergraduate Engineering Education using Learning Analytics: A Design-Based Research Project, *Paper presented at the Annual Meeting of the American Educational Research Association.*

18 Lonn, S. *et al.*, 2013, Issues, Challenges, and Lessons Learned when Scaling Up a Learning Analytics Intervention, *LAK13: Proceedings of the Third International Conference on Learning and Knowledge*, pp. 235–239.

19 Jayaprakash *et al.*, Early Alert of Academically At-Risk Students: An Open Source Analytics Initiative.

20 McKay, T. *et al.*, 2012, What to do with actionable intelligence: $E^2$Coach as an intervention engine, *LAK12: Proceedings of the First International Conference on Learning Analytics and Knowledge*, pp. 88–91.

21 Tanes *et al.*, Using Signals for Appropriate Feedback: Perceptions and Practices.

22 Jayaprakash *et al.*, Early Alert of Academically At-Risk Students: An Open Source Analytics Initiative.

23 Sclater, N., *et al.*, 2016, *Learning Analytics in Higher Education: A Review of UK and International Practice*, Jisc.

24 Tanes *et al.*, Using Signals for Appropriate Feedback: Perceptions and Practices.

25 Jayaprakash *et al.*, Early Alert of Academically At-Risk Students: An Open Source Analytics Initiative.

26 Lonn *et al.*, Issues, Challenges, and Lessons Learned when Scaling Up a Learning Analytics Intervention.

27 Krumm *et al.*, Increasing Academic Success in Undergraduate Engineering Education using Learning Analytics: A Design-Based Research Project, p. 4.

28 Whale *et al.*, Implementing Timely Interventions to Improve Students' Learning Experience, p. 911.

29 Arnold, K., 2010, Signals: Applying Academic Analytics, *EDUCAUSE Review*, 3 March, http://er.educause.edu/articles/2010/3/signals-applying-academic-analytics (accessed 11 October 2016).

30 Arnold, K. E. *et al.*, 2010, Administrative Perceptions of Data-Mining Software Signals: Promoting Student Success and Retention, *The Journal of Academic Administration in Higher Education*, 6(2), pp. 29–39.

31 Caulfield, M., 2013, A Simple, Less Mathematical Way to Understand the Course Signals, *Hapgood*, 26 September, https://hapgood.us/2013/09/26/a-simple-less-mathematical-way-to-understand-the-course-signals-issue/ (accessed 9 October 2016).

32 Caulfield, M., 2013, Purdue Course Signals Data Issue Explainer, *e-Literate*, 12 November, http://mfeldstein.com/purdue-course-signals-data-issue-explainer/ (accessed 9 October 2016).

33 Straumsheim, C., 2013, Mixed Signals, *Inside Higher Ed*, 6 November, https://www.insidehighered.com/news/2013/11/06/researchers-cast-doubt-about-early-warning-systems-effect-retention (accessed 9 October 2016).

34 Tanes *et al.*, Using Signals for Appropriate Feedback: Perceptions and Practices.

35 Jayaprakash *et al.*, Early Alert of Academically At-Risk Students: An Open Source Analytics Initiative.

36 Whale *et al.*, Implementing Timely Interventions to Improve Students' Learning Experience, p. 910.

# 12 Student-Facing Analytics

Much of the existing work in learning analytics centres on presenting data to staff and faculty so that they can intervene in some way, either directly with students or by altering the curriculum. However, an area of growing interest is the provision of analytics directly to individual students. Intervention was the subject of the previous chapter, but Kruse takes exception to this term, which she believes perpetuates a culture of students being passive subjects instead of reflective learners who can evaluate their own learning processes.[1]

Analytics can instead help to empower students rather than enslaving them.[2, 3] They can become aware of the impact of their own actions on their learning and be able to use the data to reflect on and alter their behaviour. When learners discover things for themselves, their learning is likely to be deeper than when they are told something by someone else. Kruse proposes that learning activities could also be developed around the analytics:

> helping students learn how to ask questions of themselves and their learning that will set them on a productive course of inquiry; guiding them through exercises that uncover their own metacognitive strengths and weaknesses; putting tools in their hands that bring life to their discoveries about themselves, like powerful and compelling visualizations.[4]

Ritsos & Roberts suggest that tools are required to help learners progress from novices to experts and from shallow to deep thinkers.[5] A serious challenge for many learners is that they do not have an accurate perception of where their learning is in relation to where they ought to be – or at least where the educator thinks they should be. Students may receive feedback on assignments in the form of grades and comments from the instructor but this is generally provided so infrequently that it is difficult for them to adapt their behaviour.[6] Such feedback also may reflect their skills in completing tests and assignments and not necessarily how well they are learning.

## Student Attitudes to Viewing their Analytics at the University of Melbourne

Corrin *et al.* point to the lack of research into how effective it is to provide students' own analytics directly to them. Their research at the University of Melbourne aimed to address the following questions:

- How do students interpret feedback delivered through learning analytics dashboards?
- What actions do students take in response to dashboard feedback?
- How does access to dashboard feedback influence students' motivation and performance in their course?

At the start of the semester, participants completed a survey that examined their motivation for the subject and their personal learning goals. In week seven they were shown a dashboard of their engagement and performance data and asked to comment on the data and what actions it prompted them to take. Most participants reported being more motivated towards the subject as a result of seeing the dashboard. Comments related to self-regulation (e.g. 'I'll definitely try harder' and 'it makes me want to do more'); or awareness of progress (e.g. 'it improves motivation, cause I can see where I am at and I know how I'm going so far'). A small number of students, who tended to be above average or were happy with their progress, reported that the dashboard did not affect their motivation. One student said: 'if I were doing worse I would have more motivation'.

Whether the reported increase in motivation of the students was translated into improved engagement and performance had not been ascertained by the researchers, who pointed out that this still needed to be discovered.

All participants liked the visualisations (e.g. 'if you gave me a comparison of a [numeric] mark versus class average then I wouldn't see the difference as vividly as I do here'). Many also appreciated the ability to compare themselves to their peers (e.g. 'so the first thing I notice is I'm below the class average'). However, these comparisons may also have obscured their view of how well they were progressing towards their goal in the subject. Some who had indicated that they wanted to achieve the highest grade were satisfied to see that they were only slightly above the class average at that point, the data suggesting that they were not on track for a top grade.

Another useful feature of the dashboards was a space representing what was still to come or what they had missed. Several students were helped by this to identify assessments they did not know about or had forgotten to do. This suggests that dashboards can form multiple purposes: not only to make students aware of their progress and how it compares with others but also as a kind of study guide, helping them to reflect and to plan their activities. The authors point out that it is challenging to design dashboards that include all the necessary information while remaining clear and concise enough not to be overwhelming.[7]

**The Quantified Self**

In other domains there is increasing use of personal tracking data in order to understand patterns of behaviour and progress towards goals. Mobile and wearable technologies used for applications such as fitness tracking and sleep monitoring provide examples of possible applications for enhancing learning.[8] Several features of these methods can help to change behaviour:

- The visualisation may draw attention to a pattern of personal activity that was not already apparent and prompt a change in behaviour – for example, seeing a representation of one's eating habits could lead to a better diet.[9]
- The setting of goals and targets by users (the default settings often being suggested by the app) makes them explicit and may boost motivation and enable users to reflect on their progress.[10]
- Being able to compare one's level of activity and progress with others may tap into a competitive spirit, encouraging further progress.[11]
- Being connected with others through the app can reduce isolation and help users to feel part of a broader community tackling the same issues.
- Alerts and nudges sent by the app keep the activity and goal prominent in the thinking of the user.
- Reward mechanisms such as badges, 'trophies' and congratulatory messages can engender positive feelings and spur the user on to further activity.

However, Roberts and colleagues point out that fitness apps are not identical in all aspects to educational apps. One difference is that the time period over which change can be observed is likely to be longer in learning. Metrics related to fitness may be updated every second or minute and the goals may be short term; education usually involves metrics and goals of longer duration. They are already much more mature technologies than those used in education, too.[12] Developing a person's fitness may be every bit as complex as enhancing that individual's learning but the measurement of proxies relating to fitness (e.g. steps taken or heart rate) may be easier and more accurate than ascertaining how effectively an individual is learning.

**Dashboards**

A growing range of tools provide analytics directly to learners. Verbert *et al.* examined 15 dashboards, most of which were aimed at both instructors and students, four of them being specifically designed for learners. Visualisations of the time spent on activities, social interaction and the use of documents and tools are available. Some of the tools identify popular documents and gather artefacts such as blogs or forum posts produced by students.[13]

## The Check My Activity Tool at the University of Maryland Baltimore County

John Fritz, at the University of Maryland Baltimore County, discusses the provision of a 'Check my Activity' tool for students to compare their activity in the LMS on a specific course with a summary of activity undertaken by the other students. When grades are posted by faculty, the students can view how their activity compares with others obtaining the same, higher or lower grades. They can also see to what extent other students have used individual LMS tools compared to themselves. In 2008 and 2009 Fritz and his colleagues surveyed students on three courses about their use of the tool and found that 28% of students on one of the courses were 'surprised' by how their activity compared with the rest of the class.

Subsequent adoption of the tool when it was made available to students across the institution was initially slow. A publicity campaign increased its use dramatically, however, as did placing it prominently in the gradebook of the LMS. Fritz expresses a concern that use of the tool may be 'a case of the rich getting richer' i.e. those students who are already doing well will be quick to use any tool that helps them monitor their behaviour. Research on the 2010–11 cohort of freshmen and transfer students showed that 92% of them used the LMS and of these 91.5% used Check my Activity. Those who used the tool were 1.92 times more likely to be awarded grade C or higher compared with students who did not use it.

Future enhancements planned for the tool include a view of the frequency and duration of LMS tool usage compared with others and alerts sent to individuals when their activity drops below the level associated with students who obtain the grade that they want to achieve. It also allows students to share the information with staff and to give them permission to intervene when their activity drops below a certain level.

Fritz believes that the feedback given to the students through the tool may be saying to students 'what they would not (or could not) initially hear or accept from a professor or academic advisor through a personal intervention'. The tool may also be able to build on students' 'obsessive status-checking tendencies' to provide them with feedback, which would be expensive to do via a human.[14, 15]

## Apps

Mobile apps may perform much the same function as web-based dashboards; however, they have a number of advantages:

- They are designed for viewing on mobile devices, unlike websites, which may include too much information to be viewable on a small screen.
- They can make use of the device's functionality such as touch screens and location awareness.
- Accessible through icons, they may be easier to locate than webpages.
- Users may feel more ownership over an app that has been downloaded to their personal device and be more inclined to use it.

Vendors of learning analytics products are increasingly packaging some of their functionality into apps targeted at learners, and institutions are beginning to roll out these apps to their students.

## Jisc's Student App for Learning Analytics

Responding to requests from UK institutions, Jisc specified and commissioned the building of a learning analytics app for students. Initial requirements gathering for the app involved a workshop in London where representatives from UK institutions, including students, discussed possible functionality for the app.[16] Ideas included the following:

- **How engaged am I?** This would aim to reassure students who are on track and to prompt those who are not engaging. Overall engagement could be shown and could be broken down further into, for instance, library usage, lecture attendance or LMS usage.
- **How do I compare with others?** The aim would be to motivate and inspire students to change their behaviour by showing how their engagement and achievement compares with peers and with previous cohorts.
- **My academic progress.** The aim here is to gather academic progress indicators and to identify actionable insights for the student. Timely information would aim to change their behaviour and improve achievement.
- **My assessment behaviour.** One possibility suggested was that students could see how their actions compared with those of successful students – for example, if students submit assignments just before the deadline are they more likely to fail? (Confusion of correlation and causation may be a danger here.)
- **My career aspirations.** The aim here would be to help understand whether students are on track to achieve their chosen career based on records of previous learners. This might include networking opportunities with students who have already followed a similar path.

- **Plan my career path**. A related possibility is showing what educational journey students need to take to achieve their intended career, helping them to avoid the wrong choices. For example, what do the lives of midwives look like and what was their educational journey to get there?
- **My competencies.** Enabling students to monitor their competencies and reflect on their skills development might also encourage them to engage better with the materials and with their cohort.

Other possibilities included students being able to log their emotional state, the reasons for non-attendance at classes, communication facilities, the use of geo-location data and functionality for users to grant consent for the collection and use of their data for learning analytics.

I held a subsequent requirements gathering workshop with students at the University of Lincoln.[17] Most students currently have little idea of what learning analytics is so, without leading them too much, I introduced them to the topic. It was then a challenge, as with the previous workshop, to keep the group to functionality related to the use of student data for enhancing learning, rather than straying into the many useful things that apps can do for students.

Inevitably there was a focus on **assessment**: a one-stop-shop for all of a student's results was requested. This is not of course learning analytics, but comparisons with averages could be incorporated. Meanwhile the app could show what percentage of assessments the student has completed and what grades they need to obtain in future assignments in order to receive different levels of degree award.

Providing **reading-list** functionality was also popular with the students, who suggested being presented with metrics showing how much they are engaging with the reading list on each of their modules. This could include reviews, comments and recommendations from other students. They also suggested Amazon-style recommendations for reading – 'if you liked $x$ you may like $y$'.

**How you spend your time** was another application that the students thought could be useful. The percentage of time spent by the student on various activities could be calculated from timetables, calendars, geo-location and self-declared activity. Recommendations on how much time should be spent on different activities could be another helpful feature.

**Managing event attendance** was a popular option, too. Students could be contacted about societies and social events, workshops or guest lectures, based on their interests, which they could also specify via the app. This would cut down on the amount of 'spam' messages from the university, which they reported led to many students not bothering to read their emails. Students could also push event notifications to other students via the app, based on their interests. Rating could be incorporated.

If analytics determined that they were becoming disconnected the app could **introduce students to opportunities** such as open-day volunteering. There was a suggestion that university and student-union data could be combined to suggest such opportunities based on career aspirations and interests.

Another option suggested was to use the app to **check in to lectures**, perhaps automatically using geo-location and to enter reasons (such as illness) for non-attendance. There could also be notifications on lecture cancellations.

Finally, **finding other students** with similar or complementary interests was another popular suggestion.

After consultation with more students at two further events, a design group specified the app, which was then built by Therapy Box. It incorporates the following principles:

- **Comparative** – seeing how you compare with class averages or the top 20% of performers for example may provide a competitive element or at least a reality check, driving you to increased engagement.
- **Social** – being able to select 'friends' with whom to compare your stats may add another level of engagement.
- **Gamified** – an app that includes an element of gaming should encourage uptake by some students. This may be manifested in the use of badges such as a 'Library Master' badge for students who have attended the library five times.
- **Private by default** – while data that the institution knows about you from other systems may be fed to the app, the privacy of any information you input in the app yourself will be protected. However anonymous usage information may be fed back to the app backend.
- **Usable standalone** – by students whose institutions are not using the Jisc architecture.
- **Uncluttered** – the app should concentrate for the time being on learning analytics data and not be bloated with functionality which replicates what is already present in the LMS or in other applications.

The app is being made available to all UK universities and colleges and enables integration of core learning analytics data from institutional systems through Jisc's learning analytics architecture. Initial functionality includes visualisations of engagement and attainment, consent-based comparisons with other students, an activity feed showing events generated by other students, setting targets and logging activities towards them and 'trophies' awarded when the user achieves something considered notable.

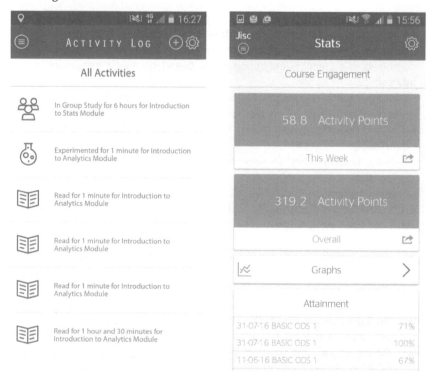

*Figure 12.1* Activity log and engagement / attainment stats from the Jisc Analytics student app.

## Conclusion

It is still early days for student learning analytics apps and dashboards. There are endless possibilities for ways in which to represent data to students and much functionality that could be built into these systems. Many institutions already provide generic student apps with features ranging from timetabling to showing where public buses are on campus in real time. It is likely that the most useful learning analytics functionality being piloted in institutions across the world will increasingly be integrated with these apps, their use becoming accepted as part of the student experience.

A concern to educators is that students will be demotivated by seeing where they are in relation to others or where they are supposed to be (this is discussed further in Chapter 20). If the analytics motivate all students to do better, it may be particularly disheartening for students who are shown to be below average to find that they are still in this position after considerable efforts to improve. Students in one study felt 'pleased, upset or ashamed by their metrics'.[18] It is possible that negative emotions may discourage some students, although, of course, they may increase the motivation of others to improve.

Conversely, some students who are shown to be doing well by the analytics may decide that they can put less effort into their studies, ultimately achieving a satisfactory rather than excellent performance. Comparison with previous cohorts has also been suggested as a possibility, however groups can vary considerably and aspects of the curriculum and how the course is taught do not remain static either from year to year.[19] All this assumes that students engage with the tools in the first place. The least engaged learners are probably also the least likely to make use of any tools provided to them.[20]

Some learners may not wish others to see how they are progressing and it may be important to protect the privacy of those who do not wish their data to be shared with others. In one study, a few students said that, while in general they liked to be able to see how their efforts compared with others, they did not want their own activity to be displayed to their peers.[21] Even if this information is not made available, it may be possible to identify individuals from anonymous data, particularly in small cohorts. In developing the Jisc Student App it was realised that if a student obtained agreement to view the analytics of all but one person in their class, they could potentially infer that person's data by examining class averages and individual scores. Rules can be built into the software, however, to restrict the data available in such situations.

Another ever present possibility with learning analytics is that learners (as well as staff and faculty) may falsely equate engagement with success or being on the right track (e.g. presentation of how many lectures a student has attended does not show whether anything has been learned). Meanwhile, it has been pointed out that the provision of too many analytics could 'kill passion' for the subject and divert student effort into assessed or measured activities rather than genuine learning.[22]

More fundamentally, perhaps, Wise discusses the problem that students are often unaware of the learning design behind the course and the purpose of a particular learning activity. They may not therefore be able to assess whether the analytics are demonstrating whether they are participating as expected. They may also not have the necessary metacognitive or self-regulating skills to use any dashboards or apps provided to them effectively.[23] A survey of 111 education professionals involved in learning analytics carried out by Greller & Drachsler found that only 21% of them thought that learners would have the competences to interpret and act on learning analytics by themselves.[24]

The situation may be compounded by the fact that each student starts from a different point and has varying skills, experience and aptitudes. This means that there may be many ways to achieve a learning outcome, rather than a single route for all students to follow. Personal goal setting, as an explicit learning activity, could therefore help students to be clear about what they need to do.[25]

Whatever the drawbacks, there is a convincing moral argument that if we know something about students (e.g. that they have a strong likelihood of dropping out) we should not withhold this information from them. Concerns about negative effects on learners may in fact be overridden by demand from students themselves as data on their learning becomes increasingly available through apps and dashboards. Educators do, however, have obligations to monitor the impact of providing the analytics to learners and to ensure that these are accurate, meaningful, informative and sensitively presented.

## References

1 Kruse, A. & Pongsajapan, R., 2012, Student-Centered Learning Analytics, *CNDLS Thought Papers*, p. 2, https://cndls.georgetown.edu/m/documents/thought paper-krusepongsajapan.pdf (accessed 9 October 2016).
2 Corrin, L. *et al.*, 2005, Loop: A Learning Analytics Tool to Provide Teachers with Useful Data Visualisations. In: Reiners, B. R. *et al.*, eds, *Globally Connected, Digitally Enabled. Proceedings Ascilite*, pp. CP:57–CP:61.
3 Wise, A. F., 2014, Designing Pedagogical Interventions to Support Student Use of Learning Analytics, *LAK14: Proceedings of the Fourth International Learning Analytics and Knowledge Conference*, p. 3.
4 Kruse & Pongsajapan, Student-Centered Learning Analytics, *CNDLS Thought Papers*, p. 4–5.
5 Ritsos, P. D. & Roberts, J. C., 2014, *Towards More Visual Analytics in Learning Analytics*, Eurographics: European Association for Computer Graphics, p. 1.
6 Roberts, J. C. *et al.*, 2015, Personal Visualization for Learning, *IEEE VIS 2015 Workshop on Personal Visualization: Exploring Data in Everyday Life*, October, p. 1.
7 Corrin *et al.*, Loop: A Learning Analytics Tool to Provide Teachers with Useful Data Visualisations, pp. 629–630.
8 Roberts *et al.*, Personal Visualization for Learning, p. 2.
9 Duval, E., 2011, *Attention Please! Learning Analytics for Visualization and Recommendation*, ACM, pp. 9–17.
10 Wise, Designing Pedagogical Interventions to Support Student Use of Learning Analytics, p. 5.
11 Lonn, S. *et al.*, 2012, Bridging the Gap from Knowledge to Action: Putting Analytics in the Hands of Academic Advisors, *LAK12: 2nd International Conference on Learning Analytics and Knowledge*, pp. 3–4.
12 Roberts *et al.*, Personal Visualization for Learning, p. 3.
13 Verbert, K. *et al.*, 2013, Learning Analytics Dashboard Applications, *American Behavioral Scientist*, 57, pp. 1500–1509.
14 Fritz, J., 2011, Classroom Walls that Talk: Using Online Course Activity Data of Successful Students to Raise Self-Awareness of Underperforming Peers, *Internet and Higher Education*, 14, pp. 89–97.
15 Fritz, J., 2013, *Using Analytics at UMBC: Encouraging Student Responsibility and Identifying Effective Course Designs*, EDUCAUSE Center for Applied Research.
16 Sclater, N., 2015, What Do Students Want from a Learning Analytics App? *Effective Learning Analytics*, 29 April, https://analytics.jiscinvolve.org/wp/2015/04/29/what-do-students-want-from-a-learning-analytics-app/ (accessed 9 October 2016).
17 Sclater, N., 2015, Gathering Requirements for a Student App for Learning Analytics, *Effective Learning Analytics*, 18 March, https://analytics.jiscinvolve.org/wp/2015/03/18/gathering-requirements-for-a-student-app-for-learning-analytics/ (accessed 9 October 2016).
18 Wise, A. F. *et al.*, 2013, Learning Analytics for Online Discussions: A Pedagogical Model for Intervention with Embedded and Extracted Analytics, *LAK13: Proceedings of the Third International Learning and Knowledge Conference*, April.

19 Sclater, Gathering Requirements for a Student App for Learning Analytics.

20 Lonn *et al.*, Bridging the Gap from Knowledge to Action: Putting Analytics in the Hands of Academic Advisors, pp. 3–4.

21 Brown, M., 2012, *Learning Analytics: Moving from Concept to Practice*, EDU-CAUSE Learning Initiative, p. 3.

22 Sclater, Gathering Requirements for a Student App for Learning Analytics.

23 Wise, Designing Pedagogical Interventions to Support Student Use of Learning Analytics, pp. 3–5.

24 Greller, W. & Drachsler, H., 2012, Translating Learning into Numbers: A Generic Framework for Learning, *Educational Technology and Society*, 15(3), pp. 42–57.

25 Wise, Designing Pedagogical Interventions to Support Student Use of Learning Analytics, pp. 3–5.

# 13  Expert Thoughts on Logistics

## Improving the Data Sources

One theme that emerges in several of the conversations with experts in learning analytics is that the data being used for learning analytics is not ideal in its current format: it is largely derived from logging systems, initially designed for tracking bugs in software and monitoring server performance rather than for understanding educational processes. Dragan Gašević suggests that we need to collect data that is measuring aspects of learning, helping us, for example, to understand levels of understanding, metacognition and the affective states of students. Alyssa Wise proposes that we consider analytics right from the start when designing systems in the future:

> We've come into the game half-way through with a lot of analytics working with the data that systems already produce – which sometimes works out well and sometimes could work out a lot better if we collected better, smarter data.

Trying to draw inferences from clickstream data, she says, is challenging. We could instead start collecting 'data that has more information in it', thus setting up the processes of inference in advance rather than subsequently. Alyssa also believes we could provide more insight by connecting different data sources together more effectively. She notes that, because the data is often aggregated, the temporal dynamic is lost. Knowing how long events take and how their timing relates to other events is important too, as learning is about changes over time.

John Whitmer has encountered a similar problem:

> The areas that are currently being exploited the most are frequency of access to online materials and resources and the relationship to student course achievements. I think much of what we're doing so far, beyond an exploratory stage, stops at how often the student accesses whatever the thing is. Our colleague, Sasha Dietrichson, the founder of X-Ray calls it 'Clickometrics'. So I think that's mostly what we're doing in learning analytics.

He believes that we need to move beyond frequency analysis and examining the quantity of experience, which is used as a proxy for effort and to begin analysing the quality of that effort and its impact on learning. We are currently looking at whether students are accessing course materials and doing well in assessments, he says, but we need to start discerning whether they are repeating something or exhibiting behaviour that suggests that they are confused or struggling. Meanwhile, we barely yet understand the impact of interventions:

> That's a whole area that we're just beginning to instrument, to collect the data around ... And I think it's always going to be the messiest because there are so many things we're looking into.

## Improving the Analytics

Whatever the underlying data sources, there is much that can be done to enhance the analytics taking place on the data. John is carrying out cluster analysis, developing different 'student types', based on how they interact. He intends to use these categories to refine the algorithms, predictions and inferences that can be drawn from student behaviour. Timothy McKay, meanwhile, says that much of what we have been doing to date is essentially high-level reporting, examining past data and trying to understand what has been happening. His university, Michigan, has assembled a team of people with the right mix of skills to bring together the appropriate datasets and work at scale, creating tools for non-data scientists to use in order to answer their own questions. He wants to develop better interventions and facilitate

> the ability to be able to gather a bunch of information about people and then ... speak to every student on campus, for example, in ways that are highly tailored to their individual circumstances and needs and desires and goals. So that kind of picking data and really putting it to use in a way that changes outcomes, doesn't just let us study the past but actually lets us change the future – that's very exciting, and I think we're just at the very beginning of different ways to do that.
>
> Other people are working on cognitive tutoring type of programs that think about the content and modelling a student's progress through content. I think there's lots of promise there for certain kinds of well-structured topics at least but being able to communicate more and more richly, more personally, to personalise education, while we're still teaching at scale – that's the thing that'll occupy me for the next few years.

## Enhancing Feedback

Doug Clow believes that we need to work harder on fine-tuning the feedback directed to students when they are struggling:

Getting a notification saying 'we've noticed you haven't been studying – is everything OK?' – that can feel really supportive, and you wouldn't want the university to not notice that you had stopped studying: that feels like being cared about. But if you get the wrong-toned message from an automated email system, saying 'You have not logged in. You are in violation of our policy' or 'you're flagged at risk of failure' – that's not going to work, and is going to come across as 'big brotherish' and [be] a self-fulfilling prophecy.

He argues too that there is a lot of potential for simple reminders and prompts. Universities should, he says, be developing strategies for the crafting and trialling of these messages, analysing what sequences of messages and what text in them has the greatest effect.

# Part IV
# Technologies

# 14  Architecture

Learning analytics brings together multiple systems, sources of data, stakeholders and processes. Modelling the various elements and how they should best fit together has been exercising the minds of a growing number of researchers and engineers. Inevitably, they do this in different ways according to their backgrounds and the systems to which they have been exposed or are developing. The uses of learning analytics vary considerably, as we have seen, and range from adaptive learning to course recommendation to early alert and student success and curriculum design. Each application requires a different configuration of data and tools, although they may draw on some of the same datasets.

There is no overall consensus as to the best way to conceptualise the components and their integration and, due to the complex nature of the market and many potential applications of analytics, a universally agreed model is unlikely to emerge. However, certain data processes are core to many learning analytics systems and one way to conceptualise the various components is to describe this data and how it flows between software applications and is transformed by them. The models that have been produced to date are generally either quite simplistic or they attempt to combine concepts such as human actors, human processes, computer systems, computing processes, types of data, data flows and data stores in complex diagrams. Some even confusingly use the same symbol for people, data and processes.

Campbell & Oblinger were two of the first researchers to examine the human and automated processes of learning analytics. They describe five discrete actions: capture, report, predict, act and refine. This is a useful starting point but it does not make explicit some key steps such as transforming the data from raw log files, for example, into something more meaningful. Meanwhile, they include stages that are not necessary for all uses of learning analytics: the analytics may not be predictive and no refinement of the process may take place. The actions of people and software are undifferentiated: the first three steps of *capturing*, *reporting* and *predicting* can be considered to be handled by the system components, while *acting* and *refining* may be largely human processes.[1]

Some of the automated processes are outlined by Bader-Natal & Lotze in their 'pipeline' for an analytics system: data collection → selection → analysis → visualisation → distribution. *Collection* gathers the data from the various sources into a single database. *Selection* draws the relevant data together to answer a specific question, normally using database queries. *Analysis* uses statistical software to answer the question. *Visualisation* displays the analysis and *distribution* ensures it is provided to the relevant stakeholder.[2]

The models described above are both primarily linear. Various authors, however, have described a more circular series of processes. Clow builds on earlier theories such as Kolb's experiential learning cycle to develop a learning analytics 'cycle' (Figure 14.1) where *learners* generate *data*, which is then processed into analytics or *metrics*, which should then lead to *interventions*. Clow believes the key is to close the loop by intervening with learners and argues that learning analytics is ineffective without doing this.[3]

The concepts of intervening somehow with learners and adapting the course in some way to benefit future learners are critical to learning analytics and are discussed at length in the chapters on curriculum design and intervention. The costs of gathering and processing data mean that any analytics project is likely to be unsustainable unless there is a demonstrable positive impact on students.

As we saw above, Campbell & Oblinger suggested that ongoing *refinement* of the analytics processes is an essential part of learning analytics. New data sources, changing curricula and teaching methods and different student cohorts require an ability to adapt predictive models continuously. This can involve refining the dataset to remove data that is found to be unhelpful, integrating new data, identifying new metrics or even selecting a different analytics method.[4] However, minimal evidence has emerged to date of such iterative improvements of learning analytics systems.[5]

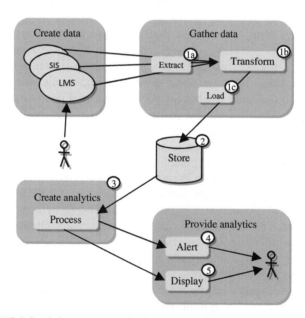

*Figure 14.1* High-level data processes in learning analytics.

Elias combines the processes from a number of different models to produce a sequence of seven distinct processes in learning analytics: select, capture, aggregate and report, predict, use, refine and share. She suggests that the selection stage at the start is required to define goals and decide which data sources should be collected to meet those goals. This is clearly an important initial step, carried out by people who are likely to have overall aims such as increasing student retention or improving student satisfaction. One consequence of working with big data, however, is that researchers do not necessarily know what they are looking for in advance. Future unanticipated uses of the data may also emerge so it may be worth collecting virtually any data relating to students and their activities, thus reducing the importance of this selection stage. Elias's final stage of sharing knowledge about what has been learned is probably another primarily human-mediated process rather than an automated one.[6]

Kraan & Sherlock developed a sequence of computer-mediated processes proposed by various researchers, including Elias:

Collection and Acquisition > Storage > Cleaning > Integration > Analysis > Representation and Visualisation > Alerting

They then reviewed the tools available for handling each of the seven steps. This model adds the processes of *storage* of the data, *cleaning and integrating it* and *alerting* users to its availability.[7]

In Figure 14.1 the main systems processes taking place on the data are modelled in a way that represents the more recent evolution of learning analytics systems. People interact with these processes at various points but the involvement of the primary stakeholders (students, staff and faculty) is required at the start and the end. From a high-level perspective data must be *created* in the first place in various systems and is then *gathered* together and *stored*. From there it can be processed to *create the analytics,* which are then *provided* to stakeholders through alerts and displays.

**Extraction and Transformation**

The first automated process is to gather data from multiple systems, transform it into something that can be worked with and, ideally, load it into a new database or data warehouse specifically designed for learning analytics. This is known as the *extract, transform and load* (ETL) process by systems engineers.

A major challenge for learning analytics is *extracting* the data (process 1a in Figure 14.1) from multiple data sources and even different hardware and software platforms.[8] Methods to collect suitable data are likely to vary according to the system containing the data. Learning management systems (LMSs) such as Moodle and Blackboard Learn have additional software modules to enable learning activity data to be extracted. Demographic and prior academic data generally will be held in a student information system (SIS) and may have to be obtained by querying the database.

Once the data has been extracted it needs to be *transformed* into a format that is usable for learning analytics. Some of the transformation processes that may be required are discussed in Chapter 9.

## Loading and Storing

Once the data has been transformed it can then be *loaded* and *stored* (processes 1c and 2) in a database or data warehouse, which is tailored for learning analytics. The US-based educational technology specifications body, ADL, developed the concept of a *learning record store* where learning activity records can be held in the Experience API (xAPI) format (see Chapter 15). The development of this format is helping to solve a problem identified by a number of earlier commentators: the lack of an agreed standard for learning-activity data accumulated in various systems. However, this format is strictly for storing records of learning activities and does not easily facilitate the storage of unstructured data that may be relevant for learning analytics such as forum postings. It is not suitable either for storing demographic or academic data.

In Jisc this problem was addressed by developing the concept of a *learning records warehouse* which incorporates a learning record store using the xAPI format and data warehousing facilities for all other relevant data which does not fit this format. The warehouse is situated in the cloud and provided to institutions as a multitenanted option – their data remains under their control and is kept separate from that of other institutions. The solution involves the usual processes of data storage such as authentication, security, backup and the dynamic scalability of a cloud-based system when faced with high demand.

## Processing

*Processing* the data (process 3) is the next stage once the data has been collected, transformed and stored. As we have seen in Chapter 9, the processor is at the heart of learning analytics. It creates the analytics, providing metrics and predictions to staff and students.

## Alerting

There may be a requirement to *alert* stakeholders (process 4) that analytics have been created or that an intervention needs to be taken. Thus, an instructor may receive a weekly email detailing students who are at risk of dropout and suggesting that contact is made with them to see if any problems can be addressed. Another example of an alert might be a notification in a student mobile app congratulating the student on being in the top 10% of 'engaged' learners on their course in the current month. Alerts may direct users to more complex visualisations during the next stage: *displaying*.

## Displaying

*Displaying* the analytics (process 5) through visualisations and dashboards is a further process common to most analytics systems. This allows students and other stakeholders to view summaries of the analytics, sometimes drilling down into successive layers of detail. Visualisations such as graphs can help to make sense of data that is less comprehensible in a textual or tabular format,[9] particularly the identification of trends over time. They can also enable the comparison of multiple statistics simultaneously.[10]

While the above processes may be manifested as individual systems, some of them are combined in some products. For example, while a 'dashboard' may be primarily used for visualising the analytics, the dashboard software may also carry out some or all of the learning analytics processing.

## Software Components

Now that we have identified the main processes of learning analytics, we can look at the key software components that are required. Some vendors are developing systems that attempt to handle all of the processes; others have created products to deal with particular functionality such as predictive modelling, visualisation of the analytics or the handling of interventions. Some of the commercial and open source solutions that have emerged are outlined in Chapter 16.

The Apereo Foundation has developed a vision for an open learning analytics platform (Figure 14.2), which includes the following elements:

- **Collection**: standards-based collection of data using the Experience API or IMS Caliper/Sensor API.
- **Storage**: a repository using the Learning Record Store standard.
- **Analysis**: a learning analytics processor that can handle data mining, data processing, predictive modelling and reporting.
- **Action**: feeding of output from the learning analytics processor to trigger alerts and so forth.
- **Communication**: dashboard for displaying the output from the learning analytics processor.

Apereo actively promotes this architecture and manifests it by integrating various freely available open-source products.[11]

Jisc's architecture for learning analytics (Figure 14.3) expands on Apereo's vision and illustrates the key components required for carrying out learning analytics, providing the data to stakeholders, obtaining students' consent for data collection and intervention, and managing any resulting interventions with learners. Data sources such as the LMS, SIS and library systems are shown at the bottom of the diagram. These include 'self-declared data' that students may wish to provide, such as e-portfolio content and records from wearable devices. The data is fed into the *learning records warehouse*

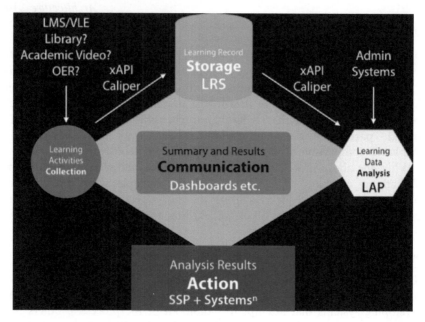

*Figure 14.2* The Apereo Foundation's vision for an open-learning analytics platform.
Apereo Foundation: https://www.apereo.org/communities/learning-analytics-initiative
CC BY 3.0 US https://creativecommons.org/licenses/by/3.0/us/

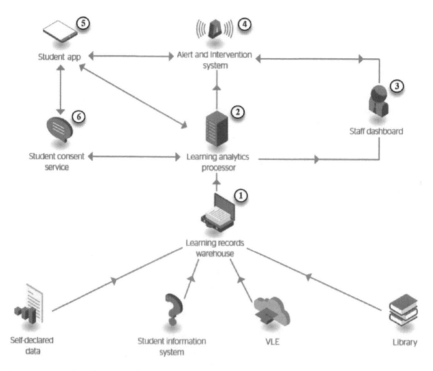

*Figure 14.3* The Jisc Learning Analytics architecture.

(component 1 in Figure 14.3). This contains a learning records store, with its data in the xAPI format. Support is built in for integration with the most common LMSs and SISs. It also contains an area for unstructured data in multiple formats.

An analytics engine or *learning analytics processor* (2) takes data from the warehouse and uses a range of models to develop predictions of future student performance. These are encoded in Predictive Model Markup Language (PMML), a standard for storage and exchange of the models (discussed further in Chapter 9).

The processor feeds a *staff dashboard* (3), which provides a wide range of visualisations of the analytics to the various stakeholders in institutions.

The *alert and intervention* system (4) sends alerts to staff and students and helps to manage the workflow around interventions. A typical scenario might be an alert sent by email to a student who is at risk, with this also being noted on the dashboard of a personal tutor. The tutor is prompted to arrange a meeting with the student, which she does and then records the details of the intervention, for example 'discovered that the student has had a problem at home and recommended seeing a counsellor'. This interaction itself creates potentially useful data for the analytics process, which can be stored in the learning records warehouse, enabling future monitoring of the effectiveness of the intervention. A senior administrator may, for example, at a later stage wish to assess to what extent the interventions taken by tutors with students flagged as 'at risk' appear to have resulted in improved student performance.

A *student app* (5), available on smartphones and also for integration into websites, provides analytics directly to students. Initial data includes engagement statistics and grades, comparisons with 'friends' selected and with class averages. There is also a facility for learners to set targets for aspects of their studies and to log their learning activities as they take place. The event stream on the app shows events such as the student meeting their study target, the awarding of badges and the study performance of 'friends'. Chapter 12 discusses the student app in greater detail.

Finally, a student *consent service* (6) enables students to decide what data they wish to share with the institution and what kind of interventions they are prepared to have – for instance, whether they are happy to be phoned by a personal tutor. The service may prove useful for new data collection or uses of analytics that students have not agreed to previously and therefore require additional consent. Concerns about privacy do seem to vary between countries: it is considered that many German students, for example, would be unwilling to give permission for their data to be used for learning analytics, even if it was anonymised. A process that enabled them to opt into data collection and provide better feedback might, however, give them more confidence.[12]

The elements of this architecture are provided freely by Jisc to universities and colleges in the UK, with the intention of helping them to develop their analytics capabilities. For some of the components both a proprietary and an open source solution are being made available. Institutions can use a subset of the framework or deploy it in its entirety. This flexible model in intended to allow the integration of new data sources as they emerge and the substitution of specific software components as required. Thus if a university has already purchased a dashboard system and has developed expertise in its use it should be able to deploy this instead of the default dashboard provided by Jisc.

## Conclusion

We have examined the main automated processes required for learning analytics and seen how some commentators view these as part of a cycle or continuum, where the analytics lead to enhancements in the provision of learning content or activity for students. I have outlined the key data processes of extracting, transforming, loading, storing, processing, displaying and alerting and described the different types of data that are being used by researchers and in large-scale institutional implementations. We have also seen how the processes are integrated as discrete software components in two open architectures.

Conceptual models of the architecture required for learning analytics by definition provide a simplified view and leave out some of the technical detail and lower-level processes. They also vary between providers, depending on the learning analytics processes for which they are attempting to provide solutions. In Chapter 16, I examine some of this software and analyse the battle for control of the market for learning analytics solutions by an increasing number of providers.

## References

1  Campbell, J. P. & Oblinger, D. G., 2007, *Academic Analytics*, EDUCAUSE.
2  Bader-Natal, A. & Lotze, T., 2011, Evolving a Learning Analytics Platform, *LAK11: Proceedings of the First International Conference on Learning Analytics and Knowledge*, ACM, pp. 180–185.
3  Clow, D., 2012, The Learning Analytics Cycle: Closing the Loop Effectively, *LAK12: Proceedings of the Second International Conference on Learning Analytics and Knowledge*, ACM.
4  Chatti, M. A., Dyckhoff, A. L., Schroeder, U. & Thüs, H., 2012, A Reference Model for Learning Analytics, *International Journal of Technology Enhanced Learning*, 4(5/6), pp. 318–331.
5  Elias, T., 2011, *Learning Analytics: Definitions, Processes and Potential*, p. 8, http://learninganalytics.net/LearningAnalyticsDefinitionsProcessesPotential.pdf (accessed 9 October 2016).
6  Ibid.
7  Kraan, W. & Sherlock, D., 2013, Analytics Tools and Infrastructure, *JISC CETIS Analytics Series*, 1(11), http://publications.cetis.org.uk/wp-content/uploads/2013/01/Analytics-Tools-and-Infrastructure-Vol-1-No11.pdf (accessed 9 October 2016).
8  Elias, *Learning Analytics: Definitions, Processes and Potential*, p. 11.
9  Dyckhoff, A. L., *et al.*, 2012, Design and Implementation of a Learning Analytics Toolkit for Teachers, *Educational Technology and Society*, 15(3), pp. 58–76.

10 Ali, L. *et al.*, 2012, A Qualitative Evaluation of Evolution of a Learning Analytics Tool, *Computers and Education*, 58(1), pp. 470–489.

11 Apereo Learning Analytics Initiative, www.apereo.org/communities/learning-ana lytics-initiative (accessed 2 October 2016).

12 Sclater, N. *et al.*, 2015, Developing an open architecture for learning analytics, *EUNIS 21st Congress*.

# 15  Standards

Learning analytics potentially requires more systems to be able to communicate with each other than any other aspect of an educational institution's IT provision. The most commonly used data sources are the learning management system (LMS) and student information system (SIS). The market-leading products in these areas are beginning to include tools to export the relevant data to learning record stores and warehouses. Add into the mix the data from library, attendance monitoring and assessment systems, however, and the number of configurations and hence data-formatting issues, quickly escalates. A survey that I carried out of 11 universities and colleges in the UK found that no two institutions had the same set of systems to draw on for learning analytics.[1] This may not matter too much for institutions deploying the analytics systems that can be acquired alongside or as part of their SIS or their LMS. However, it becomes complex and expensive to deploy learning analytics systems that gather data from multiple feeder systems unless the data is in standard formats.

## Benefits

Standards help to ensure interoperability, reusability and portability of systems and data.[2] Benefits for organisations of procuring products that comply with standards include:

- **Systems are easier to use.** There are fewer frustrations, errors, warning messages and crashes.[3]
- **Data quality is enhanced.** Data can be more understandable and is less likely to be corrupted or missing.[4]
- **Human input is reduced.** There is less need for people to re-enter or transform data.[5]
- **Preservation of data is easier.** Structures and formats for data tend to change over time but data held in a standard format is more likely to be usable in the future.[6]
- **Data can be accessed more easily.** Data held in non-proprietary formats can be accessed for learning analytics more easily and transferred to

other systems for analysis. Vendors are less able to charge institutions for access to their own data.

- **Datasets can be merged more easily.** This is particularly important for learning analytics: merging data from multiple sources will be facilitated if they are all in the same format.[7, 8]
- **Combined data leads to better validity or new insights.** The value of individual datasets may be increased greatly by merging them with others.[9]
- **Less time and money is spent on adapting systems.** Mapping between different data models becomes less arduous.[10]
- **The risk of vendor lock-in is reduced.** If an institution decides that a system it uses is no longer the best on the market, the standards, if implemented correctly, should enable it to transfer any content it has in the system to a new one.[11]
- **The market grows and innovation is encouraged.** Increased confidence from institutions that investment in a particular system will not result in vendor lock-in encourages them to buy the products, in turn developing the market. This may draw in new vendors, encouraging competition and innovation. Interoperability is particularly important for niche products such as learning record stores, which depend on standards-compliant data from multiple feeder systems and also need to be able to provide that data to predictive modelling and visualisation tools.
- **Data can be exchanged more easily with other organisations.**[12] This will be helpful for institutions wishing to carry out benchmarking of aggregated learning analytics data or, for example, for transferring data to government education departments.

## Learning Technology Standards

Interoperability standards for digital learning have been under development since the 1990s. One of the most prominent examples is the Shareable Content Object Reference Model (SCORM), which enables sequences of learning content to be packaged in a standard format and exchanged between systems. Thus a professor might use an authoring tool to create some learning content, including text, a video and a quiz. The content is then exported in a format that can be provided to students via the LMS. If the institution wishes to change its LMS, it should be possible to transfer this 'content package' to the new system.

Other standards have emerged such as IMS Global's Question and Test Interoperability (QTI) for exchanging assessment content and the Institute of Electrical and Electronic Engineers' (IEEE) Learning Object Metadata standard for describing content in a way that can be understood by multiple systems. IMS Global's Learning Tools Interoperability specification also was developed to allow the exchange of data across multiple systems and has been widely adopted by vendors.

The term 'standard' should be used with caution. Interoperability between systems can take place using a variety of technical and other methods. There are different definitions of what is considered to be a standard, particularly when the word is used outside of formal processes.[13] Official standards created by standards bodies such as the International Standards Organisation are differentiated from 'specifications' developed by organisations such as IMS Global. Specifications are usually less well-defined, more fluid works in progress, with input from multiple stakeholders. They can then evolve into standards, which are more complete and stable and should provide unambiguous guidance on how to implement them.[14, 15]

Cardinali discusses the difficulties of creating the first generation of standards for learning technology, due to the interdisciplinary nature of the requirements, the different sectors involved and the fact that not all stakeholders have a pressing financial need to complete the process. The development process, he suggests, can take between eight and ten years from conception to full adoption. Authors of specifications, Cardinali says, often hope that the documents will become de facto standards, without them having to enter the lengthy and bureaucratic standardisation process.[16]

SCORM is an example of a specification that has received widespread uptake without becoming a standard. The focus was on promotion, stewardship and certification – and there was a major financial driver in that compliance was a requirement for any company wishing to bid to provide training content for the US Department of Defense. Meanwhile, IMS Global's Learning Design specification, Cardinali argues, failed to be widely adopted because of complexity and disagreements. Achieving consensus with the right stakeholders is essential if the standard, whether official or de facto, is to succeed.[17] Those consulted should include a much broader group than the few experts who often determine the direction of the standard.[18]

## Emerging Standards for Learning Analytics

Most references in the literature and elsewhere on the internet relating to learning analytics and interoperability refer to the current *lack* of interoperability in the field; the small group of people who have written about it tend to be researchers rather than practitioners or vendors.[19] Meanwhile, existing standards have not been designed for the purposes of learning analytics,[20] though the developing specifications of the Experience API (xAPI) and IMS Caliper (see below) are an attempt to change this.

It is likely that consciousness of the importance of interoperability is low, too, among faculty and staff in institutions. Hoel & Chen interviewed eight people including students, teachers, support staff and policy makers in Norway regarding their thoughts on interoperability and learning analytics. All interviewees mentioned support for individual learners and data privacy as key concerns.[21] These are clearly more important issues to end users than technical interoperability: similarly, in order to drive a car there is no need to understand how the various components of the engine interact. However, at this early stage of the development of learning analytics, it is important for those interested in the field to understand that a lack of interoperability will hold back progress and could cause problems for institutions in the future.

## Predictive Model Markup Languages

The prediction of students' likelihood of academic success, as has been seen, is one of the main applications of learning analytics. A variety of statistical models can be used for such predictions and these can be represented using an XML-based format called Predictive Model Markup Language (PMML). PMML was developed by a vendor-led body called the Data Mining Group to enable models to be shared between applications in an interoperable format. An example of the language is given in Chapter 9.

## Student Data

Data from the SIS is key to learning analytics and ideally needs to be provided to predictive modelling systems in a standard format. The Predictive Analytics Reporting (PAR) Framework[22] is a consortium of institutions that has defined a framework to improve student retention in US higher education. The framework has recently been acquired by Hobsons. Its aim is to combine anonymised student records to achieve a more holistic perspective and hence better predictions. The PAR data model consists of elements together with definitions for concepts such as gender, permanent residence zip code, race and ethnicity. PAR attempts to overcome the many differences in the ways that institutions or the departments within them define entities such as units, modules, courses and programmes. Some of these are US-specific terms and concepts and need to be translated if they are required in international contexts. In attempt to move the UK sector forward, Jisc has developed its own Unified Data Definition for higher and further education institutions that wish to deploy its learning analytics architecture.[23]

## Learning Activity Data

In order for learning analytics to be undertaken, the activities carried out by the learner need to be captured and stored. Learning management systems and other systems, such as assessment systems, store details of user activity in a variety of formats. It can be difficult, for example, to mine the massive log files accumulated by an LMS together with attendance data or library borrowing records. A learning record store (LRS) captures the learner's activity in a consistent format and this is becoming a key conceptual element of a learning analytics solution. There are some existing commercial learning record stores available, such as Learning Locker[24], Watershed[25] and Saltbox.[26] The Apereo Foundation, meanwhile, provides its open-source OpenLRS.[27]

The leading specification for transferring learning activity data is the Experience API (xAPI).[28] Its development was sponsored by the Advanced Distributed Learning (ADL) Initiative, the organisation behind the SCORM standard for learning content, and is overseen by the US Department of Defense. xAPI uses *statements* that represent a learning activity. A simple statement consists of a noun (or *actor*), a *verb* and an *object*. Examples might be 'John borrowed Plato's Republic' or 'John completed Philosophy 101'. Such statements are the main component of a learning record store. A full code sample adapted from the xAPI specification[29] also helps to explain how it works. This example includes a *result* as well.

```
{
        "actor":{
                "objectType": "Agent",
                "name":"John Smith",
                "mbox":mailto:example.learner@adlnet.gov
        },
        "verb":{
                "id":"http://adlnet.gov/expapi/verbs/attempted",
                "display":{
                        "en-US":"attempted"
                }
        },
        "object":{
                "id":"http://example.adlnet.gov/xapi/example/simpleCBT",
                "definition":{
                        "name":{
                                "en-US":"simple CBT course"
                        },
                        "description":{
                                "en-US":"A fictitious example CBT course."
                        }
                }
        },
        "result":{
                "score":{
                        "scaled":0.95
                },
                "success":true,
                "completion":true
        }
}
```

John Smith, in the above, attempted a 'simple CBT course' and achieved a 'scaled' score of 0.95, completing and succeeding in the course. An additional *context* element, not used in the example above, can incorporate further essential information such as the relationship of the activity to other activities or the teacher's name.[30]

Other aspects to note about the xAPI specification are that:

- It does not specify what the verbs or objects are. This is left to organisations that wish to develop their own definitions.

- Content resulting from a learning activity, such as an essay or a video produced by a student, can be stored alongside it in the LRS.
- The LRS can be situated inside an LMS or can be a separate system.
- Learning tools can be separated from the LMS and operate offline, sending data when they are connected, which is potentially useful for mobile learning.[31]

The verb element describes the action performed by the learner. As well as being a text string, it includes a uniform resource identifier (URI) where the verb is defined with a description and recommended best practices. Specific communities of practice can thus extend the list of verbs or clarify their meaning.[32] This brings a high degree of flexibility but also potentially creates problems for interoperability. Wyver points out a potential issue with systems recording the same learning activity complying with the xAPI specification but implementing it in two different ways by using alternative vocabularies. One LMS may send the statement:

{Actor} {experienced} {content item, Type = article}

While the second sends the statement:

{Actor} {read} {content item, Type = webpage}

Analysing the data will require knowing that the verbs {experienced} and {read} mean the same thing, as do the activity types {article} and {webpage}. The challenge is to keep the vocabulary broad enough to be usable in most situations (and therefore interoperable) while maintaining enough specificity to be useful. Wyver notes that the xAPI community has already collected sets of reusable vocabulary; however, many terms require further refinement.[33] Jisc is deploying xAPI in its learning analytics architecture for UK higher and further education, developing a vocabulary or 'recipe' in order to ensure that learning activity data is described consistently. It commissioned Blackboard to develop a building block for the Blackboard Learn LMS to output xAPI statements and has also adapted a plug-in for the Moodle LMS to do the same.

In 2014 ADL submitted the xAPI specification for standardisation with IEEE. This was rejected because a more modular structure was requested and the European IEEE members wished it to incorporate further details on privacy.[34] The specification is gaining increasing prominence, however, and appears to be becoming a de facto standard for learning activity records. It is now being stewarded by the Data Interoperability Standards Consortium, which hosts regular 'camps' in different parts of the world for organisations and individuals interested in the development of xAPI to come together.[35]

IMS Global is the organisation behind successful specifications for transferring data such as Learning Tools Interoperability (LTI) and Question and Test Interoperability (QTI). The organisation is developing a 'learning measurement framework' called Caliper Analytics,[36] which brings together a number of specifications to create 'learning events' that can be stored in an analytics store. Some of the concepts are similar to those in xAPI, with a learner activity being stored in a learning record store. A learning event in Caliper consists of a *learning context* (e.g. a person or a course) + *action* + *activity context*, which maps onto xAPI's *actor* + *verb* + *object* concept. Whereas xAPI allows others to define their own learning event vocabularies, IMS Caliper defines a standard set of 'learning activity metrics', for example *Reading > annotations* and *Social > connections*, which could be used for analytics.

Caliper is also tackling privacy issues and the workgroup intends to create a 'privacy nutrition label' to describe the information collected, how it is used and with whom it is shared.[37]

Many in the learning analytics community were concerned that the two specifications might create divergent groups of products. The specifications have emerged from different communities and while xAPI is open to all, IMS Global is a membership organisation, with development of the specification and viewing of its initial versions only available to members. At the Learning Analytics and Knowledge Conference Hackathon in 2016, participants developed the 'Edinburgh Statement', which outlined plans to maintain close collaboration through 'an ongoing and open dialogue amongst all vendors, practitioners and organisations influencing the learning analytics landscape'.[38]

## Testing the Interoperability of Three Learning Record Stores

In 2005 three vendors of learning record stores (LRSs) – Watershed, Saltbox, and Learning Locker – carried out extensive interoperability testing across their systems with the aim of:

- testing and improving interoperability across the three systems;
- ascertaining whether the specification was adequate;
- finding gaps in the conformance testing;
- promoting the benefits of learning record stores to the wider community;
- developing collaboration between competing vendors to drive forward the market.

The vendors integrated an LMS, several feeder systems providing learning activity records and instances of each of their three LRSs. They then saw what happened when sharing statements from one LRS to another. The participants note a number of situations where the exchange of learning activity records might be required. Institutions might want to transfer data out of or into an LRS, migrate to a new system, or push statements to a non-LRS system such as a business intelligence system or a certification tool. There also might be multiple LRSs within one institution – an easily imaginable situation in many universities where IT support is provided by individual faculties or departments. Another scenario is enabling learners to take their records with them when they transfer to a new institution.

The experiment was considered successful overall, with statements being transferred across the different systems, each of which had followed the xAPI specification and used the conformance suite. However, various issues emerged: some statements did not work at all and the process was 'fragile'. These were attributed to bugs in the LRSs and no ambiguities in the specification were found regarding the sharing of statements. Once the bugs had been fixed, the second attempt went 'extremely smoothly'. The authors recommend that all LRS vendors should test them against other LRSs in this way and also with multiple activity providers – the 'feeder' systems that provide the statements, such as LMSs and library systems. Vendors of those systems also need to test their interoperability with real LRSs rather than simply relying on conformance testing.[39]

## Conclusion

The reality is that systems differ widely in their functionality and data structures and are likely to implement standards in subtly or significantly different ways. One perhaps paradoxical aspect of interoperability is that, despite the claims of vendors that their systems are interoperable, it may be fundamentally against their commercial interests to facilitate the easy transfer of data to a competitor's system.[40] It can also be costly to implement the standards. Checking that products have been conformance tested and certified by independent bodies thus may become increasingly important for organisations planning to procure products in the learning analytics arena. At the moment, however, learning analytics standards are 'work in progress'[41] and it may take several years before the return on investment in their development can be demonstrated.

Most evolving standards for learning analytics are technical documents relating to the transfer of user, activity or contextual data and have little to do with learning or pedagogy. One danger is that by satisfying ourselves that the systems we procure are 'standards compliant', we validate the expenditure on them without evidence that learning is being enhanced at all. The standard itself may simplify complex issues and be portrayed as something desirable in itself rather than an abstraction that does not completely represent the learning experience.[42] Standards for transferring data across learning analytics warehouses, predictive engines and dashboards are only part of the solution for learning analytics. As has been noted earlier in this book, the subsequent steps of intervening on the basis of the analytics and then evaluating the effectiveness of the interventions are essential too.

## References

1 Sclater, N., 2014, *Learning Analytics: The Current State of Play in UK Higher and Further Education*, Jisc.

2 Frieson, N., 2005, Interoperability and Learning Objects: An Overview of E-Learning Standardization, *Interdisciplinary Journal of Knowledge and Learning Objects*, 1, pp. 23–31.

3 Cooper, A., 2014, *Learning Analytics Interoperability – The Big Picture in Brief*, Learning Analytics Community Exchange.

4 Ibid.

5 Ibid., p. 2.

6 Ibid.

7 Ibid., p. 3.

8 Cooper, A. & Hoel, T., 2015, *Data Sharing Requirements and Roadmap*, Learning Analytics Community Exchange, p. 8.

9 Cooper, *Learning Analytics Interoperability – The Big Picture in Brief*, p. 2.

10 Cooper & Hoel, *Data Sharing Requirements and Roadmap*, p. 14.

11 Cooper, *Learning Analytics Interoperability – The Big Picture in Brief*, p. 2.

12 Ibid., p. 3.

13 Cooper, A., 2015, *Specifications and Standards – Quick Reference Guide*, Learning Analytics Community Exchange.

14 Frieson, Interoperability and Learning Objects: An Overview of E-Learning Standardization, p. 4.

15 Varlamis, I. & Apostolakis, I., 2006, The Present and Future of Standards for E-Learning Technologies, *Interdisciplinary Journal of Knowledge and Learning Objects*, 2, pp. 59–76.

16 Cardinali, F., 2015, *Towards Learning Analytics Interoperability at the Workplace (LAW Profile)*, Learning Analytics Community Exchange, pp. 3–6.

17 Ibid., pp. 6–7.

18 Blandin, B., 2004, Are E-Learning Standards Neutral? *Proceedings CALIE 04: International Conference on Computer Aided Learning in Engineering Education*, p. 6.

19 Cooper, *Specifications and Standards – Quick Reference Guide*.

20 Cooper & Hoel, *Data Sharing Requirements and Roadmap*, p. 15.

21 Hoel, T. & Chen, W., 2014, Learning Analytics Interoperability – Looking for Low-Hanging Fruits, *Proceedings of the 22nd International Conference on Computers in Education*, pp. 4–8.

22 PAR: www.parframework.org/ (accessed 2 October 2016).

23 Jisc Unified Data Definitions: https://github.com/jiscdev/analytics-udd (accessed 2 October 2016).

24 Learning Locker: https://learninglocker.net/ (accessed 2 October 2016).

25 Watershed LRS: https://www.watershedlrs.com/ (accessed 2 October 2016).

26 Saltbox: www.saltbox.com/ (accessed 2 October 2016).

27 Apereo OpenLRS: https://github.com/Apereo-Learning-Analytics-Initiative/OpenLRS (accessed 2 October 2016).

28 Experience API: https://www.adlnet.gov/xapi/ (accessed 2 October 2016).

29 xAPI specification: https://github.com/adlnet/xAPI-Spec (accessed 2 October 2016).

30 Corbi, A. & Burgos, D., 2014, Review of Current Student-Monitoring Techniques used in Elearning-Focused Recommender Systems and Learning Analytics. The Experience API & LIME Model Case Study, *International Journal of Interactive*

*Multimedia and Artificial Intelligence: Special Issue on Multisensor User Tracking and Analytics to Improve Education and other Application Fields*, 2(7), pp. 44–52.

31 Blanco, Á. d. *et al.*, 2013, E-Learning Standards and Learning Analytics. Can Data Collection Be Improved by Using Standard Data Models? *Global Engineering Education Conference (EDUCON)*, pp. 1255–1261.

32 Ibid., pp. 1258–1259.

33 Wyver Solutions Ltd, 2015, Choosing Your xAPI Vocabulary, www.wyversolutions. co.uk/2015/05/18/choosing-your-xapi-vocabulary (accessed 9 October 2016).

34 Hoel, T. & Cooper, A., 2015, *Standards to Support Learning Analytics, 2015*, Learning Analytics Community Exchange, p. 6.

35 Data Interoperability Standards Consortium: http://datainteroperability.org/ (accessed 2 October 2016).

36 Caliper Analytics: https://www.imsglobal.org/activity/caliperram (accessed 2 October 2016).

37 Hoel & Cooper, *Standards to Support Learning Analytics*, p. 4.

38 The Edinburgh Statement for Learning Analytics Interoperability: https://docs. google.com/document/d/18VJ9hVcfk9sOzs2MEeZ59Q5RSz1jZnUHzSWFSed nEXg/ (accessed 2 October 2016).

39 Downes, A., Shahrazad, A. & Smith, R., 2015, *Sharing between LRSs: A Collaborative Experiment in Practical Interoperability*, Rustici Software.

40 Sclater, N. *et al.*, 2002, Interoperability with CAA: Does it Work in Practice? *Proceedings of the Sixth CAA Conference.*

41 Hoel & Cooper, *Standards to Support Learning Analytics*, p. 2.

42 Marshall, S., 2004, E-Learning Standards: Open Enablers of Learning or Compliance Strait Jackets? *Beyond the Comfort Zone: Proceedings of the 21st Ascilite Conference*, pp. 596–605.

# 16 Products

Chief information officers and other senior leaders have become used to continual approaches from vendors, keen to cash in on the interest that has developed around the potential for analytics to solve their pressing institutional issues. A growing range of products is marketed as having learning analytics capabilities. However, the field is new, the technologies and functionality are evolving rapidly and many systems are as yet unproven at scale. There are numerous new entrants to the marketplace, as well as established players that are incorporating analytics capabilities within systems initially developed for other purposes. Some vendors offer 'complete' solutions, even customising predictive models for individual courses at an institution, and other companies are concentrating on niche products as part of an overall learning analytics architecture, or simply ensuring their offerings can provide the user activity data required for analytics.

Given the wide variety of potential applications for learning analytics, including early alert, course recommendation, adaptive learning and curriculum design, no single platform can meet all possible requirements. Procuring a system will therefore initially require deciding in which of these areas the institution wishes to focus its activity. For many, the most pressing need is addressing poor retention rates and they may be looking to purchase an early alert system. Other organisations will be more interested, for example, in enhancing overall learner attainment and using the data to identify which parts of the curriculum should be enhanced, or to assess the effectiveness of adaptive learning software.

There is no simple way to categorise these systems and their functionality can overlap considerably. Meanwhile, vendors are continually adding new features, which means that their systems cannot be restricted to a particular category. However, they can be roughly grouped as:

- **Learning management system (LMS)-based engagement reporting tools.** Users increasingly expect their LMS to be able to report on student engagement and reporting functionality is being incorporated into the main LMSs.
- **Learning management system-centric analytics systems.** Learning management system vendors are selling additional, more comprehensive

analytics products, which attempt to draw data not only from the LMS but from other systems such as the student information system (SIS).

- **Student information system-centric analytics systems.** SIS vendors have also realised that their systems can be at the centre of the learning analytics ecosystem, so they have built products to integrate data from other systems, such as the LMS.
- **Business intelligence (BI) systems.** Often already in use at institutions for business planning purposes, these are increasingly acquiring functionality and visualisations for carrying out learning analytics.
- **Platform-independent solutions.** A few companies offer solutions for various aspects of learning analytics such as student success and curriculum enhancement. These sit outside the LMS, SIS or any existing BI system and can usually be customised to the institution's requirements.
- **Application-specific products.** Adaptive learning systems, early alert systems and course recommender systems are examples of new products providing specific functionality, which again sit outside the LMS and SIS (though they may be delivered to students via the LMS).
- **Niche components.** Learning record stores, dashboards for learning analytics, student apps and alert and intervention systems are examples of components that are sometimes sold as products in their own right to fulfil a single part of a learning analytics architecture.
- **Learning activity provider systems.** Vendors of 'feeder' systems that provide the data for learning analytics (e.g. library systems or attendance monitoring systems) are beginning to incorporate functionality to export learning activity data.

## LMS Engagement Reporting Tools

A few products sit within the LMS, look at LMS data only and provide simple indications of a student's progress, raising flags when the student appears to be at risk.[1] These tools are aimed at instructors and sometimes also at the students themselves. Some of them send email alerts to students and faculty. The products include Blackboard *Retention Centre*, which is an integral part of the Blackboard *Learn* LMS and the Moodle plug-in *Engagement Analytics*. Such tools are likely to evolve into more sophisticated systems, perhaps drawing in learning activity data from 'feeder' systems. Student apps providing some LMS functionality will also increasingly incorporate analytics.

## LMS-Centric Analytics Systems

Blackboard's *Analytics for Learn* (Figure 16.1) combines data from its *Learn* LMS platform with data from the SIS to enable more extensive reporting and analysis on individual students and groups of students, including student

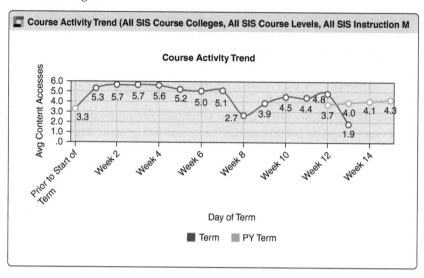

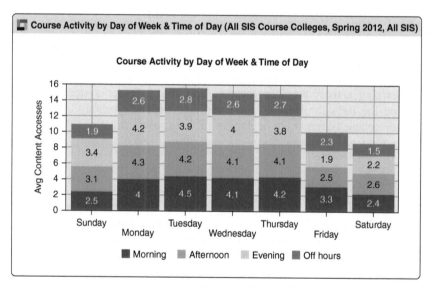

*Figure 16.1* Visualisation of course activity in Blackboard's Analytics for Learn.
Image is the property of Blackboard and has been used with the permission of Blackboard

performance and engagement, academic adoption, tool and content use and insights into course design and pedagogic effectiveness. The system is closely bundled with a business intelligence tool. Much of the functionality could indeed be described as business intelligence, although low-level drilling down to individual student records is available.

Other LMS vendors have developed similar functionality in separate products that draw data from the LMS and other systems. D2L, for example, has *Brightspace Insights*, which provides views of how tools are used across an organisation and enables analysis of the patterns of behaviour that contribute to learner success by instructors and higher-level administrators.

## SIS-Centric Analytics Systems

While LMS vendors would no doubt like their systems to be at the heart of an institution's learning analytics efforts, some SIS vendors are also attempting to position their own systems as *the* place for organisations to analyse data on students and their learning. Ellucian's *Student Retention Performance* tool, for example, was developed to help identify at-risk students, examine retention and degree completion rates and analyse the effectiveness of retention strategies. In the UK, Tribal developed a learning analytics product alongside their SIS, *SITS:Vision*, with the University of Wolverhampton and now provides this through Jisc's learning analytics architecture.

## Business Intelligence Systems

Many institutions have already developed expertise in using business intelligence (BI) software to analyse higher-level aspects of educational provision such as recruitment, financial planning or meeting government reporting requirements. Specifically, this might involve calculating graduation rates per course, analysing student surveys or assessing the academic success of minority groups. While much of this data is the same as that used for learning analytics, business intelligence usually involves examining it at a more aggregated level. However, some institutions are using BI systems for applications that could be considered learning analytics and enable drilling down to individual student records.

One such system is *Qlik*, which enables multiple data sources to be loaded and joined into a single model and is stored in machine memory for rapid processing. Dashboards can then be developed to visualise and interrogate the data by different users in the organisation. Figure 16.2 shows a dashboard which integrates data on student activity, such as lecture attendance, exam attendance, assignment submission, logins to the LMS and the campus network, library usage, time spent on learning material, social participation and attainment. Each metric can be weighted based on historical data. Overviews are provided of at-risk students, which can be broken down and displayed by criteria such as academic level, gender, age or ethnicity.

One reseller of Qlik, BME Solutions, has developed a range of educational applications for the product, potentially removing much of the development burden from institutions. Interestingly, automated email alerts for at-risk students have been integrated with Qlik, meaning it cannot be categorised simply as business intelligence or dashboard software but is straying into the territory of alert and intervention systems.

Most of the SIS-centric and LMS-centric systems are themselves built on top of BI systems. While Blackboard's Analytics for Learn is built on the

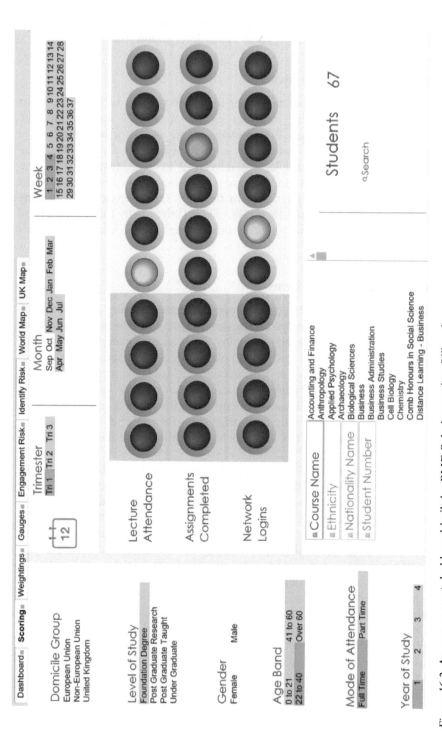

*Figure 16.2* An engagement dashboard built by BME Solutions, using Qlik software.

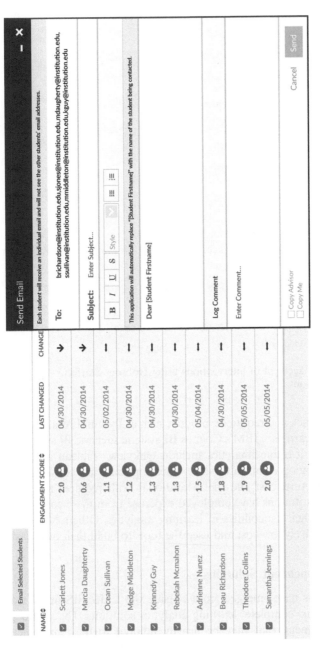

*Figure 16.3* List of students with very low engagement and the ability for instructors to email them all directly from Civitas Learning's Inspire for Faculty product, part of its Student Success Platform.

Source: Civitas Learning, Inc

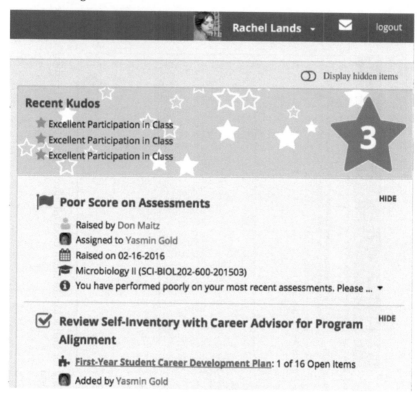

*Figure 16.4* Management of interventions using Hobsons Starfish.
Starfish by Hobsons

Microsoft BI stack and requires a product such as Pyramid Analytics to view the data, Desire2Learn uses IBM's Cognos BI system. Generic BI systems currently being used for learning analytics include Qlikview, Tableau and Cognos, all already widely adopted at universities. These options vary considerably in complexity, architecture, cost and the institutional skills required for their deployment. Some institutions have employed expertise from these companies to help them develop their capabilities in learning analytics. Others have adopted the systems at relatively low cost and used the tools to build their own dashboards.

## Platform-Independent Solutions

A few solutions have emerged from outside the LMS, SIS or BI worlds and are promoted as 'complete' learning analytics solutions. The vendors of these systems recommend that they be heavily tailored to the requirements of an institution, with predictive models sometimes developed by the vendor using historical data on a course-by-course basis. Examples include DTP SolutionPath in the UK, whose product, StREAM, focusses on academic progression, with customisable dashboards for tutors, students and others, alerts and a student app. Civitas Learning, based in the US, meanwhile, provides its *Student Success Platform* to help institutions address issues relating to retention, progression, performance, satisfaction, graduation, engagement and learning efficacy (Figure 16.3).

Hobsons *Starfish* (Figure 16.4) is another widely used platform-independent solution that addresses student success and engagement, including functionality to identify students at risk and to manage interventions.

## Application-Specific Products

A range of new products is emerging to provide individual learning analytics applications, such as early alert, recommender systems and adaptive learning. Some of these are tightly integrated with other systems or draw on their data. For example, Ellucian's *Course Signals*, the early alert tool originally pioneered by Purdue University, can be integrated with and displayed within an LMS. It combines engagement data with data drawn from the SIS to make more accurate predictions of student success than using LMS data alone. Blackboard has purchased *Blue Canary* and rebranded it as *Blackboard Predict*, a predictive analytics system for student success, which draws data from Blackboard *Learn* and an SIS and is made available to users from within *Learn*. A further product, Blackboard *X-Ray Analytics*, is integrated with *Moodle* and enables the identification of at-risk learners and monitors the quality of learner contributions and their social cohesion by analysing discussion forums.

The evolving tools for course recommendation and adaptive learning were discussed earlier in their respective chapters. Market reviews of adaptive learning products have also been carried out by Tyton Partners[2] and Brown.[3] It is not difficult to foresee a requirement to combine data on student use of application-specific products, such as adaptive learning systems, with other aspects of their learning and engagement into dashboards giving a more complete picture. Thus application-specific products may themselves become 'feeder' products – providers of learning activity data to more comprehensive student success systems. Whether users will prefer to access the analytics from within these systems or from a single all-embracing system will ultimately depend on their usefulness and usability.

## Niche Components

Learning analytics architectures specify a range of core components such as predictive engines, dashboards and alert and intervention systems. Some vendors have produced niche products that deliver this functionality. Learning record stores available include HT2's *Learning Locker*, *Wax LRS* from Saltbox and *Watershed LRS*. The Apereo open source learning analytics suite includes an Open Learning Record Store, Learning Analytics Processor and Open Dashboard. These have been integrated into Jisc's learning analytics architecture by Unicon and Marist College, together with Tribal's learning analytics processor and dashboard and a student app built by Therapy Box. The idea behind the architecture is that institutions will be able to select the best components for their requirements and to be able to replace them if better products emerge (see Chapter 14).

## Learning Activity Provider Systems

Systems other than the LMS and SIS contain potentially valuable data for learning analytics. Examples include attendance monitoring systems, library and reading list software and e-book readers. One system for downloading and viewing e-books, VitalSource *CourseSmart Analytics*, provides data for presentation within an LMS on aspects of student e-book access and calculates an 'engagement index', which can be presented within the LMS.

Extracting the data from multiple systems using their own proprietary formats and transforming it into consistent formats, usable by a predictive engine, is likely to be a complex and expensive task for institutions. As learning analytics develops, systems customers will increasingly require systems to make their learning activity data available in the emerging standard formats.

## Conclusion

An institution's choice of learning analytics products may be determined to some extent by the systems it has already deployed. For example, if it has invested significantly in Blackboard Learn as its institutional LMS it is unlikely to use analytics tools developed for Moodle. Institutions can carry out limited learning analytics at low cost by deploying one of the LMS-based engagement reporting tools. The choice for more sophisticated analytics based on multiple data sources may be whether to:

- buy into an analytics system developed by a trusted vendor of an LMS, SIS or BI system already deployed at the institution;
- procure one of the platform-independent solutions together with consultancy from the vendor to tailor it to local requirements; or
- piece together the individual components of a learning analytics architecture, perhaps using an existing BI system and deploying individual commercial or open-source tools as required.

The institution will also need to decide whether it has the expertise to go it alone or needs to purchase consultancy from one of the increasing number of vendors eager for business in this area. Also worth considering is that a number of the products available are components of wider BI offerings, which cover other activities such as student recruitment and fundraising. It may be that the commissioning of a learning analytics solution should be part of a wider exercise to develop better use of analytics and data-informed decision making across the institution.

## References

1 Sclater, N., 2014, Learning Analytics: What Types of Product are Available? *Effective Learning Analytics*, 2 October, https://analytics.jiscinvolve.org/wp/2014/10/02/learning-analytics-what-types-of-product-are-available/ (accessed 9 October 2016).
2 Tyton Partners, 2013, *Learning to Adapt: Understanding the Adaptive Learning Supplier Landscape*.
3 Brown, J., 2015, *Personalizing Post-Secondary Education: An Overview of Adaptive Learning Solutions for Higher Education*, S+R.

# 17 Expert Thoughts on Technologies

I asked each of my panel of 20 experts what they thought the main challenges were around technologies and data. In many cases their answers centred on issues around ethics and privacy and concerns around human adoption, rather than relating to the technologies specifically. Physicist and astronomer, Timothy McKay feels, encouragingly, that:

> A lot of the technical challenges are a little hard but they're a lot less hard than many of the technical things I've done in my science career.

However difficult the technical issues are, the deployment of learning analytics will mean organisations having to integrate new systems. Even at relatively small institutions, says Josh Baron:

> the amount of data we're collecting per student is so much that you need ... really big data systems at your institution ... So understanding how to deploy and support and run those systems I think is going to be a barrier for places. But not an insurmountable barrier.

## Data Access

Abelardo Pardo identifies the problem of colleagues often being unable to access the data, even though it is being captured. He believes that educational technology products should have easy access through an API to the data collected, enabling enterprise systems to talk to them and transfer the data to the institution's data warehouse. Alyssa Wise reports hearing of many situations where people cannot view their LMS data, either because it is hosted elsewhere or because the technical mechanisms are simply not in place to access it. She feels it is important to be able to query the LMS database directly rather than to use the 'pre-packaged stuff that they're rolling out' and this should be 'without having to have a PhD in computer science'. Mark Milliron, meanwhile, refers to the current situation of many systems as 'data jail':

Where you're having cloud-based providers or digital providers who are housing data off-premises from the institution, and they see that data as a commodity, and they want to sell it back to the institution ... Actually it's that institution's data, it's their students' information, so often they can't even bring the data back to federate it with other data sources because they'd have to pay for it. A lot of folks are now trying to write into their purchasing requirements 'you can't hold our data in jail anymore'. We've got to solve that because often the data in itself is OK but when combined with other data sources becomes amazing.

Stephanie Teasley found it easy to get started with analytics at Michigan as the institution owned the data and held it on campus, but she has found the data from MOOCs more difficult to get hold of and messier. She worries about institutions failing to understand the contracts they are signing with vendors and what they are potentially giving away. She recommends collaborations such as Unizin,[1] where institutions have greater power to negotiate contracts with vendors as a collective group and can more easily insist on unfettered access to their own data.

## Standards, Open Architectures and Open-Source Systems

Mark Glynn refers to Jisc's efforts to develop common architectures and data structures in the UK and is 'slightly jealous' that Irish institutions are not able to benefit from a similar national collaboration. Rebecca Ferguson discusses one institution in Ireland that is embarking on its third learning analytics solution, has wasted hundreds of thousands of euros on previous options and is having to relabel its data again because it cannot be transferred seamlessly between the systems. She is concerned, too, about the possible divergence in the emerging standards for learning analytics:

> It sounds as if we're going down different standardisation routes at the moment – we don't want to end up with a sort of VHS vs Betamax, half of us doing one thing and half of us doing the other. Why aren't we doing the same thing in the first place?

Abelardo Pardo wants to see the tools available being much more interoperable, with better guidance on how academics can use the data available to them. A series of recipes would recommend the appropriate, data-driven interventions, with new vocabularies to describe these. Alan Berg, too, is concerned about interoperability and would like data to flow freely, ensuring that users have control over it. He also thinks that a reference implementation of an open learning analytics architecture, such as the standards-based one that Jisc is building, and consolidating the data dictionaries will be essential to encourage adoption by institutions and competition in the marketplace. Data standardisation would also help students who move from one institution to another, something that is particularly prevalent in Australia, notes Shane

Dawson. This would increase flexibility and microcredentialing of courses and would enable the collection of data from more informal workplace-based activities.

Recognising that deploying open-source systems is not free, Josh Baron nevertheless suggests that this may be a way for some institutions to move forward with learning analytics relatively cheaply. He also expresses a concern that the knowledge maps that are increasingly being developed for adaptive learning systems are currently all proprietary. Referring to disadvantaged students in the US, as well as students in developing nations, he says:

> If we're living in a world where some people have access to those knowledge maps and the technology to get individual personalised tutors from them, and then there's a whole population who don't have any access ... that doesn't sound like a good thing to me. And again I think that's why there needs to be more of an effort to create open options for people so that this technology can spread in a way it might not if that option's not out there.

## Tools

While the data may become increasingly accessible and available in standardised formats, its presentation to students, staff and faculty still often leaves a lot to be desired. Doug Clow mentions the approaches of some designers of learning analytics dashboards such as 'well let's just throw it in because it looks cool' or 'we can measure it so let's have it in there in case it's useful later'. Kirsty Kitto suggests that:

> People measure what they can measure; they don't measure what they ought to be measuring. There's no such thing as a model-free dataset ... if people don't appreciate that there's some sort of underlying reason that the data was originally collected, and respect that, then they'll end up with a really dumb flow of consequences.

Dragan Gašević adds that most of the tools are designed for data scientists:

> Many people don't see why we have all these charts – maybe just a checklist of things that people need to address is more than sufficient.

Cathy Gunn, too, would like to see new tools that can

> combine and present raw data in readable format, and make complex analysis techniques accessible to teachers who aren't data scientists ... Many excellent systems are either available or under development, but many are still too complex or inflexible to appeal to the average teacher.

Currently, not all institutions have a single learning environment on which to perform analytics – there are often multiple systems in place, particularly in large research-led universities. Alyssa Wise, who has worked at one such institution, would like to see the systems there consolidated – instructors would be able to choose from a limited but consistent set of tools. These would have been well designed both for learning and for gathering the 'smart data' she would like to see being captured.

## Reference

1  Unizin: www.unizin.org (accessed 2 October 2016).

# Part V
# Deployment

# 18 Institutional Readiness

The successful implementation of an institution-wide learning analytics project requires the organisation to be 'ready' in various ways. Initiatives that are not properly prepared run the risk of alienating important stakeholders, destroying confidence in the potential for learning analytics and, not least, wasting significant resources. Yet it is common to find that institutions are quite unprepared for the changes required to their processes. Fritz notes that 'the lack of a cohesive vision for academic analytics in higher education often means that individual campuses are building the plane while they fly it'.[1] Even small-scale learning analytics projects or pilots at departmental level require a number of areas to be considered and dealt with in advance.

Various researchers have analysed the elements that need to be in place. As far back as 2005, Goldstein & Katz found three significant factors that were present in institutions that had successfully implemented what they termed 'academic analytics': effective training, the commitment of leadership and staff with strong analytical skills.[2] More recently, Pressler recommends deploying the McKinsey 7S Framework for preparing and implementing organisational change, which examines: shared values, strategy, structure, systems, style, staff and skills.[3] Bichsel uses a similar set of categories in analysing an institution's maturity for implementing learning analytics: culture/process, data/reporting/tools, investment, expertise and governance/infrastructure.[4] Meanwhile Norris & Baer propose five areas to analyse:[5]

- technology infrastructure, tools and applications, including the combination of data, information, reporting and analytics capabilities;
- policies, processes and practices – and ensuring that a 'data-driven mindset' is built into processes;
- skills of faculty, staff, students and other stakeholders – and their focus on enhancing student success;
- culture and behaviours of institutions – moving from simple reporting to developing a culture of evidence to drive interventions;
- institutional leadership – there must be executive commitment to financial investment in new solutions and practices and to changing the culture and behaviours.

## The Learning Analytics Readiness Instrument

Arnold *et al.* developed a 'Learning Analytics Readiness Instrument' using a 90-item survey, which assessed:

- **governance and infrastructure** – including technical infrastructure, institutional policies, governance and oversight;
- **ability** – the wide range of skills necessary for a learning analytics initiative and adequate access to those skills;
- **data** – the types of data available, their validity and reliability, storage, access, ownership etc.;
- **culture** – acceptance of data-driven decision making, support from stakeholders and a shared vision;
- **process** – the stakeholders, project management and processes.

Thirty-three individuals in nine institutions were surveyed, all either faculty or staff based at large research universities in the US Midwest. Participants responded to statements such as 'my institution has a culture that accepts the use of data to make decisions' and 'my institution has professionals with knowledge and expertise in manipulating data from multiple sources and platforms to conform to institutional specifications'. Analysis of the responses showed that readiness for learning analytics differed widely across institutions, even among this group of relatively similar institutions.[6]

The EDUCAUSE Analytics Maturity Index for Higher Education (Figure 18.1) measures six different dimensions of readiness, based on responses to a series of questions. This model has been refined over several

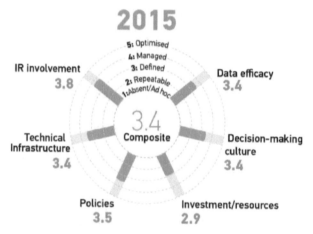

*Figure 18.1* EDUCAUSE Benchmarking Service; EDUCAUSE Analytics Maturity Index for Higher Education, 2015.

years and the key areas are now defined as: information resources involvement, technical infrastructure, policies, investment/resources, decision-making culture and data efficacy. In each of these dimensions institutional readiness is rated as *absent/ad hoc, repeatable, defined, managed* or *optimised.*

Arnold and her colleagues suggest that, while informative, such ratings may not provide nuanced enough guidance to institutions and that they should be backed up with more in-depth discussion.[7]

## Assessing Readiness for Learning Analytics at UK Universities

A large-scale programme in the UK, funded by Jisc, has employed Blackboard and Unicon to visit universities in order to evaluate their preparedness for learning analytics. Consultants from these two companies carry out a readiness assessment during a three-day campus visit, using broadly similar methodologies. They interview stakeholders and hold workshops during which participants are asked to identify their goals for a learning analytics initiative and to discuss issues such as institutional culture and technical infrastructure. Unicon provides a programme that is customised to the requirements of the institution, while Blackboard believes that a somewhat more standardised agenda is appropriate. As well as helping to ensure all necessary prerequisites are considered, the visits have the additional benefits of catalysing the learning analytics initiative and bringing together stakeholders who rarely have opportunities to meet, but whose cooperation will be essential in the anticipated project.

A subsequent report issued to the institution describes its readiness according to certain criteria and recommends actions. In the Blackboard methodology, more than 20 evidence statements are mapped onto a number of rubrics. The institution is assessed on 'four pillars of readiness': culture, processes, people and technology, each of which is rated as one of:

- not ready with recommendations
- ready with recommendations
- ready.[8]

Sheila MacNeill, whose institution, Glasgow Caledonian University, was assessed in this way, summarises the visit on her blog:

I was pleasantly surprised that we got such [a] good score in terms of our cultural readiness. The validation of having an external report from a nationally recognised agency such as Jisc is also incredibly useful for those of us on the ground to remind/cajole (hit people [on] the head – oh wait that's only in my dreams) with in terms of what we should be doing next.

However, MacNeill also expresses her frustrations at the difficulty for the institution in prioritising learning analytics over other pressing developments such as improving the admissions process, or updating the SIS and finance systems.[9]

Andy Ramsden, the Strategic Consultant involved from Blackboard, was surprised to find a number of similarities across the very varied universities where he has carried out readiness assessments:

- a strong vision and belief in the importance of learning analytics from senior managers in order to enhance the student experience;
- interest in better reporting and dashboards, rather than simply predictive analytics at this stage;
- interest in enhancing both progression and attainment;
- the agent of change seen primarily as the personal tutor mediating the data rather than automated, unmediated, student-facing dashboards.[10]

## Leadership

Norris & Baer argue that commitment and leadership from the most senior level in the institution is critical for the implementation of learning analytics.[11] A study of learning analytics at Australian universities, carried out by Colvin *et al.*, consulted 28 experts in the field: a major theme to emerge was the importance of senior leaders in setting the strategic direction and indicating the institution's commitment.[12] Apart from this, which leadership attributes are important for ensuring the successful roll-out of learning analytics initiatives? Kotter proposes that effective leadership involves eight steps:

1. Establish a sense of urgency.
2. Create a guiding coalition.
3. Develop a change vision.
4. Communicate the vision for buy-in.
5. Empower broad-based action.
6. Generate short-term wins.
7. Never let up.
8. Incorporate the changes into the institutional culture.[13]

However, being expert in the art of leadership in a generic way may not be enough. Arnold *et al.* suggest that leaders should possess domain knowledge too: 'Absolutely vital to success was having a leader with a deep scholarly understanding of learning analytics principles and practices and the mechanics of creating predictive models.'[14]

In reality, leadership is likely to have to occur at multiple levels in the organisation. A member of the senior executive may be required to provide overall sponsorship and to ensure that adequate funding is secured and that there is buy-in from stakeholders. This person is unlikely, though, to have the in-depth knowledge of learning analytics and predictive modelling that Arnold and colleagues suggest is required. A project leader, fully supported and empowered by the senior sponsor, with an understanding of the issues and the time to devote to running the project, may also have to be identified.

The ability for leadership to be effective will vary depending on the type of institution. Norris & Baer found that for-profit institutions in the US had the most effective leadership in learning analytics and had 'largely achieved enterprise-wide commitment to pervasive student success practices and behaviour change.' They also acknowledge that data and case studies are particularly hard to come by in this sector.[15] This was confirmed to me by an ex-employee of a for-profit university who had witnessed a particularly comprehensive and effective approach to learning analytics but was prevented from talking publicly about the details.

Organisations may have an uphill struggle to achieve any kind of large-scale institutional change, particularly where faculties, schools or departments have high levels of autonomy. Initiative fatigue is a serious issue in some universities and colleges and learning analytics may be perceived by overworked faculty and staff as yet another project being foisted on them by leaders keen to make their mark before abandoning the institution for their next career move. When I asked faculty in one institution I visited about the importance of strong leadership in the success of learning analytics, the response was: 'Promotion by the Vice Chancellor in this place would be the kiss of death for the project.' Evidence of success by advocates 'on the ground', especially students and faculty, might ultimately, therefore, have more impact than pronouncements by senior management.

## Culture and Vision

The leader clearly needs to be aware of the organisational culture to be effective in convincing others of the initiative's benefits. This requires an understanding of shared values, the beliefs held about what is in the best interests of the institution, its students and employees. A learning analytics initiative can and probably should be built around the institutional mission or strategic plan. Widening participation might, for example, be a shared value of the organisation – ensuring equality of access for different ethnic groups or disabled students and providing additional support for those groups if they are considered to be disadvantaged in some way. If it can be shown how analytics can help to fulfil this agenda then the project may have more chance of acceptance.

**Discovering the Importance of Culture when Implementing Learning Analytics in a Canadian University**

Learning analytics and a range of research instruments were used by Macfadyen & Dawson to assess the uptake of learning technologies across a Canadian university. They note that, while issues of functionality, scalability and reliability are important, it can be tempting to focus exclusively on the technology. They argue that the development of a pedagogical vision is also essential: 'A focus on technological issues merely generates "urgency" around technical systems and integration concerns, and fails to address the complexities and challenges of institutional culture and change.'

These researchers believe that learning analytics failed to inform the development of a strategic vision for learning technology at their institution. They suggest that higher education does not give enough attention to the importance of culture within institutions and that resistance to innovation and change needs to be considered from the start.[16]

Learning analytics differs from some other change initiatives or information technology projects in its potential for the misuse of personal data in multiple ways. 'Many myths surrounding the use of data, privacy infringement and ownership of data need to be dispelled and can be properly modulated once the values of learning analytics are realized.'[17] It may help to propose solutions to some of the legal and ethical issues in a policy document, agreed by the key stakeholders, particularly those most directly affected by learning analytics, who are likely to be students and faculty. Jisc's Code of Practice for Learning Analytics, as discussed in Chapter 20, provides what amounts to a checklist of the key issues to be considered. This states early on that learning analytics 'should be for the benefit of students'. Other important principles include being open and transparent at all stages of learning analytics, ensuring that the processes are valid and robust, upholding the privacy of student data and enabling individuals to access all the data held about them.[18] Being explicit around such principles and enshrining them in a policy that has the approval of students, faculty and staff, will help to build confidence in the initiative.

## Strategy and Investment

The McKinsey framework considers that strategy should include gaining and maintaining competitive advantage. Indeed, the main drivers for learning analytics often relate to cost/benefit or return on investment.[19]

The savings resulting from retaining learners who might otherwise have dropped out can be a powerful argument for justifying expenditure on a learning analytics initiative. While consideration of the bottom line is vital for most educational institutions, there are often other concerns at the strategic level such as 'student success' (e.g. improving grades and graduate employment rates), increasing student satisfaction or improving the relationship between faculty and students. Ultimately, of course, improvements in each of these may have a financial impact on the institution as well. In Chapter 19 I examine more closely the goals and benefits that institutions have proposed for their projects.

There is a danger that learning analytics is seen as a temporary project and that budgets are not built into long-term operating costs. Competitor analysis may therefore be useful before embarking on a large-scale initiative. Much can be learned from how other organisations are implementing learning analytics, by reviewing publications or arranging visits.[20] Some institutions may consider that their projects in this area give them competitive advantage, so may be less forthcoming. However, the learning analytics community comprises many innovative researchers with a mission to improve education overall and a willingness to share their experiences.

## Structure and Governance

The organisational structure that is put in place for the initiative – who reports to whom and who is responsible for the various tasks – will be key to its success. Learning analytics projects can be particularly threatening for individuals as they cut across existing roles and power structures. There may be a requirement to change aspects of institutional and IT governance to incorporate the project and the new processes resulting from it. Data ownership for learning analytics is inherently distributed and particular stakeholders may hold onto data for reasons of procedure, privacy or ethics. As well as the crucial process of establishing who owns the relevant data, it may also be necessary to redefine the human and technical entities that supply or input data, process it, output it or consume it.[21]

Governance around the processes of defining the metrics and algorithms and interpreting the analytics is also required. Who in the organisation decides what metrics should be selected and which statistical techniques are deployed? Who should be tasked with making sense of the analytics[22] and who takes the decisions over the intervention strategy?

Not to be underestimated are personal or political reasons for obstructing the initiative and an unwillingness to give up the perceived power associated with the control over data. This can be a serious impediment to organisational change. However, some institutions report that one of the benefits of an institutional learning analytics initiative is the breaking down of silos and the forcing of data owners to cooperate for the benefit of the institution and ultimately of the students.[23] Meanwhile, control of the initiative itself and the associated processes and staffing may become subject to political infighting. Involvement in learning analytics because of its novel, innovative and cross-cutting nature, can be a way for individuals to differentiate themselves from others and to further their careers.

There are mixed views as to whether individuals or parts of the organisation can really 'own' data. While individual employees may feel they have been given the power of data ownership, the ultimate legal entity entitled to collect, use, copy, transfer or destroy the data is usually the institution itself. Furthermore, there is an argument that students should be the owners of the data pertaining to themselves. It may be appropriate to give students the power to change personal information such as their addresses themselves. However, allowing them to amend learning activity records such as learning management system (LMS) accesses or library visits makes less sense and may result in inaccurate analytics.

## Technology and Data

Assessing technological readiness is another task that many organisations should put effort into before embarking on an institutional learning analytics project. The procurement of a new system requires analysis of the needs of different stakeholders, addressing ease of use, functionality and fit with existing systems. Various new tools may be required.[24] Norris & Baer found that most large institutions were selecting systems from multiple vendors, based on beliefs that the area is still developing and that it is sensible not to be locked into one provider.[25] Other institutions are developing their own systems or carrying out customisations to the analytics software purchased.

Local knowledge of the potential data sources is critical and is likely to require both technical and pedagogical expertise. Those familiar with the data sources in the SIS may not be used to working, for example, with the LMS data. It is important to identify staff who understand the data that is collected from students and why some of it might be missing or incomplete.[26] In particular, in-depth knowledge about which LMS tools are used by different courses and instructors may be required.

The existing data sources and systems may not be adequate or properly understood. More fundamentally, the data may not even be being collected in a systematic way that allows it to be incorporated into a learning analytics solution. In some institutions, for example, attendance data is collected in a variety of formats, ranging from paper to spreadsheets maintained by individual instructors. Reliable historical data is unlikely to be obtainable in this case to 'train' a predictive model. Similarly, there may be significant problems in accessing data held in systems hosted by third parties, such as some library systems.

## Skills

Powell & MacNeill suggest that institutions need to ensure they have appropriate skills available in three broad areas:

- **Handling data** – gathered from different sources which may be not well integrated and formatted and could be of poor quality.

- **Interpretation and visualisation** – presenting information accessibly and informatively.
- **Actionable insights** – enabling teachers and learners to take actions based on the analytics.[27]

Expertise will be required 'to develop and validate predictive models; integrate, coordinate and use data inputs from multiple data systems; help interpret the meaning of significant predictive variables as well as determine appropriate interventions based on the strength of models; and develop data visualisation tools and other means of synthesizing data for mass consumption'.[28] Such skills do not exist within most organisations and the expertise of a data scientist may have to be brought in from elsewhere. There will also be a requirement for skills in project management and evaluation.

Once the analytics are in place, will staff, faculty and students have the skills to interpret and act on them? Understanding the visualisations or presentation of the information may not be straightforward.[29] Norris & Baer point to the often discussed 'talent gap' for data professionals with the skills to interpret the analytics – they suggest that comprehensive development and certification of individuals' skills in analytics and overall institutional competence need to be put in place.[30]

Siemens *et al.* come to the same conclusion from the analytics initiatives they surveyed – that there is a shortage of skills and capabilities and in particular of people able to apply analytics in a pedagogical context. They believe that this is one reason why most of the case studies they discuss have failed to translate innovations into institution-wide practices. Offering courses in analytics they suggest would help to resolve this issue.[31]

In one pilot project discussed by Arnold and colleagues, faculty were selected based on their enthusiasm for identifying at-risk student behaviour using predictive data. They were given support in assessing the predictions and validating their accuracy, as well as developing an intervention strategy. The authors believe that it is essential for faculty to be able to interpret the data and the predictions confidently.[32] Another study suggested that those who are already engaged in online teaching are more able to perceive the benefits of learning analytics tools and are therefore more likely to adopt them.[33]

## Conclusion

Learning analytics projects may turn out to be the drivers for sorting out longstanding issues such as unclear data governance or poor systems integration, as well as deeply rooted cultural or organisational challenges. They may also highlight the lack of use or inconsistency of use of systems such as the LMS. A readiness assessment carried out in advance of procurement and development of systems can help to highlight potential areas of institutional weakness that should be addressed first. Broad areas for consideration should include: leadership, culture and vision, strategy and investment, structure and governance, technology and data and skills. Many of these, particularly the skillsets required, will need to be considered not just for the duration of a learning analytics project, but on an ongoing basis after the initiative has been embedded in institutional processes.

## Assessing Readiness for Learning Analytics in Leading US Institutions

Norris & Baer surveyed 40 leading institutional practitioners and 20 solution providers. Their findings indicate that institutions are at one of three stages in their adoption of learning analytics.

The first stage is 'static reporting', where institutions have a culture of reporting but are beginning to try out analytics tools. They believe that around 3,000+ institutions in the US are at this stage. Their second level is 'dynamic analysis and intervention' where there is a stronger emphasis on evidence-based decision making, early use of analytics applications such as predictive analytics, more developed data governance and some professional development offered in the area. They think that around 800 to more than 900 institutions in the US are at this stage. They call the third level 'optimisation', where strong leadership prioritises analytics as a key area for institutional strategy. In the 30–50 institutions they suggest have reached this level, a culture of performance measurement and enhancement is emerging, the use of predictive analytics is mature, the use of analytics is pervasive and leadership is focussed on using it to enhance student success and other measures of institutional effectiveness.

The researchers found that most institutions take two to three years to advance from level 1 to level 2 and a further three to five years to reach level 3. However, they suggest that institutions starting from scratch could change more quickly than this now as there is so much to be learned from the ones that are most developed.[34]

Assessing an institution's overall readiness for learning analytics may depend on who is being surveyed. Oster *et al.* found that information technology professionals are likely to rate their institution's preparedness higher than deans, faculty and researchers, for example. Achieving a common understanding of readiness is important.[35] Patience is also necessary. Unicon's readiness assessment process suggests that two to three years are required to implement a full-scale learning analytics solution. Not many institutions have yet spent this amount of time on their projects; Siemens *et al.* in their wide-reaching survey of analytics initiatives were unable to identify a single example of an institution that had implemented an institution-wide learning analytics strategy. They do suggest that some for-profit institutions such as the University of Phoenix have well-developed strategies in this area. However, as learning analytics is seen as a competitive differentiator, they do not generally publish details of these in the literature.[36]

# References

1  Fritz, J., 2011, Classroom Walls that Talk: Using Online Course Activity Data of Successful Students to Raise Self-Awareness of Underperforming Peers, *Internet and Higher Education*, 14, pp. 89–97.

2  Goldstein, P. J., & Katz, R. N., 2005, *Academic Analytics: The Uses of Management Information and Technology in Higher Education*, EDUCAUSE Center for Applied Research, p. 15.

3  Pressler, E. J., 2014, Logging into Learning Analytics, *Current Issues in Emerging eLearning*, 1(1), p. 48.

4  Bichsel, J., 2012, *Analytics in Higher Education: Benefits, Barriers, Progress, and Recommendations*, EDUCAUSE Center for Applied Research, pp. 22–23.

5  Norris, M. D. & Baer, L. L., 2013, *Building Organizational Capacity for Analytics*, EDUCAUSE, pp. 31–32.

6  Arnold, K. E. *et al.*, 2014, An Exercise in Institutional Reflection: The Learning Analytics Readiness Instrument (LARI), *LAK14: Proceedings of the Fourth International Conference on Learning Analytics and Knowledge*, pp. 163–167.

7  Ibid.

8  Ramsden, A., 2016, Notes from JISC's Fifth Learning Analytics Network Meeting (UEL), *Andy's Blog*, February 4, https://andyramsden.wordpress.com/2016/02/04/notes-from-jiscs-5th-learning-analytics-network-meeting-uel/ (accessed 9 October 2016).

9  MacNeill, S., 2016, Clawing My Way Up through the Trough of Disillusionment with Learning Analytics, *howsheilaseesIT*, February 9, https://howsheilaseesit.wordpress.com/2016/02/09/clawing-my-way-up-through-the-trough-of-disillusionment-with-learning-analytics/ (accessed 9 October 2016).

10  Ramsden, Notes from JISC's Fifth Learning Analytics Network Meeting (UEL).

11  Norris & Baer, *Building Organizational Capacity for Analytics*, p. 38.

12  Colvin, C. *et al.*, 2016, *Student Retention and Learning Analytics: A Snapshot of Australian Practices and a Framework for Advancement*, Australian Government Office for Learning and Teaching.

13  Kotter, J., 1995, Leading Change: Why Transformation Efforts Fail, *Harvard Business Review*, 73(2), pp. 59–67.

14  Arnold, K. E. *et al.*, 2014, Building Institutional Capacities and Competencies for Systemic Learning Analytics Initiatives, *LAK14: Proceedings of the Fourth International Conference on Learning Analytics and Knowledge*, pp. 257–260.

15  Norris & Baer, *Building Organizational Capacity for Analytics*, p. 38.

16  Macfadyen, L. P., & Dawson, S., 2012, Numbers are Not Enough: Why E-Learning Analytics Failed to Inform an Institutional Strategic Plan, *Educational Technology and Society*, 15(3), pp. 149–163.

17  Arnold *et al.*, Building Institutional Capacities and Competencies.

18  Sclater, N. & Bailey, P., 2015, *Code of Practice for Learning Analytics*, Jisc.

19  Bichsel, J., 2012, *2012 ECAR Study of Analytics in Higher Education*, p. 13, https://library.educause.edu/resources/2012/6/2012-ecar-study-of-analytics-in-higher-education (accessed 9 October 2016).

20  Campbell, J. P. & Oblinger, D. G., 2007, *Academic Analytics*. EDUCAUSE, p. 15.

21  Elouazizi, N., 2014, Critical Factors in Data Governance for Learning Analytics, *Journal of Learning Analytics*, 1(3), pp. 211–222.

22  Ibid., p. 218.

23  Sclater, N., 2014, *Learning Analytics: The Current State of Play in UK Higher and Further Education*, Jisc.

24  Arnold *et al.*, Building Institutional Capacities and Competencies for Systemic Learning Analytics Initiatives.

25  Norris & Baer, *Building Organizational Capacity for Analytics*, p. 38.

26  Arnold *et al.*, Building Institutional Capacities and Competencies for Systemic Learning Analytics Initiatives.

27  Powell, S. & MacNeill, S., 2012, Institutional Readiness for Analytics, JISC CETIS Analytics Series 1(8), http://publications.cetis.org.uk/wp-content/uploads/2012/12/Institutional-Readiness-for-Analytics-Vol1-No8.pdf (accessed 9 October 2016).

28  Arnold *et al.*, Building Institutional Capacities and Competencies for Systemic Learning Analytics Initiatives.

29  Greller, W. & Drachsler, H., 2012, Translating Learning into Numbers: A Generic Framework for Learning, *Educational Technology and Society*, 15(3), 42–57 (p. 45).

30  Norris & Baer, *Building Organizational Capacity for Analytics*, p. 43.

31  Siemens, G. *et al.*, 2013, *Improving the Quality and Productivity of the Higher Education Sector: Policy and Strategy for Systems-Level Deployment of Learning Analytics*, Society for Learning Analytics Research.

32  Arnold *et al.*, Building Institutional Capacities and Competencies for Systemic Learning Analytics Initiatives.

33  Ali, L. *et al.*, 2012, A Qualitative Evaluation of Evolution of a Learning Analytics Tool, *Computers and Education*, 58(1), pp. 470–489.

34  Norris & Baer, *Building Organizational Capacity for Analytics*, pp. 40–41.

35  Oster, M. *et al.*, 2016, The Learning Analytics Readiness Instrument, *LAK16: Proceedings of the Sixth International Learning Analytics and Knowledge Conference*, p. 7.

36  Siemens *et al.*, *Improving the Quality and Productivity of the Higher Education Sector*, p. 11.

# 19  Project Planning

In the previous chapter I examined how an institution can assess its readiness for implementing a large-scale learning analytics initiative. This chapter outlines some of the more detailed areas of activity to consider in the planning stages. It is not intended to be completely comprehensive and will certainly need to be tailored for each institution's unique circumstances.

Institutional learning analytics projects have much in common with other initiatives aimed at achieving organisational change and in order to be successful should be closely aligned with, or even explicitly part of, the organisational mission. Several areas might differentiate them, however, and they may not have been encountered in previous projects. For example, there is likely to be a need to:

- consult and obtain unprecedented buy-in from a wide variety of stakeholders across the institution, including the senior executive;
- draw data from established silos, cutting through existing ownership structures;
- deal with a range of ethical objections, particularly relating to the potential misuse of students' personal data;
- procure a number of new systems at once and undertake considerable local technical integration and customisation work.

## Objectives

While procuring or developing a system may be the focus of initial efforts, establishing the business and educational objectives is likely to be a better starting point for a learning analytics project. These can differ greatly between institutions, based on their size, structure, the nature of their student cohorts and their approaches to learning and teaching.

In her survey of the use of analytics (in general) at US institutions, Bichsel notes its most popular perceived benefits among respondents:

1. Understanding student demographics and behaviours.
2. Optimising the use of resources.

3.  Recruiting students.
4.  Helping students learn more effectively/graduate.

Other benefits reported by Bichsel largely relate to improved organisational efficiency.[1] *Learning* analytics, perhaps, most closely relating to benefits 1 and 4 above, may thus be in continual competition for resource with other areas such as recruitment and finance.

Powell & McNeill list the following business objectives, which could be considered for a learning analytics project, specifically:

*   for individual learners to reflect on their achievements and patterns of behaviour in relation to others;
*   as predictors of students requiring extra support and attention;
*   to help teachers and support staff plan supporting interventions with individuals and groups;
*   for functional groups such as course teams seeking to improve current courses or develop new curriculum offerings.[2]

## Motivations for Learning Analytics at UK Institutions

In a study I carried out for Jisc in late 2014, I interviewed staff and faculty about their learning analytics initiatives at a wide variety of institutions. At one end of the spectrum, the University of Edinburgh has a distributed management structure and a strong research culture, resulting in a number of learning analytics projects across its highly varied schools and departments. At the other end, Bridgwater College was taking a centralised approach to student support using systems to track student performance and enable more effective management of teaching staff (which would be anathema to faculty at many institutions).

Motivations for carrying out learning analytics varied considerably among the institutions that I visited. Most mentioned a desire to enhance the student learning experience in various ways such as improving achievement and reducing the number of resits, providing better feedback and empowering students to become more reflective learners. Some institutions had significant issues with retention and saw learning analytics as a way to identify students at risk of attrition; for others this was not considered a significant problem.

Learning analytics is also regarded as a way of enhancing teaching, sometimes by encouraging the more timely marking of student work and helping to build better relationships between students and staff. For several institutions the focus was on putting the analytics tools in the hands of staff who work directly with learners and providing them with actionable insights into student performance. A frequently stated aim of learning analytics is to help identify students at risk before it is too late to intervene.

A number of institutions mentioned the variety of levels of achievement between different ethnic groups or genders and how they are using analytics to identify and attempt to provide additional support to individuals from under-performing groups. Derby University uses analytics to ensure that its decision making on supporting black and minority ethnic students is evidence based. It has developed a recipe book for academic staff, which appears to have improved the performance of students from these minority groups.

Educational institutions in the UK are required to provide data on the attendance of foreign students to the immigration authorities. This requirement was imposed after it became clear that some foreigners were obtaining student visas as an easy way to enter the country, perhaps never even attending the institution with which they were signed up. This required capturing attendance data in various ways and it became evident that the data could also be of use in identifying domestic students who were struggling academically.

Other national policies are also motivating learning analytics initiatives. The UK's National Student Survey provides data from each university on the student experience. It can help institutions identify and address issues of concern to learners such as inadequate feedback. Manchester Metropolitan University attributes a 9% increase in student satisfaction over two years to its efforts to reorganise its curriculum based on better analysis of student requirements, in particular through student surveys.[3]

It is clear that learning analytics is likely to mean different things both across institutions and within the institution itself; it will be important to establish a common language and to define what is meant by the term itself at the institution. It may also be appropriate to concentrate on a more meaningful overarching concept such as 'student retention' or 'curriculum enhancement' and to refer to the initiative by a name more related to the ultimate objective than the 'learning analytics project'. It will be important to establish how the institution will know whether the goal has been achieved. So, if the aim is 'increasing student satisfaction', a means to measure this such as the results of student surveys needs to be in place. A difference in worldviews between the academic and business sides of the institution may mean that agreeing these measures is tricky.

## Drivers and Goals for Learning Analytics at Nottingham Trent University

At Nottingham Trent University, the key strategic driver is enhancing the academic experience for its 28,000 students, particularly engagement with their course. Earlier institutional research had identified that up to a third of students had considered withdrawing at some point during their first year. These 'doubters' were less confident about coping with their studies, less engaged with their course, formed weaker relationships with peers and tutors and were ultimately more likely to withdraw early. This apparent detachment from teaching staff meant that tutors were at risk of putting effort into assisting those who requested support, rather than those who most needed it.

Three detailed goals were developed for the initiative:

- to enhance retention;
- to increase a sense of belonging within the course community, particularly with tutors;
- to improve attainment.[4]

## Identifying the Purposes for Learning Analytics at the University of Technology, Sydney

The University of Technology, Sydney, has an overarching vision to become a 'data-intensive university' and believes that 'access to data can enrich all aspects of the university and provide a springboard for creation and innovation'.[5] The purposes identified for learning analytics in particular were to:

- provide information to reduce student attrition;
- help understand the factors affecting low pass rates in 'killer subjects', i.e. those with high failure rates;
- provide a dashboard to students showing their study and engagement patterns;
- better understand how different types of interventions affect student success;
- help to develop more personalised adaptive learning.[6]

Colvin *et al.* interviewed 32 senior leaders at Australian universities to find out about their experiences and views of learning analytics. They grouped these institutions into two clusters. Cluster 1 institutions tended to think of learning analytics as a tool for measuring efficiency gains and addressing student retention issues. This was conceptualised as a phenomenon distanced from learning and teaching. Cluster 2 institutions, however, saw learning analytics as part of a bigger picture and were using it to help to understand student learning and to inform curriculum design. They perceived retention as a product of the broader learning, teaching and student engagement practices of the organisation. Institutions in this cluster typically had significant input from senior leadership with sponsorship at the Vice Chancellor and Deputy

Vice Chancellor levels. Few of the Cluster 1 institutions, however, had input from their Vice Chancellor.[7]

## Stakeholders

Ensuring a successful institutional initiative is likely to require early consultation with stakeholders. This will help to establish appropriate goals, achieve better buy-in and be more likely to ensure that adequate resources and time are allocated.[8] Elouazizi suggests that supporting and empowering the key stakeholders is critical, as the project is likely to require 'unprecedented collaboration efforts both vertically and horizontally across the organisation'.[9]

A balance must be created between the expectations and obligations of the stakeholders.[10] Moreover what one might consider a benefit – for example, a programme director obtaining data on teaching effectiveness – others might think of as a threat (the instructors, perhaps, in this case).[11] The needs of individual learners may even be in conflict with the interests of other stakeholder groups such as academic administrators.[12]

Greller & Drachsler make the distinction between *data subjects*, the suppliers of data – mainly the students – and *data clients*, the users of the data who are meant to act upon the analytics. They argue that it is important to differentiate between these two groups in order to understand how learning analytics impacts on individuals. However they recognise that this categorisation is over-simplistic, as learners may not only supply data but also view analytics on their learning.[13] In addition, the actions of lecturers and other personnel are relevant in the analytics, particularly if the effectiveness of interventions is being measured.

Greller & Drachsler list the main stakeholders as students, teachers and the institution, mentioning researchers, service providers and government agencies as further possibilities. They also consider that computers themselves can act as stakeholders, for instance by triggering notifications to students based on their analytics.[14] Arguably, though, it is more straightforward to consider the human stakeholders as separate from the technology.

Figure 19.1 shows the key stakeholders that are likely to be required for an institutional learning analytics project, their primary roles and some of the entities with which they interact – the project, systems, data and dashboards. The names of these positions will vary between institutions, as will the composition of their roles. For example 'instructor' and 'academic' are not represented but people in these positions may act in the 'teacher', 'personal tutor' or 'course designer' roles outlined below.

- **Executive.** The executive board of the institution will be interested in indicators that impact on the reputation and financial position of the institution, such as graduation rates and student satisfaction. Support from members is critical if the initiative is to be a success. They will need to agree to the project, authorise the budget and continue to

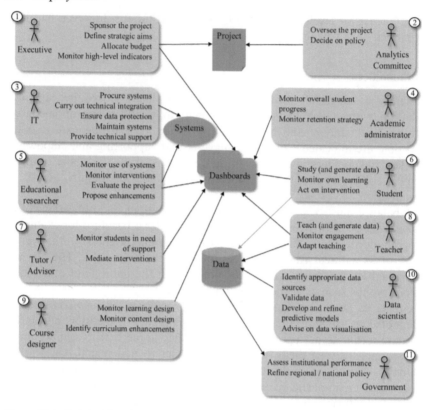

*Figure 19.1* Stakeholders in a learning analytics project and their roles.

oversee and support it, even when the novelty has worn off. A champion at this level with accountability for the initiative is generally appointed.

- **Analytics committee.** A high-level representative group responsible for strategic decisions regarding learning analytics may be required. This might be a new body or an existing committee responsible for learning and teaching. The senior executive champion for the initiative is likely to be on this group. Student representatives will help to ensure buy-in from the student body and that their opinions are taken into account when developing policies and processes.
- **Information technology (IT).** The IT department is likely to take primary responsibility for procuring, maintaining and supporting the systems and underlying technical infrastructure, as well as ensuring legal compliance, in particular for the protection of personal data.
- **Academic administrator.** These are people such as heads of department, programme directors and deans who wish to monitor aspects of educational provision across multiple instructors and courses, perhaps evaluating the effectiveness of their programmes and the teaching, student drop-

out rates and retention strategies.[15] Student affairs departments may be responsible for some of these activities as well.

- **Educational researcher.** There will be a requirement for staff or faculty with detailed knowledge of the curriculum and of educational issues. This may involve monitoring how students and others use the systems, designing interventions and assessing their effectiveness. Other tasks may include evaluating the project overall and proposing changes to the curriculum, teaching methods or systems. These roles may be carried out to some extent by instructors or by those more dedicated to educational research.
- **Student.** It is all too easy to forget the critical role of students in agreeing to the collection of their data and being subject to interventions, in generating the data through their learning activities, in monitoring their own learning through the analytics and in acting on any interventions taken. For this reason students should be included in the design of the learning analytics initiative and the associated processes – particularly the interventions – and in discussions around ethics and data protection issues.
- **Tutor/advisor.** This is another stakeholder whose roles will be constituted differently depending on the organisation and may be known by terms such as 'academic advisor'. Academic and pastoral support roles may or may not be carried out by the same person. This is a critical stakeholder, though, however the roles are designated. Someone needs to be designated to receive alerts and to monitor the students who are flagged as in need of additional support. This is the person who will intervene by contacting students and attempts to help them overcome any issues that are leading to lack of engagement or academic progress.
- **Teacher.** The individual involved in the teaching of students through lectures, tutorials, labs or online facilitation is likely to have an interest in monitoring the engagement of their cohorts through dashboards and potentially taking 'on the fly' interventions to address aspects of the curriculum which the analytics suggest could be enhanced.
- **Course designer.** Those involved in developing the courses, including the teaching methods, learning content, assessments, interface design and the educational technologies deployed, may have an interest in any analytics that point to improvements that could be made to the course. People with such a role may include instructors, instructional designers or educational technologists.
- **Data scientist.** Detailed knowledge of the existing data sources will be required, as well as being able to ensure the data itself is valid. Other roles of this stakeholder include understanding how to transform the data into formats suitable for learning analytics, developing and refining predictive models and advising on data visualisation. Many institutions are likely to lack some or all of these skills and will need to employ outside expertise, though internal knowledge of data sources and formats will almost certainly be required.

- **Government**. There is normally a requirement to pass data such as numbers of students and graduation rates to regional or national government departments responsible for education. Data deriving from analytics may be added to this in order to assess institutional performance in areas such as teaching quality or retention. Government, of course, also sets the agenda in areas such as data protection legislation.

## Concerns of Stakeholders

Resistance to a large-scale learning analytics can be expected from various stakeholders across the institution. Faculty, in particular, will be concerned about the impact on their time and their ability to carry out research and teaching activities.[16] They may also fear that the analytics will be used to measure their own performance and allow comparisons with peers and that their autonomy may be reduced. They are likely, too, to have legitimate concerns about the potential negative impacts on their students.[17]

Members of the executive board will be concerned that funding for analytics is spent appropriately and receives adequate return on investment. Given media scare stories about security breaches in education and other industries they are also likely to want reassurance that personal data is being properly protected.[18] Academic administrators meanwhile may have personal conflicts of interest, which militate against the success of the initiative. Deans and heads of department are often drawn from senior faculty members and may not wish to burden themselves and their colleagues with additional tools and processes.[19]

Information technology departments are required to store and process data and to maintain systems in conformance with laws and institutional policies. Essential though this is, the policies can conflict with innovation and exploration. Information technology staff are particularly likely to be wary about the additional workload requirements imposed on them in implementing new systems and they can be so distanced from any impact on the student that their buy-in cannot be guaranteed.[20] It may also be advisable to separate responsibility for defining the datasets required from responsibility for the technical infrastructure and from responsibility for the interventions taken as a result of the analytics.[21]

Most stakeholders are likely to be concerned about impacts on their workload, changes to their working practices and adverse impacts on the students and may present resistance in varying degrees to the initiative. Meanwhile some of their perspectives will be more aligned with institutional priorities than others and their suggestions for what analytics could achieve may be unrealistic.[22] Establishing what the benefits and workload implications are for each stakeholder is likely to pay dividends. It is important, too, to manage expectations carefully and not to overpromise on the expected benefits, as well as to involve those most affected by new systems and processes in their design.

### Involving Counselling Staff in Developing a System to Identify At-Risk Students at New York Institute of Technology

New York Institute of Technology (NYIT) had a problem with levels of attrition, with graduation levels of only 50%, and wished to intervene early with at-risk students. Using the expertise of the counselling staff who support students, the Institute developed a model and dashboard that are now able to identify students at risk with a high degree of accuracy.

The project involved mining the data, developing the predictive model and producing the analytics in a format that was helpful to the counselling staff. It was essential to involve these stakeholders from the outset: it was concluded that unless they were willing and able to incorporate the new systems and processes into their day-to-day work the project would not be a success. The processes of identifying students at risk of attrition needed to be as automated as possible, without time-consuming manual interventions.

The problem definition originated from those responsible for supporting students. An external IT solution provider worked with NYIT staff to identify the relevant data. The IT provider gathered and prepared the data and deployed and evaluated the model. The design process was iterative, with counselling staff involved at every stage.[23]

## Communication and Awareness Raising

One area that will be critical to the success of the initiative is adequate communication and awareness raising at the early stages and throughout the project. Arnold and her colleagues discuss the focus on holding awareness workshops for the academic community at two different universities and the early involvement of faculty in planning and visioning the project. Conversations required complete transparency and, while highlighting the benefits, also required a degree of pragmatism: 'Overnight success and silver bullet solutions in the realm of learning analytics [are] highly unlikely.'[24] Diaz & Fowler recommend specifically that successful projects at other institutions are promoted in order to combat the initial resistance and scepticism that is likely to be encountered.[25]

Early communication and consultation with stakeholders can also create advocates for the project. Those who believe that their input is valued and are included in the process, are likely to feel a greater sense of ownership and to be able to communicate more effectively with colleagues. They may also be more inclined to adopt the new tools and processes.

## Workstreams

An institutional learning analytics initiative will have a number of subprojects or workstreams. At a high level these may relate to the learning analytics processes outlined in Chapter 14 and may include:

- **Systems.** Procuring systems, customising them and integrating them with existing technologies and data sources are likely to require significant effort.
- **Ethics and legal issues.** Best handled early on, a well-researched and constructed policy will help to deal with the numerous ethical and legal objections likely to be raised by faculty, students and staff.
- **Skills.** Training may need to be provided in areas such as predictive modelling and intervention management. Some skills may have to be procured externally.
- **Data preparation.** This may consist of identifying data sources and transforming the data into formats appropriate for predictive modelling.
- **Predictive analytics.** Developing predictive models, training them with historical data and creating appropriate visualisations may be required. Vendors may provide some of this expertise and larger institutions may wish to develop their own capacities in the area.
- **Interventions.** A further workstream might involve creating an intervention strategy, ensuring staff have the right skills and time available to intervene and evaluating the success of the interventions.

## Budget

Setting the budget for a learning analytics initiative will depend on a range of factors in the institution. Estimating the cost of buying in new systems may be difficult in advance of a procurement exercise. Evaluating the relative merits of each product may be complex as well, due to the widely differing types of system available, the immaturity of the market, the lack of transparency as to how the predictive analytics are calculated, a dearth of reference sites and the sometimes unverifiable claims of vendors.

Senior managers may have a tendency to concentrate on the costs of procuring software and therefore seriously underestimate the real costs of implementing an institutional learning analytics project, particularly those for deploying existing staff and faculty and any training and reskilling required. It may also be necessary to recruit new staff for roles such as project managers, data scientists and tutors to act on the analytics, or to backfill existing staff whose skills are needed for the project. There is an inherent unwillingness in many institutions to accept that some existing activities will need to cease in order for existing staff to focus on new activities related to learning analytics. Senior managers may also be so concerned with initial costs that they lose sight of the ultimate objectives of the initiative and the longer-term benefits.

## Timescales

Learning analytics projects, again due to their organisational and technical complexities, are likely to take longer than more straightforward IT projects implementing, for example, a new payroll system. In addition it may take months or years after the end of the initial project before tangible benefits are seen in improved educational outcomes. There may also be dependencies with other institutional initiatives, which lead to delays – or simply more pressing projects that emerge due to unforeseen circumstances such as IT problems or changes to legislation or government policy. Large-scale analytics projects should be seen as long-term initiatives, helping to develop a more data-informed mindset across the organisation. They should not be expected to provide immediate 'fixes'.

Arnold *et al.* point to specific areas to manage closely: '(a) tracking task completions, (b) development of processes and workflow, (c) coordinating communication for key deliverables and dates and (d) ensuring that the work that is conducted [is] in line with the overall directions set by the group.'[26] All of these are familiar requirements from other large-scale initiatives and it should be feasible to apply them in the context of a learning analytics project. Agile methodologies should be considered as they enable the rapid development of partial solutions with user involvement, helping to maintain visibility and momentum, as well as allowing frequent reprioritisation of developments as requirements evolve.

## Underestimating the Time Required for Learning Analytics: The Experience at St Louis University, Missouri

Buerck & Mudigonda analyse why their learning analytics initiative at St Louis University was not as successful as it should have been. Firstly, the stakeholders were not able to keep to the planned schedule. While they do not say so explicitly, this is presumably because they did not give the learning analytics work a high enough priority in competition with other demands on their time. Commitment to the initiative from senior levels may help to ensure that the work is prioritised by existing staff – but only if other duties can be scaled back without serious consequences.

The time required to complete all the tasks required for an initiative involving predictive analytics was, with hindsight, seriously underestimated. This included developing automated processes for collecting data from multiple sources, cleaning and formatting the data and building the predictive models. In particular, understanding the data and metadata across multiple databases using naming conventions unique to each vendor 'was a stupendous task requiring a significant amount of time and collaboration among various departments'. The researchers themselves had the statistical analysis skills to produce student profiles; however, they could not obtain the datasets in a format they could use properly. Furthermore, they could not fully understand the metadata nor obtain permission to access all of the relevant data.

The model that was produced for one course showed that student access to learning content and the gradebook correlated with their final grade. However, this was considered an unsurprising finding that did not provide any useful insights that could be used to support learners.

A second learning analytics initiative attempted to learn from the earlier experiences but to work at the departmental rather than institutional level. Blackboard's *Retention Center* became available at this point, enabling alerts to be triggered when various aspects of a student's participation or achievement fall below a specified level. An associated dashboard for instructors provides visualisations of student performance and enables them to intervene as appropriate. This considerably simplifies the processes of identifying at-risk students and of intervening. The fact that Retention Center processes the data automatically avoids the need for all the processes described earlier. What this experience shows, perhaps, is that, as learning analytics systems become increasingly commoditised, ubiquitous and easy to use, it should become easier to roll them out.[27]

## Risks

As with any sizeable project, developing a risk register and managing those risks closely as the project progresses is advisable. Risks may include:

- **Insufficient staff time available.** All aspects of the project will require input from stakeholders who are already busy across the institution.
- **Insufficient skills available.** Training staff may be time-consuming and expensive. Recruiting staff with appropriate skills (e.g. data scientists) may be difficult, particularly as these skills are currently in high demand in industry as well as education.
- **Poor quality data.** It may not be apparent on commencement of the project that the data sources are inadequate or that data is not collected consistently across the institution. Learning analytics can be the catalyst for re-examination of various aspects of data handling, such as its collection, ownership and retention policies. The project may also demonstrate the inadequacy of existing attendance monitoring systems or the lack of effective use of the LMS.
- **Conflicts with other strategic priorities.** Senior management and staff at other levels may feel that other priorities are more pressing, particularly as the benefits of learning analytics may take months or years to become evident.
- **Delays due to institutional governance processes.** Projects can be held up, for example by a key committee meeting taking place only once per semester – if this deadline is not met, aspects of the project may be delayed by months.
- **Roles are not re-envisioned appropriately.** New roles such as carrying out interventions and evaluating their effectiveness may not be properly allocated or resourced.

## Conclusion

The experiences at St Louis suggest that institutions might wish to consider beginning with smaller, departmental-level pilot projects before scaling them up to the institutional level. Elouazizi also recommends starting on a small scale as governance and business processes are likely to be disrupted by larger-scale initiatives.[28] The study of Australian institutions by Colvin and colleagues concluded that programmes involving small projects that can be rapidly evaluated and scaled up appeared to be more effective than some of the grander institutional initiatives.[29] However some organisations have taken a centralised and comprehensive approach and there is a strong argument that, in order to achieve tangible benefits, the initiative needs significant investment and involvement from across the institution from the start. Ferguson asserts that engaging in 'piecemeal, simplistic and non-systemic approaches to learning analytics implementation will struggle to gain traction across an institution'.[30]

The NYIT case study suggests that it is helpful to have those who will be involved in the use of new software and processes closely involved in their design. This is a step that is often missed when institutions develop or procure systems. Whatever scale the initiative is launched at, pilots of new systems and processes are advisable, as they help to identify issues that are much easier to address with small numbers of users, than during a full institutional deployment. Pilots may also create valuable advocates among students and staff, sometimes providing a more powerful voice than that of senior management for obtaining buy-in amongst peers.

Institutional learning analytics initiatives can fit into existing project-planning processes, including defining objectives, stakeholder management and communication, the specification of subprojects, budgets, timescales and risks. What is likely to make them unique is the variety of stakeholders to be involved at all stages, the challenges to existing structures and ownership of data, systems and processes and the time and patience needed to realise tangible benefits.

## References

1 Bichsel, J., 2012, *Analytics in Higher Education: Benefits, Barriers, Progress, and Recommendations*, EDUCAUSE Center for Applied Research, p. 11.
2 Powell, S. & MacNeill, S., 2012, Institutional Readiness for Analytics, *JISC CETIS Analytics Series*, 1(8), p. 4.
3 Sclater, N., 2014, Learning Analytics: The Current State of Play in UK Higher and Further Education, Jisc, pp. 3-4, http://repository.jisc.ac.uk/5657/1/Learning_ana lytics_report.pdf (accessed 9 October 2016).
4 Sclater, N. *et al.*, 2016, *Learning Analytics in Higher Education: A Review of UK and International Practice*, Jisc.
5 Ferguson, R. *et al.*, 2014, Setting Learning Analytics in Context: Overcoming the Barriers to Large-Scale Adoption, *Journal of Learning Analytics*, 1(3), pp. 120–144.
6 Ibid., pp. 139–140.

7 Colvin, C. *et al.*, 2016, *Student Retention and Learning Analytics: A Snapshot of Australian Practices and a Framework for Advancement.* Australian Government Office for Learning and Teaching, p. 13.

8 Diaz, V. & Fowler, S., 2012, *Leadership and Learning Analytics*, EDUCAUSE Learning Initiative, p. 2.

9 Elouazizi, N., 2014, Critical Factors in Data Governance for Learning Analytics, *Journal of Learning Analytics*, 1(3), pp. 211–222.

10 Ibid., p. 214.

11 Ibid., p. 217.

12 Powell & MacNeill, Institutional Readiness for Analytics, p. 4.

13 Greller, W. & Drachsler, H., 2012, Translating Learning into Numbers: A Generic Framework for Learning, *Educational Technology and Society*, 15(3), pp. 42–57.

14 Ibid., p. 46.

15 Elouazizi, Critical Factors in Data Governance for Learning Analytics, p. 217.

16 Campbell, J. P. & Oblinger, D. G., 2007, *Academic Analytics*, EDUCAUSE, p. 10.

17 Macfadyen, L. P. & Dawson, S., 2012, Numbers are Not Enough: Why E-Learning Analytics Failed to Inform an Institutional Strategic Plan, *Educational Technology and Society*, 15(3), pp. 149–163.

18 Campbell & Oblinger, *Academic Analytics*, p. 12.

19 Arnold, K. E. *et al.*, 2014, Building Institutional Capacities and Competencies for Systemic Learning Analytics Initiatives, *LAK14: Proceedings of the Fourth International Conference on Learning Analytics and Knowledge*, pp. 257–260.

20 Macfadyen & Dawson, Numbers are Not Enough, p. 160.

21 Elouazizi, Critical Factors in Data Governance for Learning Analytics, pp. 219–220.

22 Diaz & Fowler, *Leadership and Learning Analytics*, p. 2.

23 Agnihotri, L. & Ott, A., 2014, Building a Student At-Risk Model: An End-to-End Perspective, *Proceedings of the Seventh International Conference on Educational Data Mining*, p. 209.

24 Arnold *et al.*, Building Institutional Capacities and Competencies for Systemic Learning Analytics Initiatives.

25 Diaz & Fowler, Leadership and Learning Analytics, p. 3.

26 Arnold *et al.*, Building Institutional Capacities and Competencies for Systemic Learning Analytics Initiatives.

27 Buerck, J. P. & Mudigonda, S. P., 2014, A Resource-Constrained Approach to Implementing Analytics in an Institution of Higher Education: An Experience Report, *Journal of Learning Analytics*, 1(1), pp. 129–139.

28 Elouazizi, Critical Factors in Data Governance for Learning Analytics, p. 219.

29 Colvin *et al.*, *Student Retention and Learning Analytics*, p. 22.

30 Ferguson *et al.*, Setting Learning Analytics in Context, p. 126.

# 20 Ethics

This book has described some of the many potential benefits for institutions and individuals of learning analytics. However, the increasing amount of data being accumulated about learners and their activities also creates opportunities for its misuse. Analysing this data brings further risks: concerns have been expressed in particular about the validity of predictive analytics and its possible misinterpretation by users. The various ethical objections that are raised have the potential to impede or halt the implementation of learning analytics. Without addressing such issues there may be a backlash from users[1, 2] who feel threatened in various ways – for example, by their privacy being invaded or their autonomy being put at risk. Such concerns may be part of an overall sense that the increasing use of surveillance in all aspects of human activity is a threat to our way of life.

Dealing with the ethical challenges relating to the use of IT is not simply advisable but also helps institutions to develop an ethical mindset where 'bad' things are less likely to occur.[3] Negative publicity about the use of IT frequently results from failures to deal with ethical issues. This is particularly relevant in learning analytics, where the nature of the algorithms and how the results are presented and acted upon can have a significant impact on a student's academic success and hence future employment prospects. When new systems are introduced there may be pressures to cut corners and disregard ethical dilemmas that arise. Information technology staff may also feel that if the data is held remotely in the cloud, ethical issues will be more distant and can safely be ignored.[4]

### Facebook 'Mood Experiment': The Dangers of Not Considering the Ethical Dimension when Analysing Users' Data

In 2014 Facebook carried out its infamous 'mood experiment', which placed positive and negative items and images in the timelines of 700,000 users to determine whether these altered their moods. This resulted in objections from many people and detrimental media coverage of Facebook. It is possible that users might have been particularly upset by the intention to manipulate their emotions rather than simply to analyse their activity.

Mike Shroepfer, Chief Technology Officer at Facebook, suggested that the company should have considered non-experimental ways to carry out the research, involved a wider and more senior group of people on the review panel and communicated better regarding why and how they were doing it. He pledged to tighten up processes at Facebook for studies involving personal issues such as emotions.[5]

Some of the issues emerging in the literature and in dialogue within institutions are ethical in nature; others will be more determined by legal considerations. There is a complex interplay between the ethics and the legalities: the laws themselves are built upon a morality that attempts to treat individuals and groups fairly. In turn our perception of fairness is often built upon accepted legal practice. It is not therefore possible entirely to separate ethical practice from compliance with the law. This chapter, however, explores the challenges of learning analytics that are primarily ethical in nature, while the following two chapters examine issues that, while also having an ethical dimension, are of legal concern to institutions: transparency and consent; and privacy and data protection.

A growing body of literature is emerging that outlines the questions being raised in institutions as they embark on analytics programmes. A few of them have written, or are currently developing, new policies for the ethical use of student data.[6] Others consider that their existing computing regulations, procedures and working practices are adequate. Berg argues, though, that without a code of ethics and agreed practices, institutions may act in an ad hoc way, thus reducing consistency and fairness for students. He suggests that senior management may have a different perspective to teachers and asks who should be able to decide what is done with the analytics. His solution is that a code of practice would be the arbitrator.[7] Several organisations and initiatives have investigated and codified the issues, notably Jisc in the UK and the Learning Analytics Community Exchange (LACE) Project across the European Union.[8]

## Developing a Code of Practice for Learning Analytics

Jisc, an educational charity responsible for many aspects of the IT infrastructure for universities and colleges in the UK, was tasked by its stakeholders with providing guidance on the legal and ethical issues of learning analytics, seen as a major barrier to its uptake. In order to find out what ethical issues were of most concern, on behalf of Jisc, I carried out an analysis of the literature relating to learning analytics and big data in higher education, relevant legislation and various codes of practice in related areas, drawing material from 86 publications.[9] From this review I developed a taxonomy of 85 distinct legal, ethical and logistical issues, validating these at a workshop in Paris[10] with invited experts from the Apereo Foundation[11] and the LACE Project.

The issues were grouped into nine categories: ownership and control, consent, transparency, privacy, validity, access, action, adverse impact and stewardship. These then formed the basis for Jisc's Code of Practice for Learning Analytics[12] which was published to help institutions develop their own ethical policies in the area. Forty-five of the issues documented have an ethical dimension.

Educational institutions are in a unique position in the huge influence they have potentially over an individual's current wellbeing and future career prospects. While the organisations are subject to financial pressures and some are, of course, for-profit institutions, they are fundamentally concerned with research and/or with educating individuals rather than being driven primarily by the need to provide dividends to shareholders. They can make strong moral arguments that the collection and use of data on learning and learners is for the benefit of their students (or at least to help the institutions so that they can better serve future cohorts). Through transparent working practices, backed up by ethical policies, they can ensure that the data is used for altruistic, educational purposes rather than to snoop on users or to target customers with commercial products.

## Ethical Approaches

There is little in the growing literature around learning analytics that refers to philosophy and ethical theory. Applied ethics is not a familiar area for most practitioners and it is worth examining what is behind our notions of what makes a practice ethical. Pardo & Siemens define ethics in the digital context as 'the systematisation of correct and incorrect behaviour in virtual spaces according to all stakeholders'.[13] Harris and colleagues, in an attempt to help IT staff assess ethical issues, suggest using the four questions put by Mason *et al.*, which are themselves based on the two main ethical traditions of *teleology* and *deontology*:

- Who is the agent (and what are their motives, interests and character)?
- What action was taken or is being contemplated?
- What are the results or consequences of that action?
- Are those results fair or just?[14, 15]

Willis points to two further philosophical traditions. The first is *utilitarianism*, which suggests that actions should be based on what does the most good for the most people. *Moral utopianism* similarly suggests that people should act in a way that betters others. These stances can be applied to learning analytics: interventions should be targeted where they will benefit the most people and should be aimed at helping students to learn and develop themselves.[16]

Learning analytics brings together individuals from various disciplines with different ethical approaches. Slade & Prinsloo take a *socio-critical* standpoint, discussing power relations between students, their institutions and other stakeholders such as funding bodies. They position learning analytics as a 'transparent moral practice', where students are participants in the various processes.[17]

Ethical decision making is based on people's worldviews (including their epistemology and values), their individual positions on methodology, the academic and political environment and the assumptions of individual disciplines.[18] Often somewhat lofty and obscure, ethical systems become more meaningful when given a set of principles.[19] Many of the fundamental ideas within codes of ethics come from documents such as the UN Declaration of Human Rights and the Nuremberg Code. These include human dignity, autonomy, protection, safety and the minimisation of harm.[20]

## Obligation to Use Learning Analytics

Universities already collect vast amounts of data on students and their activities. Some of this is essential for educational purposes, some is required for reporting to government and much of it is collected automatically in log files from the systems that students use, such as learning management systems (LMSs). If data about students and their learning is being collected anyway it is arguably irresponsible *not* to use it to enhance educational processes and to attempt to improve the academic prospects and ultimately the life chances, of individuals. Slade & Prinsloo argue that to ignore data that might help an institution to achieve its goals seems 'short-sighted in the extreme'.[21] There is also a risk that students could take legal action against institutions that failed to offer them additional support, despite knowing that they were at risk.[22]

## Flawed or Inadequate Data

The biggest technical challenge for learning analytics may be poor-quality or insufficient data. Users often 'pollute' databases with erroneous or incomplete data.[23] Teachers who wish, for example, to view their LMS from the perspective of a student might set up a test account, which is then included in the analytics for the course, skewing the results. Another challenge is 'enmeshed identities' where students are working together online. The data cannot then differentiate between an authenticated individual and other members of the group.[24] A related issue that may cause complications is when a person is both a student and an employee of the institution. Meanwhile, when data is collected against identifiers such as IP addresses or cookies and attributed to an individual there is a danger that it does not actually relate to that person at all.[25]

Drawing conclusions from a single data source can be dangerous and it is generally better to use data from multiple sources.[26] Two of the primary data sources used for learning analytics, the LMS and the student information system (SIS), capture only a fraction of the learning that takes place and the contextual information; work is needed to integrate data from other sources which will provide 'analytics opportunities that far exceed single data points'.[27] This does not, however, mean that it is worth gathering data from every possible source. Some will have only a marginal effect on the predictions and may not justify either the expense or the intrusiveness of collecting them.

## Invalid Predictions

Some researchers have expressed concerns that the analytics may be invalid and asked how institutions can avoid drawing misleading conclusions from spurious correlations.[28] There is an ongoing confusion in the minds of the public and even within universities between causation and correlation. One of main rationales behind predictive learning analytics is that there is a relationship between engagement in learning activities and student success. The argument is that if you can measure learner engagement you can then predict subsequent retention and grades.

Engagement, however, does not necessarily *cause* success. Nor is more engagement always associated with greater success. Extremely high levels of individual engagement may in fact be due to weaker students failing to understand concepts and having to work much harder than others, without necessarily reaping the benefits of their efforts in final grades. Conversely, exceptional students may be able to pass a course with minimal engagement in learning activities. It has also traditionally been possible to succeed in many courses by studying the relevant texts off campus and without any recorded evidence of engagement other than the submission of assignments and the taking of examinations.

### Mistaking Correlation with Causation at Rio Salado College, Arizona

Data can very easily be misinterpreted and subsequent interventions can be ill-thought-out. At Rio Salado College, a correlation was identified between logins on day one of a course and subsequent student success. An assumption was made from this finding that if students were encouraged to log in on their first day they would be more likely to succeed. A welcome email was consequently sent to a future cohort of students, recommending that they log into the course website.

Unfortunately the email turned out to have no impact. An alternative theory of the relationship between the early logins and success is that motivated learners are more likely to succeed and also to log in on the first day of the course.[29]

Putting blind faith in the algorithms, particularly when they are sold as part of black-box solutions by external providers, may not be advisable from an ethical point of view either. Claims of high levels of accuracy in the predictive analytics by vendors may be impossible to validate and the algorithms may not be easily transferable to new institutional contexts. Organisations therefore need to find ways to confirm the validity of the predictions, perhaps by employing new staff or consultant data scientists on a temporary basis.

One solution is that new independent bodies will emerge to validate the algorithms provided in commercial software. However, it seems likely that commercial sensitivities will make vendors reluctant to sign up to such outside inspection. An alternative scenario is that open-source algorithms will become increasingly prominent and validated through their use by multiple institutions. The mystery of the algorithms themselves and their commercial value, may be reduced over time. Vendors may decide instead to compete on other aspects of their products such as functionality, user interface, robustness, support and price.

## Loss of Autonomy

Could student autonomy in decision making be undermined by predictive analytics?[30] A course-recommender system might interfere with a student's career choice, for example, by suggesting future courses that are predicted to result in her achieving better grades but might not lead to her preferred job. What should she do if the suggestions are in conflict with her study goals?[31] The institutional philosophy may value high grades and rapid progress but this might not necessarily be in the student's best interest or what she wants.[32] The algorithms may even 'reflect and perpetuate current biases and prejudices' in the organisation.[33]

Adaptive learning systems bring the potential to 'infantilise' students by spoon-feeding them with automated suggestions, making the learning process less demanding.[34] It is important that automated processes do not give students the impression that everything is ordered and controlled: ultimately they should be able to decide for themselves whether to take up the suggestions made to them.[35] A further concern is that, as increasing numbers of decisions are based on algorithms, we could be judged on what are predicted to be our future actions rather than what we actually do.[36] In the longer term, analytics may create 'echo chambers', where intelligent software reinforces our own attitudes and beliefs by introducing us to similar people and suggesting courses and learning resources that match our preferences rather than challenging us.[37] Similarly, some academics are concerned that adaptive systems will take away *their* autonomy in how to teach a course.

**Recommender Systems at Arizona State and Austin Peay: Helpful or Undermining of Student Autonomy?**

Johnson discusses course-recommender systems where students are encouraged to do what people 'like them' have done before. Arizona State University's eAdvising system attempts to identify students whose skills do not match up to their ambitions. Johnson claims that learners are being thought of as mere collections of skills to be matched to an outcome rather than as individuals. He suggests that such systems undermine students' autonomy and condemns the university's processes to compel struggling students to change their major as 'coercive', denying them the opportunity to take their own decisions.

The 'softer' approach of the course recommendation system at Austin Peay State University, Tennessee, he feels, encourages students to conform to the values and behaviours that the institution considers to be most likely to result in success.

Such interferences may be valid on the basis of preventing the wastage of public money or guiding students who are not mature or informed enough to take sensible decisions. However, every violation of autonomy should, Johnson argues, be justified. A way forward, he suggests, may be to design systems that encourage autonomy and help students to make decisions for themselves, without institutional paternalism.[38]

## Demotivation

Information about where students are placed relative to their cohort has the potential to impact positively on motivation levels, building on their spirit of competitiveness. The attitudes and behaviours of successful learners can also be used an as example for lower-achieving students.[39] However, while some learners who are labelled 'at risk' might be motivated to do better, particularly if they are equipped with the skills and life circumstances to be able to do so, increased awareness may have adverse consequences for less fortunate students.[40] Predictions given to students may become self-fulfilling prophecies, which cause them to give up on a course they are predicted to fail. As the algorithms and metrics become more fine-tuned and trusted, will this effect intensify?[41]

Some commentators have expressed a concern that the labelling of students as 'at risk' could lead to them losing confidence and ultimately dropping out.[42, 43] While this might be a possibility for some, the argument returns that *not* telling students that they are at risk when the institution knows this is unethical.

## Negative Impacts of Continual Monitoring

Perhaps more insidious, the knowledge that their activities are being continuously monitored may lead to some students changing their behaviour, either consciously or unconsciously. For example, if students are aware that their e-book usage is being analysed they may feel the need to annotate the text more frequently or to spend longer on each page. While this could result in improved learning, it could also lead to increased stress levels and even non-participation by learners who feel that their every move is being monitored. It is possible, however, that students are already aware that most of the things they do online are being recorded and may therefore be unconcerned about the capturing of data about their learning activities.

## Manipulation of the Analytics by Students

It may be that some students, once they know that their learning activities are being monitored, will begin to 'game the system' in an attempt to improve their scores and ratings.[44] A lecturer at one university I spoke to had asked a student why he was standing at the door of the library, continuously slotting his ID card into the entry system. 'I'm just trying to improve my library engagement score', was the surprising response. Another possibility is that students will try to break the system or at least to have some fun by presenting themselves as more active than their peers by appearing to engage in extreme ways. The more analytics that are presented to students through apps and dashboards, the more likely this is to occur. The fact that gaming strategies are being built into student learning analytics apps in an attempt to make them more engaging might simply exacerbate the problem. Systems could be designed, though, to spot such behaviour and adjust for it accordingly. Ryan Baker writes:

> It has been my dream, and continues to be my dream, that intelligent tutoring systems that incorporate detectors of – say – gaming the system, and adapt in real-time when students game the system, will one day be commonplace.[45]

Another observer reported to me that he had seen a number of students at one English university queuing up to swipe their cards inside a lecture theatre, then immediately leaving, presumably to avoid a boring lecture by retreating to somewhere more amenable such as a café or home. This is an institution where attendance at lectures is a requirement and the data is used for learning analytics. Turning an organisational blind eye to such behaviour, or to the incentive that the institution has created to act in this way will make a mockery of attempts to develop valid predictions.

A further possibility that has been suggested is that students who wish to obtain additional support may deliberately manipulate the data. If the factors that lead to the triggering of an intervention are known, a student might act in a way that ensures that this occurs.[46]

## Human versus Computer Mediation of the Results

Given the possibility for misinterpretation of the analytics, demotivation or simply erroneous predictions, some people have expressed the belief that results and predictions should always be presented to students by a human, rather than through an automated process. The initial aim at Nottingham Trent University, for example, was that the dashboard should help to build the relationship between students and personal tutors.[47] This concern, on the surface a laudable one, might, however, be based on a narrow understanding of what learning analytics is and in addition perhaps a desire to preserve existing faculty–student relationships. A fear that their roles may be automated and that a computer could not possibly intervene with the required empathy and detailed knowledge of a student's circumstances might also be behind this approach.

There is no doubt that human contact with students will remain highly beneficial, if not essential, in many academic and pastoral situations. However, there will be significant resource implications for most institutions in providing the ideal levels of support for students which analytics might suggest are required. Visualisations of their learning activity, comparisons with other students, target setting and logging of activities and gentle nudges and suggestions from mobile apps are likely to play an increasing role in the learners' lives; none of these necessarily require human mediation.

## Obligations Resulting from the Analytics

A regularly expressed ethical question is whether there is an obligation on the institution to act on the basis of the analytics.[48, 49, 50] Indeed this is a strong argument for capturing student data in the first place, for developing the analytics and using it as the basis for interventions: if we have new ways of knowing that students could do better, is it not our duty to inform them and attempt to stop them from withdrawing or to guide them to greater levels of academic achievement?

Just what is done to intervene with students whom the data suggests could be assisted, is, of course, dependent on multiple considerations (and is the subject of Chapter 11). It may be, in fact, that the best course of action is to advise a learner, who is predicted to fail, to withdraw from the course straight away.[51] At Marist College the presentation of analytics to students appeared to result in greater dropout, however this was seen as a positive outcome – those who might have failed were able to withdraw earlier and thus switch to a different course where they may have had more chance of success.[52]

> **An Ethical Dilemma: Should Students who are Predicted to Fail be Recruited in the First Place?**
>
> The Open University in the UK has an open-access policy and mission that have traditionally encouraged anyone to sign up for courses, whether they have prior qualifications or not. However, the analytics may point to a new recruit with a certain demographic and academic history being highly likely to fail or drop out. Should the institution accept such students in the first place, particularly when there are significant financial implications of attrition for both the individual and the university?
>
> What though if the analytics are wrong? The institution was founded on being able to offer a 'second chance' to aspiring learners who may not have

had an earlier opportunity to experience higher education: refusing to sign them up potentially conflicts with its mission.

A way forward that was suggested was to direct such learners to shorter 'access' courses, which give them an experience of higher education and allow them to decide whether they should then embark on a full degree course.

Other authors have questioned whether students themselves have an obligation to act on the analytics.[53, 54] When I put this to employees at two different institutions, one respondent replied 'absolutely not' and that students are adults and should be able to decide for themselves whether to take the advice the analytics are offering them. Another interviewee felt that the analytics should be seen in the broader context of the support offered to students and their overall academic responsibility to draw from the resources available.[55]

## Prejudicial Categorisation and Treatment of Students

Another issue that has emerged is that the labelling of students from automated processes could affect staff and faculty perceptions, resulting in different or negative behaviours towards them.[56, 57] It might also reinforce discriminatory attitudes and actions by profiling students based on their race, gender or some other categorisation such as campus-based rather than distance students.[58, 59] Learners may be particularly concerned that data displayed about mental health or learning difficulties could negatively affect attitudes towards them, perhaps reducing opportunities to obtain placements with employers. Among students, too, knowledge of the labels assigned to them may exacerbate social power differentials and their status in relation to each other. Those in the 'most engaged' category might want to stay together and be less willing to associate with those that the analytics flags as struggling. If used ethically though, learning analytics and big data could actually help to identify and address issues of prejudice and differential treatment.[60]

## Reduction of the Individual to a Metric

Oversimplification of a learner's progress is one of the most frequently expressed objections to learning analytics. Any algorithm or method will, by definition, be reductive in that it attempts to create a manageable set of metrics.[61] However students are individuals not numbers and institutions need to be wary of simplistic metrics which ignore personal circumstances and reduce their learning activities to a number or traffic light.[62] In addition, as much of the data related to learning is held outside the institution, or is not even captured digitally in the first place, it is impossible to create a holistic picture of a student's studies.[63]

Systems are unlikely to be able to report whether a student has failed to hand in an assignment because she has split up with her boyfriend, is struggling with a particular concept, or has recently had to take on time-consuming paid work to fund her studies. There are potential solutions to this problem however. In requirements gathering I carried out for the Jisc student app at the University of Lincoln, students expressed a strong interest in being able to note the reasons for failure to submit an assignment or to attend a lecture, so it did not adversely affect their engagement scores.[64]

## Triage

One issue which has both ethical and logistical implications is that of 'triage'. In war situations this occurs when doctors are faced with a number of patients with different injuries but have limited resources and need to decide whom to treat first. Do they attend to those who are most injured out of compassion, even though they are certain to die, or do they concentrate their efforts on those with a chance of recovery?

While medical triage is not entirely analogous to education, institutions do need to work out whom to concentrate their limited resources on.[65] There may be considerable expenditure on supporting students with low levels of engagement or academic progress, while ignoring the better achieving ones. Does it make sense to spend money on learners who are strongly predicted to drop out,[66] or should resource be targeted at those who are struggling academically but are still predicted to have a chance of success? Ellis suggests that learning analytics tends to be directed towards learners who are struggling with course materials or are at risk of attrition; meanwhile, the literature also points to potential benefits of analytics for excellent students who need additional challenges. She believes that learning analytics is in danger of ignoring the needs of the majority of students who fall between these two extremes.[67]

It will always be impossible to target resources with complete accuracy: students cannot simply be categorised as 'not needing help', 'may pass with additional support' and 'destined to fail whatever additional support is provided'. The aims of the analytics initiative are clearly important: is it primarily aimed at reducing attrition or at improving levels of academic achievement? Meanwhile, if this kind of thinking is built into policies and processes, how transparent should an institution be about how it allocates resource to different groups? Transparency is argued by Slade & Prinsloo to be key to justifying the provision of or exclusion from additional services for individual students.[68]

## Conclusion

Concerns about ethical issues have emerged as possibly the biggest barriers to the uptake of learning analytics in educational institutions. As one of the primary reasons for the existence of universities and colleges is to enhance the minds and employment prospects of their students, it should not be difficult to argue that deploying learning analytics is in the interests of both the learner and the organisation. However, given the amount of data that is collected about students and their activities and the possibilities for misinterpretation and misuse, there are numerous opportunities for institutions, employees and students to engage in practices which are regarded as unethical. These are heightened by media scare stories of the misuse of personal data and a growing consciousness that algorithms could be reducing personal autonomy in other areas of human existence.

The acceptance and uptake of learning analytics systems and processes is likely to be easier in institutions that have analysed the issues of concern to their stakeholders and put in place clear and transparent policies and practices to address them. The possibility that a new issue will suddenly emerge among students or faculty and hinder efforts to deploy learning analytics, is ever present and vigilance in monitoring stakeholder concerns and ensuring ongoing ethical practices is advisable.

## References

1 Greller, W. & Drachsler, H., 2012, Translating Learning into Numbers: A Generic Framework for Learning, *Educational Technology and Society*, 15(3), pp. 42–57.
2 Siemens, G., 2012, *Learning Analytics: Envisioning a Research Discipline and a Domain of Practice*, ACM, pp. 4–8.
3 Duquenoy, P., Dando, N. & Harris, I., 2010, *Ethics in the Provision and Use of IT for Business*, Institute of Business Ethics.
4 Ibid.
5 Schroepfer, M., 2014, *Research at Facebook*, Facebook.
6 Open University, 2014, *Policy on Ethical Use of Student Data for Learning Analytics*, www.open.ac.uk/students/charter/essential-documents/ethical-use-student-data-learning-analytics-policy (accessed 9 October 2016).
7 Berg, A. M., 2013, *Towards a Uniform Code of Ethics and Practices for Learning Analytics*, https://ict-innovatie.uva.nl/2013/09/13/towards-a-uniform-code-of-ethics-and-practices-for-learning-analytics/ (accessed 9 October 2016).
8 Learning Analytics Community Exchange: www.laceproject.eu/ (accessed 2 October 2016).
9 Sclater, N., 2015, A Taxonomy of Ethical, Legal and Logistical Issues of Learning Analytics v1.0, *Effective Learning Analytics*, Jisc.
10 Ibid.
11 Apereo Foundation: https://www.apereo.org/ (accessed 2 October 2016).
12 Sclater, N. & Bailey, P., 2015, *Code of Practice for Learning Analytics*, Jisc.
13 Pardo, A. & Siemens, G., 2014, Ethical and Privacy Principles for Learning Analytics, *British Journal of Educational Technology*, 45, pp. 438–450.
14 Harris, I. *et al.*, (2008) *Helping ICT Professionals to Assess Ethical Issues in New and Emerging Technologies*, University of Pavia, British Computer Society.
15 Mason, R. O. *et al.*, 1995, *Ethics of Information Management*, Sage Publications, Inc.
16 Willis, J. E., (2014) *Learning Analytics and Ethics: A Framework beyond Utilitarianism*, EDUCAUSE.

17 Slade, S. & Prinsloo, P., 2013, Learning Analytics: Ethical Issues and Dilemmas, *American Behavioral Scientist*, 57(10), pp. 1509–1528.

18 Markham, A. & Buchanan, E., 2012, Ethical Decision-Making and Internet Research: Recommendation from the AoIR Ethics Working Committee (Version 2.0), https://aoir.org/reports/ethics2.pdf (accessed 9 October 2016).

19 Pistilli, M. D. & Willis, J. E., 2013, Ethics, Big Data and Analytics: A Model for Application, *EDUCAUSE Review*, 6 May, http://er.educause.edu/articles/2013/5/ethics-big-data-and-analytics-a-model-for-application (accessed 12 October 2016).

20 Association of Internet Researchers (2012), *Ethical Decision-Making and Internet Research*.

21 Slade & Prinsloo, Learning Analytics: Ethical Issues and Dilemmas.

22 Kay, D. *et al.*, 2012, *Legal, Risk and Ethical Aspects of Analytics in Higher Education*, Jisc Cetis.

23 Greller & Drachsler, Translating Learning into Numbers.

24 Ibid.

25 Information Commissioner's Office, 2014, *Big Data and Data Protection*, https://ico.org.uk/media/1541/big-data-and-data-protection.pdf (accessed 12 October 2016).

26 Bollier, D., 2010, *The Promise and Peril of Big Data*, Aspen Institute.

27 Siemens, *Learning Analytics: Envisioning a Research Discipline and a Domain of Practice*.

28 Bollier, *The Promise and Peril of Big Data*.

29 Johnson, J. A., 2014, The Ethics of Big Data in Higher Education, *International Review of Information Ethics*, 7, pp. 3–10.

30 Ibid.

31 Ferguson, R., 2012, Learning Analytics: Drivers, Developments and Challenges, *International Journal of Technology Enhanced Learning*, 4(5/6), p. 304.

32 Johnson, The Ethics of Big Data in Higher Education.

33 Slade & Prinsloo, Learning Analytics: Ethical Issues and Dilemmas.

34 Ellis, C., 2013, Broadening the Scope and Increasing the Usefulness of Learning Analytics: The Case for Assessment Analytics, *British Journal of Educational Technology*, 44(4), pp. 662–664.

35 Pistilli & Willis, Ethics, Big Data and Analytics: A Model for Application.

36 International Working Group on Data Protection in Telecommunications, 2014, *Working Paper on Big Data and Privacy: Privacy Principles under Pressure in the Age of Big Data Analytics*, http://dzlp.mk/sites/default/files/u972/WP_Big_Data_final_clean_675.48.12%20%281%29.pdf (accessed 9 October 2016).

37 Ibid.

38 Johnson, The Ethics of Big Data in Higher Education.

39 Ellis, Broadening the Scope and Increasing the Usefulness of Learning Analytics.

40 Swenson, J., 2014, Establishing an Ethical Literacy for Learning Analytics, *LAK14: Proceedings of the Fourth International Conference on Learning Analytics and Knowledge*, ACM, pp. 246–250.

41 Willis, J. E. & Pistilli, M. D., 2014, Ethical Discourse: Guiding the Future of Learning Analytics. *EDUCAUSE Review*, http://dzlp.mk/sites/default/files/u972/WP_Big_Data_final_clean_675.48.12%20%281%29.pdf (accessed 9 October 2016).

42 Slade, S. & Galpin, F., 2012, Ethical Issues in Learning Analytics, *American Behavioral Scientist*, 57(10), pp. 1510–1529.

43 Pistilli & Willis, Ethics, Big Data and Analytics: A Model for Application.

44 Bollier, *The Promise and Peril of Big Data*.

45  Baker, R., 2016, Stupid Tutoring Systems, Intelligent Humans, *International Journal of Articial Intelligence in Education*, 26(2), pp. 600–614.
46  Slade & Prinsloo, Learning Analytics: Ethical Issues and Dilemmas.
47  Sclater, N. *et al.*, 2016, *Learning Analytics in Higher Education: A Review of UK and International Practice*, Jisc.
48  Campbell, J. P. *et al.*, 2007, Academic Analytics: A New Tool for a New Era, *EDUCAUSE Review*, 42(4), pp. 40–57.
49  Prinsloo, P., 2013, Ethics and Learning Analytics as a Faustian Pact: Between Orwell, Huxley, Kafka and the Deep Blue Sea (PowerPoint presentation), http://linus.up.ac.za/telematic/sahela2013/day2-9h30-sahela2013-paul_UNISA_ethics_and_learning_analytics_as_a_fuastian_pact.pdf (accessed 9 October 2016).
50  Pistilli & Willis, Ethics, Big Data and Analytics: A Model for Application.
51  Slade & Prinsloo, Learning Analytics: Ethical Issues and Dilemmas.
52  Jayaprakash, S. M. *et al.*, 2014, Early Alert of Academically At-Risk Students: An Open Source Analytics Initiative, *Journal of Learning Analytics*, 1(1), pp. 6–47.
53  Pistilli & Willis, Ethics, Big Data and Analytics: A Model for Application.
54  Campbell, DeBlois & Oblinger, Academic Analytics: A New Tool for a New Era.
55  Sclater, N., 2016, *How Do You Decide Whether to Intervene with Students Based on their Learning Analytics?* [Podcast]. Jisc.
56  Campbell, DeBlois & Oblinger, Academic Analytics: A New Tool for a New Era.
57  Pistilli & Willis, Ethics, Big Data and Analytics: A Model for Application.
58  Swenson, J., 2014, *Establishing an Ethical Literacy for Learning Analytics*, ACM, pp. 246–250.
59  MacCarthy, M., 2014, Student Privacy: Harm and Context, *International Review of Information Ethics*, 21, pp. 11–24.
60  Polonetsky, J. & Tene, O., 2014, The Ethics of Student Privacy: Building Trust for Ed Tech, *International Review of Information Ethics*, 21, pp. 25–34.
61  Greller & Drachsler, Translating Learning into Numbers: A Generic Framework for Learning.
62  Campbell, DeBlois & Oblinger, Academic Analytics: A New Tool for a New Era.
63  Slade & Prinsloo, Learning Analytics: Ethical Issues and Dilemmas.
64  Sclater, N., 2015, What Do Students Want from a Learning Analytics App? *Effective Learning Analytics*, 29 April, https://analytics.jiscinvolve.org/wp/2015/04/29/what-do-students-want-from-a-learning-analytics-app/ (accessed 9 October 2016).
65  Campbell, DeBlois & Oblinger, Academic Analytics: A New Tool for a New Era.
66  Pistilli & Willis, Ethics, Big Data and Analytics: A Model for Application.
67  Ellis, Broadening the Scope and Increasing the Usefulness of Learning Analytics.
68  Slade & Prinsloo, Learning Analytics: Ethical Issues and Dilemmas.

# 21  Transparency and Consent

Ensuring the acceptance among stakeholders of learning analytics may require transparency and the obtaining of consent – telling users about what is going on and ensuring that it is acceptable to them. These issues should be considered from an ethical perspective but are also required by law in many countries. This chapter examines why learning analytics processes should be carried out transparently and discusses issues around obtaining consent for the collection of personal data and the carrying out of interventions based on the analysis of that data.

## Transparency

Being open and transparent with students, faculty and staff about what data is being collected and what is being done with it is important both from an ethical and a legal standpoint. The management of student perceptions of learning analytics is also critical to its successful adoption.[1] Secret processes and opaque and unaccountable algorithms can hide arbitrary or unfair decision making.[2] However, transparency in the use of big data helps to prevent abuses of institutional power, makes individuals feel safer in sharing their data and can result in better predictions.[3] Legal requirements for transparency vary in different countries and states but it is advisable to provide clear information to stakeholders, particularly students and faculty. They should be made aware of the purposes of the learning analytics, exactly what data is being collected to achieve these purposes and what is involved in the analytics and intervention processes.

> ### Ensuring Transparency Regarding the Data Collected
>
> The Open University makes clear to staff and students, in a policy document, the categories of data potentially available for learning analytics. These are: personal information provided by the student, the student's study record, sensitive information such as ethnic origin and disability, details of contacts between the student and the university, interactive content generated by the student, system-generated data such as accesses to the learning

management system (LMS), data derived from other data, and data generated internally such as student use of a library subscription service.

Provisions are made for the use of anonymised data both internally, for instance forum posts, and from external datasets such as social networking sites – but only to generate information on cohorts rather than individuals. Data types out of scope for learning analytics are also listed, such as data on student complaints.[4]

As discussed in the previous chapter, it may be important for the predictive algorithms and metrics to be verified by experts and properly explained, as these could have significant impacts on individuals. Arguably, the greater the implications of a particular decision or prediction, the greater right a person should have to question how that conclusion was reached.[5] Analytics may be more effective, too, if stakeholders can see and understand the metrics, while poor interpretations of analytics are also more likely to be noticed and challenged.[6] Proprietary systems, where the algorithms are kept hidden due to commercial sensitivities, bring the real threat that institutions will be challenged because they are taking decisions that affect students, based on methods that they do not understand. On the other hand the complexities of the underlying statistical models may not be easily understood by anyone other than data scientists. The solution may be to attempt to explain in a clear and accessible way how the analytics work and how decisions to intervene are being taken.

### How Important is it to Explain the Detail of Processes, Algorithms and Metrics to Stakeholders?

In a series of interviews I carried out with UK institutions leading in the field of learning analytics I asked Anne-Marie Scott at the University of Edinburgh whether she thought it was important to be able to explain the processes, algorithms and metrics of learning analytics to faculty, staff and students. She replied:

> I think it's useful for transparency. I think we always hit interesting questions, when perhaps it's commercial software, around explaining algorithms. I think for some of our staff, particularly those who are active in the field or in related fields, a good portion of establishing the credibility of what we're doing can be done by being very thorough in our explanations of these things. But I think that there's a difference between explaining them and being clear about them, and people having to understand them to actually use whatever it is we produce or offer to them. I certainly think that, at scale, there is no way that you could train up our entire staff and student body in such a way that they could get to grips with the nitty-gritty detail of it. So I think the explanations

have to be available, but they mustn't be a mandatory part of using whatever it is that's provided.

I also asked Sharon Slade, Senior Lecturer at the Open University Business School, how important she felt it was to explain how the analytics works to the students. She said:

I don't think we anticipate being able to explain in detail to students and staff how those models work ... We do need to be able to explain what we're doing, and why, and be able to demonstrate that the purposes are robust.[7]

## Student Input to Analytics Processes

Should students have a say in what data is collected about them, how it is used for analytics and what interventions should be taken with them?[8] The answer, based on the ideas presented in Chapter 19, would be a resounding 'yes'. Apart from the ethical imperative of involving students in decisions about new processes that may have a significant impact on their education, there are clear benefits in consulting these key stakeholders. The analytics and interventions are likely to end up being more effective, as well as more accepted; student advocates can also help support further roll-out of the technology. How the consultations can best take place, though, is another matter: involving students in decision making is not always straightforward. Student union members may have their own agendas and may not be truly representative of their peers, or they may have limited time to engage in the complexities of learning analytics. It may also be important to secure representation from students who have most to gain from learning analytics, such as first-year students who are struggling.

## Informed Consent

It is not clear to what extent students are aware of how much personal data is being recorded about them by their institutions, although they are increasingly used to being monitored in other parts of their lives.[9] Highly personal information about many aspects of our existence can be derived from our emails, our online searches, our likes and postings on social networks and the people with whom we associate. Our physical location at all times is monitored through phone networks and multiple apps on our smartphones and, as online and cashless payments increasingly replace the use of physical currency, everything we purchase is recorded and analysed. This data is then used to build highly personal profiles in order to target us with advertising, an arguably more insidious purpose than anything a university or college is likely to want to do with its students. The possibilities for surveillance, breaches of privacy and other misuse of this vast data source by the state, as well as commercial interests, are immense.

Universities and colleges can make a convincing case that they have no need for much of the data we so freely and unthinkingly provide to other agencies. They should at all times ensure that what is collected is stewarded carefully and used only for the purposes of enhancing education. Should students therefore be asked for their consent to collect the data required for learning analytics in the first place and subsequently for it to be used for learning analytics?[10] This has been one of the main questions to be asked in the emerging learning analytics initiatives at university campuses and in the growing body of literature surrounding the use of big data in education. There is a belief in some institutions that they are legally covered for learning analytics because of the computing regulations and other consent forms they ask students to sign at the start of their studies. This is more than a just legal issue, though: we need to ask '*Should* we be carrying out the analytics?' as well as '*Can* we?'

Claims have been made that students should be asked for their *informed* consent[11, 12] to collect and use their data, in similar ways to experiments in medicine and social science carried out on human subjects. In other words, learners should be made fully aware of what data is being collected and to what uses it will be put before giving their permission. Informed consent is a basic principle of scientific research on humans.[13] It can demonstrate credibility and accountability on the part of researchers and, by extension, the institution. Traxler & Bridges describe informed consent as referring to students' 'understanding of the nature, extent, duration and significance' of their participation.[14] When requesting informed consent it is important to use language that is respectful and easy to understand and participants should be allowed to ask questions about the research at any stage. In conventional research the subjects should be told that their participation is voluntary and that withdrawal does not incur any penalty. They should also be informed about the possible consequences of non-participation or withdrawal.[15]

The apparent reasonableness of applying the principles of informed consent ignores the fact that learning analytics deployments may not be in the form of short-term scientific experiments on discrete groups of subjects. They may instead be carried out with students across an entire institution indefinitely and as part of the normal business of the organisation. In a period of rapid technological development in the field of learning analytics it is also unlikely that consent given for the use of their data at the commencement of their studies by a student will remain relevant and appropriate by the time they graduate several years later.[16]

Declining to participate in learning analytics could have a negative impact on academic success, so a student may not feel they have much choice in agreeing to be monitored. The concept of *voluntary* informed consent[17] is commendable but not necessarily achievable by institutions that wish to make extensive use of learning analytics. It can be argued that requesting consent for the collection of much of the data to be used for learning analytics is unnecessary and impractical: education in increasingly digitised institutions would be logistically impossible without holding this data.

Governments may moreover require that attributes such as race or gender are collected so that they can monitor the provision of education to minority groups. They might also expect some data to be retained by institutions indefinitely. Asking students to agree to the collection of this data is not providing them with a real choice if their education would have to be terminated immediately by refusing their consent. However, there are certain types of data, currently not used for mainstream learning analytics, where permission for collection may be required because its use without consent could be regarded as intrusive: for example location data, data from external social media sites, records of confidential discussions with a personal tutor, or 'sensitive' data, such as race, religion or sexuality.

## Consent and the Law

Whether students should be asked for their data to be collected and for interventions to be taken based on analysis of that data, is complex both ethically and logistically. It is also subject to legal restrictions in many jurisdictions, many of them ambiguous and yet to be tested in the courts. The European Data Protection Directive, which is enacted separately in the laws of each of the 28 member states, is highly relevant to the collection of data for learning analytics. Personal data can be processed if the data subject has 'unambiguously' given consent. A tightening up of the legislation in the new European Data Protection Regulation will result in greater obligations on institutions in all European Union countries that are relying on consent from students as justification for the collection and use of their data.[18] However, there are other situations such as protecting the 'legitimate interests' of the organisation, which can be used to justify the collection and processing of data in certain circumstances.

Federal laws in Canada also require organisations to obtain the 'meaningful consent' of individuals before collecting and using their personal information.[19] However, institutions may be less restricted in other parts of the world: in Australia for example the Federal Privacy Act permits organisations to gather personal data *without* consent, though users must be notified that it is being gathered and informed about the purposes for which it will be used. Any data collected must, though, be regarded as 'reasonably necessary' for one or more of the organisation's activities or functions. Moreover, the right to gather data without consent in Australia does not apply in the case of 'sensitive' data, which would require the prior agreement of the data subject.[20]

Rubinstein, a US-based commentator, claims that European law fails to acknowledge the 'impending big data tsunami', which she believes will overwhelm principles such as informed choice. The distinction between personal and non-personal data is not necessarily sustainable in the world of big data, and new rights such as the 'right to be forgotten', Rubinstein argues, may be impractical and conflict with rights of free expression.[21]

There is another fundamental problem here for educational institutions: unlike traditional research where a hypothesis is made and where evidence is then sought to prove or disprove it, the analysis of big data may involve the identification of patterns that cannot be anticipated in advance. Thus, there may be unknown future uses for the analytics to which individuals cannot consent. Despite this, the UK's Information Commissioner states unambiguously that: 'The complexity of big data analytics is not an excuse for failing to obtain consent where it is required.'[22]

The official US government approach differs markedly from the European philosophy. This is important because some of the main learning analytics products available are developed primarily in the US and will be potentially unusable in many other countries unless appropriate privacy safeguards are built in. Also, any American company wishing to provide hosted learning analytics services for a European organisation needs to comply with EU data protection legislation. The overall environment in the US generally relies on utilitarian approaches, which weigh up the possible benefits against the risks and costs. Meanwhile, in Europe, basic human rights are so fundamental that it may be difficult to justify potential breaches of them despite apparent benefits to society or industry.[23] In summary: the US approach tends to permit the use of personal information unless a law prohibits it, partly because of the protections for freedom of expression in the First Amendment.[24] Many other countries, however, are imposing laws that require informed consent to be obtained from users before gathering and processing their personal data.

## Privacy Policies

Prinsloo and Slade suggest that despite most universities having policy frameworks to safeguard data privacy and regulate access, the frameworks do not generally address the specific ethical challenges of learning analytics. They find that institutions often provide a large number of documents relating to legal and ethical issues that the student is required to navigate. It is difficult to consider this to be *informed* consent when few students will have the time or inclination to read these documents.[25]

Complex terms of contract and long-winded privacy notices send out the wrong message to students. One study suggests that people will not read privacy policies if they perceive that the cost of reading them is greater than the benefit of doing so and that users tend to scan the documents for particular information rather than read them comprehensively.[26] Facebook's privacy policy itself is reported to contain more words than the US Constitution and, while users are able to change their privacy settings, they are presented with over 50 toggles, which result in over 170 privacy options.[27]

Adding to the confusion, providers regularly change their privacy policies and may or may not make that clear to the user.[28] There is a fundamental imbalance meanwhile in the relationship between the provider, which offers a lengthy set of terms on a take-it-or-leave-it basis, and the user, who has little time to read the document.[29] However, the UK Information Commissioner's Office challenges organisations to be 'as innovative in [the provision of privacy notices] as they are in their analytics and to find new ways of conveying information concisely'.[30]

Users of online services may have control over what information they share but are highly unlikely to understand the complexities of how their data is being processed subsequently. Arguably the granting of consent is meaningless if learners have no conception of the way their data is being used – or could potentially be misused. The paradox is that any document that properly explains the complexities is unlikely to be understood or read, while summaries are likely to be oversimplistic. Meanwhile, some organisations may attempt to give an impression of transparency that can hide what is really going on.[31]

## The Logistics of Requesting Consent

So how can consent best be granted by students? The ticking of a box at the end of a lengthy agreement in a small font in complex legal language is unlikely to be satisfactory. Even if they do read the policies, it can be difficult for students to work out what is actually being done with their personal information. A checkbox for opting *into* data collection, which requires a positive action, is more likely to be considered valid, at least in European law, than one for opting out.[32] However users may fail to check the box, thus denying themselves the benefits of learning analytics and creating gaps in the dataset and logistical problems for the institution.

Another issue that may arise if students are asked to consent to the collection of their data is that they may subsequently change their minds. Should they be allowed to withdraw their consent part of the way through their studies? Logistical difficulties would be presented for the institution in this scenario: mechanisms would need to be provided for the withdrawing, as well as the granting, of consent and consequently there would be gaps in the dataset. However, it could be argued to be unfair to allow some students to opt out initially but not to allow those who participate for a while subsequently to withdraw their consent.

## Consent for Interventions

A requirement to request consent potentially comes in not at the data collection stage but when the data is used and in particular when an intervention is taken with the student as a result of the analytics. A typical intervention would be at-risk students being contacted by a tutor when it appears that they are at risk of dropping out, based on their attendance data combined with other indicators such as low prior educational attainment. Some commentators have suggested that students should provide their prior consent to be 'intervened with' in this way by their institutions. Cormack argues that universities should put in place a two-stage process where data collection and analysis is justified on the basis of the legitimate interests of the organisation, while student consent should be sought for subsequent interventions based on the analytics.[33] However, as decision making becomes increasingly driven by big data in all realms of society, learning analytics too will become ever more integrated into the way that faculty monitor and run their courses. This, in turn, will influence the perceptions of students as to what is normal practice in education; giving them opportunities to consent may become increasingly unnecessary or confusing.

## Opting Out

Various researchers have asked whether students should be able to opt out of data collection and learning analytics.[34, 35, 36] Consent is arguably meaningless if there is no realistic option to opt out. Most smartphones apps request consent to access a range of data, such as the user's contacts or image gallery, for which there is sometimes no apparent requirement. Refusing access to any of this data usually means the app cannot be used at all. Similarly, allowing students to opt out of certain data collection in education may make it impossible for them to continue to participate in their studies. Institutions have always recorded attributes of learners, such as their name and date of birth; they also need to document what courses their students are studying and what grades they obtain. There may be legal reasons why this data should be held indefinitely by the institution: there are certainly business ones for it to be gathered in the first place.

With the increasing use of online learning there is significantly more data being collected about individuals. Learning management systems and other software that provides learning content, assessments and communication facilities often *cannot function* without logging the activities of users. Allowing students to opt out of this data being recorded might make it impossible for them to take part in courses with an online component. Arguably, then, it simply does not make sense to ask learners to consent to the collection of such data. 'Allow us to collect data about your learning activities or quit your studies now' is not a meaningful or fair choice that can be put to students. However, institutions do cover themselves already in this way by expecting learners to agree to computing regulations and other policies when signing up with the institution. Meanwhile, at least under current European law, organisations can claim that some forms of data collection and use are in their *legitimate interests* – that they are essential for the functioning of their business and that consent does not therefore have to be obtained.

One reason why opting out of data collection may not be realistic is the impact it has on other students. Single students removing themselves from the dataset may have little impact. However, if significant numbers of students opt out, the statistics will be less representative and the analytics of lower value. Opting out could be seen as a selfish act that denies the full benefits of learning analytics to those who want them. Opting out could also have a detrimental effect on the individual. Should students be allowed to deny themselves the benefits available to other students, such as the provision of feedback or interventions, when they look to be at risk of academic failure?

Pardo & Siemens point out that, in medical research, analysing patients' records can have benefits for society as a whole and that in learning contexts, too, absolute confidentiality may not always be in the best interests of the wider group.[37] Slade & Prinsloo propose that the benefits for many may outweigh the rights of individuals who wish to withhold their data for reporting purposes, for example to funding bodies. However, students should, they believe, be able to opt out of having their learning *personalised*, assuming they are made aware of the consequences.[38] Such decisions may be highly contextual though: personalised learning may evolve to such an extent that opting out on an individual basis simply does not make sense in the context of the pedagogy: this is already the case where adaptive learning software has been introduced as an integral part of the course.

## New Uses for the Data

What happens, then, if an innovative learning analytics project emerges or software is deployed that does something with student data which has not been done before? An argument can be made that students should be asked for their consent when additional sources of data are to be collected or new uses for learning analytics are to be rolled out. The fact that the new use for the data is in the legitimate interests of the institution may be relevant here too but it can still be argued that it has an ethical, if not legal, duty at least to inform students about this new use of their personal data.

## Unknown Future Uses of the Data

One of the features of big data is that hypotheses are often unknown in advance of data collection. Findings are made once the dataset has been accumulated and patterns in the data discovered. It is unlikely that all the purposes to which student data could be put in any institution are currently known. Furthermore, storing it well into the future could bring unforeseen benefits to future cohorts. Thus asking students to consent to a restricted set of potential uses for their data may limit the possibilities for learning analytics in the future. Asking them, instead, for renewed consent when a new purpose for their data emerges is another option. However, this is likely to be complex and unsatisfactory, requiring the contacting of individuals who may even have left the institution. Many may fail to respond or deny the use of their data for the new purpose, thus leaving problematic gaps in the dataset.

## Conclusion

The ethical and logistical challenges in requesting students' permission to use their data for learning analytics are complex. Legislation requiring the requesting of consent by students is evolving rapidly and varies across different jurisdictions. Data protection officers in institutions may emphasise the legal aspects of what should be done regarding consent, while faculty may be more concerned with the ethical issues and doing what is 'right'.

Gaining and retaining the trust of learners that their data is being collected for legitimate reasons, used appropriately and stewarded carefully, is essential. Students may accept the intrusive collection and use of their data by online retailers and social networking sites because they consider the benefits of using these services to be greater than the resulting loss of privacy, though it is likely that they are unaware of the full extent of this profiling. To reduce fears and misunderstandings about learning analytics, institutions should ensure that the mechanisms of personal data collection and use, and consequent benefits for their students, are well documented, promoted, explained and understood.

Requesting consent may be covered in existing institutional policies and computing regulations. Ensuring that this consent is fully informed, though, is highly problematic, particularly when there is no realistic possibility of opting out. The collection of more sensitive data may require explicit consent from students. If interventions are planned that could potentially be regarded as intrusive, such as making suggestions to students based on location, then it is advisable, if not legally required, to seek their consent. Legislation is evolving rapidly in this area and institutions will need to ensure that they stay on top of any changes – across all of the legislatures where they operate.

## References

1 Slade, S. & Prinsloo, P., 2013, Learning Analytics: Ethical Issues and Dilemmas, *American Behavioral Scientist*, 57(10), pp. 1509–1528.

2 MacCarthy, M., 2014, Student Privacy: Harm and Context, *International Review of Information Ethics*, 21, pp. 11–24.

3 Richards, N. M. & King, J. H., 2014, Big Data Ethics, *Wake Forest Law Review*, 19 May, http://ssrn.cohttp://ssrn.com/abstract=2384174 m/abstract=2384174 (accessed 9 October 2016).

4 Open University, 2014, *Policy on Ethical Use of Student Data for Learning Analytics*, www.open.ac.uk/students/charter/essential-documents/ethical-use-student-data-learning-analytics-policy (accessed 9 October 2016).

5 Crawford, K. & Schultz, J., 2013, *Big Data and Due Process: Toward a Framework to Redress Predictive Privacy Harms*, Social Science Research Network.

6 Clow, D., 2012, The Learning Analytics Cycle: Closing the Loop Effectively, *LAK12: Proceedings of the Second International Conference on Learning Analytics and Knowledge*.

7 Sclater, N., 2016, *How Do You Deal with Student Consent when Using Learning Analytics?* [Podcast], Jisc.

8 Willis, J. E. & Pistilli, M. D., 2014, Ethical Discourse: Guiding the Future of Learning Analytics, *EDUCAUSE Review*, http://er.educause.edu/articles/2014/4/ethical-discourse-guiding-the-future-of-learning-analytics (accessed 9 October 2016).

9 Slade & Prinsloo, Learning Analytics: Ethical Issues and Dilemmas.

10 Campbell, J. P. & Oblinger, D. G., 2007, Academic Analytics, *EDUCASE Review*, 42(4), pp. 40–57.

11 Esposito, A., 2012, Research Ethics in Emerging Forms of Online Learning: Issues Arising from a Hypothetical Study on a MOOC, *The Electronic Journal of E-Learning*, 10(3), pp. 315–325.

12 Slade & Prinsloo, Learning Analytics: Ethical Issues and Dilemmas.

13 American Sociological Association, 1999, *Code of Ethics*, www.asanet.org/mem bership/code-ethics (accessed 9 October 2016).

14 Traxler, J. & Bridges, N., 2005, Mobile Learning – the Ethical and Legal Challenges, *Mobile Learning Anytime Anywhere*, Learning and Skills Development Agency.

15 American Sociological Association, *Code of Ethics*.

16 Cormack, A., 2016, A Data Protection Framework for Learning Analytics, *Journal of Learning Analytics*, 3(1), pp. 91–106.

17 British Educational Research Association, 2011, *Ethical Guidelines for Educational Research*, https://www.bera.ac.uk/researchers-resources/publications/ethical-guide lines-for-educational-research-2011 (accessed 9 October 2016).

18 European Commission, 2014, *Progress on EU data protection reform now irrever-sible following European Parliament vote.* Press release, 12 March, http://europa.eu/ rapid/press-release_MEMO-14-186_en.htm (accessed 9 October 2016).

19 Office of the Privacy Commissioner of Canada, 2013, *Guidelines for Online Con-sent*, https://www.priv.gc.ca/en/privacy-topics/collecting-personal-information/con sent/gl_oc_201405 (accessed 9 October 2016).

20 Office of the Australian Information Commissioner, 1988, *Privacy Act*, Australian Government.

21 Rubinstein, I. S., 2013, Big Data: The End of Privacy or a New Beginning? *International Data Privacy Law*, 3(2), pp. 74–87.

22 Information Commissioner's Office, 2014, *Big Data and Data Protection*, https:// ico.org.uk/media/1541/big-data-and-data-protection.pdf (accessed 9 October 2016).

23 Ess, C. & Association of Internet Researchers, 2002, *Ethical Decison-Making and Internet Research*, 22 November, http://aoir.org/reports/ethics.pdf (accessed 9 October 2016).

24 Schwartz, P. M., 2010, *Data Protection Law and the Ethical Use of Analytics*, The Center for Information Policy Leadership.

25 Prinsloo, P. & Slade, S., 2013, An Evaluation of Policy Frameworks for Addressing Ethical Considerations in Learning Analytics, *LAK13: Proceedings of the Third Conference on Learning Analytics and Knowledge*, pp. 240–244.

26 McDonald, A. & Cranor, L. F., 2008, The Cost of Reading Privacy Policies, *I/S: A Journal of Law and Policy for the Information Society, Privacy Year in Review Issue*, 4(3), http://lorrie.cranor.org/pubs/readingPolicyCost-authorDraft.pdf (accessed 9 October 2016).

27 Rayport, J. F., 2011, What Big Data Needs: A Code of Ethical Practices, *MIT Technology Review*, 26 May.

28 Pardo, A. & Siemens, G., 2014, Ethical and Privacy Principles for Learning Analytics, *British Journal of Educational Technology*, 45, pp. 438–450.

29 President's Council of Advisors on Science and Technology, 2014, *Big Data and Privacy: A Technological Perspective*, May, https://www.whitehouse.gov/sites/default/ files/microsites/ostp/PCAST/pcast_big_data_and_privacy_-_may_2014.pdf (accessed 9 October 2016).

30 Information Commissioner's Office, *Big Data and Data Protection*.

31 Office of the Privacy Commissioner of Canada, 2012, *The Age of Predictive Analytics: From Patterns to Predictions*, August, https://www.priv.gc.ca/en/opc-actions-and-decisions/research/explore-privacy-research/2012/pa_201208/ (accessed 9 October 2016).

32 Kay, D., Korn, N. & Oppenheim, C., 2012, *Legal, Risk and Ethical Aspects of Analytics in Higher Education*, Jisc Cetis.

33 Cormack, A Data Protection Framework for Learning Analytics.

34 Campbell & Oblinger, Academic Analytics.

35 Prinsloo, P., 2013, *Ethics and Learning Analytics as a Faustian Pact: Between Orwell, Huxley, Kafka and the Deep Blue Sea* (PowerPoint presentation), https://www.priv.gc.ca/en/opc-actions-and-decisions/research/explore-privacy-research/2012/pa_201208/ (accessed 9 October 2016).

36 Slade, S. & Galpin, F., 2012, *Ethical Issues in Learning Analytics* (PowerPoint presentation), http://www.slideshare.net/SharonSlade/ethical-issues-in-learning-analytics.

37 Pardo & Siemens, Ethical and Privacy Principles for Learning Analytics.

38 Slade & Prinsloo, Learning Analytics: Ethical Issues and Dilemmas.

# 22  Privacy and Data Protection

Protecting the data of individuals and preserving their privacy is not only essential for the acceptance and long-term viability of learning analytics but is a legal requirement in most jurisdictions. Despite claims from leading figures in the IT world such as Mark Zuckerberg that privacy is no longer a 'social norm',[1] there appears to be a growing consciousness of the importance of protecting personal information. Edward Snowden's revelations about the surveillance carried out by the US National Security Agency and its UK counterpart, GCHQ,[2] created a public outcry, with ongoing repercussions for government agencies throughout the world collecting personal data.

Companies, too, are concerned that their customers may stop using their services unless reassurance can be given that their privacy is being protected.[3] Apple's court battles to resist orders to help the FBI hack into the iPhone of a shooting suspect[4] show just how important privacy is now perceived to be to the commercial interests of corporations. Educational institutions also risk significant reputational damage and legal challenges if they do not succeed in protecting user data. A breach of security at the University of Greenwich resulted in personal details of students such as their addresses, mobile phone numbers, signatures and even mental health issues being made available on the institution's website. Such incidents in Europe could result in fines of €10 million from 2018, when new legislation comes into force.[5]

Learning analytics brings additional challenges for the protection of individuals' privacy. The analysis of big data from multiple sources can enable far more to be learned about students than was anticipated when the systems were put in place to gather that data. Potential threats to privacy include:

- **Invasion of private communications**: Students engage in communications with peers, faculty and others using multiple tools, some provided by the institution, others not. The conversations may be valuable for learning analytics; however, using them, unless students have given their consent, has serious privacy implications.
- **Invasion of privacy at home**: A student's 'virtual home' now includes a range of internet-based tools, storage of documents in the cloud and multiple devices, all of which create data that could be relevant for learning analytics.

- **Use of inferred sensitive facts**: Analytics can infer highly sensitive facts from multiple data sources such as suggesting sexual preferences or aspects of personality or health of which individuals may not even be aware themselves.
- **Intrusive tracking**: The technologies may enable the tracking of a student's physical location as they move around campus or even outside the campus. Without proper safeguards, this information could be misused for marketing purposes, or abused by stalkers.
- **Loss of anonymity**: Arguably, learners should have the right to remain anonymous in many circumstances during their studies, particularly when learning outside formal contexts.
- **Loss of private association**: Students should be able to associate with each other in private if they wish, without their every interaction being monitored.[6]

There are significant potential benefits for institutions in treating the data used for learning analytics with the utmost care. It should help to develop trusting relationships with students and reassure faculty that the institution is acting correctly. There should be reduced reputational and financial risks from security breaches. Clear institutional policies around data protection should also result in fewer questions, complaints and disputes about the use of personal data.[7] All of these should consequently assist with the deployment and adoption of learning analytics.

## The Legal Context

Privacy is not a simplistic, binary concept and data is not necessarily restricted to either the public or the private domain – in fact, most of the information held about us is an intermediate state between completely private and completely public. Information, moreover, is of little use unless it is shared in some way.[8, 9] *Data protection* is the term that tends to be used for restricting access to data and information in Europe, while *privacy* is more commonly used in the US and elsewhere. It has been suggested that 'information rules' – the rules that govern how we should treat personal information – might be a more appropriate and less emotive term to use than 'privacy'.[10]

The laws regarding the collection and processing of personal information vary considerably and reflect the legal, social and cultural values in each jurisdiction.[11] There is minimal case law to provide for the specific context of learning analytics[12] but many existing legal restrictions on the collection and processing of data need to be considered. Institutions should already be familiar with laws for protecting personal data, so should have most of the necessary policies and processes already in place.[13]

The interests of big business have arguably been more influential in the development of laws relating to data in the US than in Europe. However, US citizens are becoming increasingly concerned about their own privacy rights, the biggest example in the educational domain being the inBloom initiative.

> ## inBloom: The Risks of Failing to Deal with Users' Concerns about Privacy
>
> In 2011, an initiative, later rebranded as 'inBloom', was set up to help school teachers develop a better picture of student progress. In 2013, the programme received $100 million from the Bill and Melinda Gates Foundation and the Carnegie Corporation of New York and nine US states agreed to use inBloom to store student data.[14]
>
>> *inBloom* was a highly ambitious, though flawed attempt, to move from a rather inefficient, bureaucratic and often paper-bound set of records to an easy-to-use, accessible, cloud-based system that seamlessly moved with the child through her school years, as she changed classes, years, schools and even localities.[15]
>
> Privacy advocates and parents of the pupils to be affected by inBloom began to raise concerns about possible commercial exploitation of their children's personal data. They discovered that some of the data that was anticipated to be collected included information on the nature of family relationships and learning disabilities.[16] The media storm that followed meant that a few months later six of the participating states had dropped out of their contracts and by April 2014 the programme was closed completely.[17]

In the US, the key piece of legislation is the Family Educational Rights and Privacy Act 1974 (FERPA), which allows students to access the information held about them by universities and to have some control over that data. However, this federal law is more concerned with students giving their consent for the disclosure of their personal data to third parties than with the use of student data within the institution and its collection in the first place. In 2008 and 2011, FERPA was expanded somewhat, allowing educational officials, contracted vendors and state authorities to access student data.[18]

Recognising that US legislation is inadequate in this space, the White House released a report in 2014 calling for further revisions to FERPA and arguing that:

> federal government must ensure educational data linked to individual students gathered in school is used for educational purposes, and protect students against their data being shared or used inappropriately.[19]

Subsequent to the inBloom debacle, California enacted a law that restricts how schoolchildren's data can be used by educational technology companies.

They are now unable to use students' text messages, photos, locations or other data relating to them for selling, disclosing or marketing purposes. In a pledge developed by the Future of Privacy Forum, a Washington-based think tank, 14 industry players, including Microsoft, though notably excluding Apple and Google, committed themselves not to use students' data to target them with advertisements or to compile profiles on individuals – unless authorised by their parents.[20]

In Europe the key legislation is the Data Protection Directive,[21] which is enacted separately in the laws of each member state. In the UK, the Data Protection Act 1998 builds on eight key principles from the European Directive, requiring that data should be:

- processed fairly and lawfully;
- obtained only for specific lawful purposes;
- adequate, relevant and not excessive for those purposes;
- kept accurate and up to date;
- kept for no longer than is necessary for those purposes;
- processed in accordance with the data subject's rights;
- kept safe from unauthorised or unlawful processing, accidental loss, destruction or damage to the data;
- not transferred outside the European Economic Area unless that country has equivalent levels of protection for processing personal data.

Similar protections for personal data were built into the Privacy Act 1985 in Canada, the Privacy Act 1988 in Australia and the Privacy Act 1993 in New Zealand. All of this legislation provides vital protections for individuals in relation to their personal data, but potentially holds back the development of learning analytics, often due to the strict interpretation of the laws by institutional officers wishing to protect their organisations. Technology and society have moved on considerably since these Acts were first put into place: there have been claims that they are no longer entirely appropriate for today's context and new laws are consequently emerging.

One of the key stated benefits of big data is that patterns can be discovered and conclusions drawn that were never anticipated. This tends to conflict with traditional scientific method, where a theory is postulated and the data is then sought to confirm or contradict it. It also challenges the privacy principle in the European Directive that data cannot be used for purposes incompatible with the original purpose(s). As big data is also about maximisation, it conflicts with the concepts of relevance and data minimisation, principles that are intended to ensure that only the data required is stored and that it is deleted, when it is no longer of use for its original purpose. The point about big data is that its value is related to possible future uses as well as current purposes. Organisations will not wish to delete data that could be a future source of insights and revenue: it may thus become increasingly difficult for authorities to enforce the requirement to delete personal data.[22]

The EU General Data Protection Regulation was proposed 'to strengthen privacy rights and boost Europe's digital economy',[23] and will create a single law applicable across member states, without the need for separate national legislation. The following principles, each of which is of relevance to learning analytics, are included in the proposal:

- **A right to be forgotten**. When individuals no longer want their data to be processed and there are no legitimate grounds for retaining it, the data should be deleted. This principle was the subject of a lengthy legal battle between the European Commission and Google.[24]
- **Easier access to your own data**. A right to data portability will allow users to transfer their personal data between service providers, though only that which the individuals themselves have provided. There may be value in students being able to take this with them when moving to a new institution.
- **Putting you in control**. When consent is required to process an individual's data, they must be asked to give it explicitly. This may have implications for institutions that assume that current computing regulations or other policies are sufficient for learning analytics.
- **Data protection first, not an afterthought**. 'Privacy by design' and 'privacy by default' will also become essential principles in EU data protection rules – this means that data protection safeguards should be built into products and services from the earliest stage of development and that privacy-friendly default settings should be the norm. Again, this will have significant implications for European institutions wishing to deploy learning analytics.

The relative strictness of European data protection legislation affects perceptions of what data should be collected about students and what should be done with it. Concerns about privacy are certainly holding back the development of learning analytics in countries such as Germany and the Netherlands, where memories of historic excessive state monitoring and control may still have an influence.

## Sensitive Data

Some types of data are arguably more 'sensitive' than others: race, political beliefs, sexual orientation or religion, for example. The potential for invasions of privacy or misuse of such data leading to discrimination is such that legislation in some jurisdictions (e.g. EU, Australia) has a special definition for these attributes and requires them to be treated with particular care. Some of this information may be irrelevant for learning analytics but there is a strong legal case for requesting students' consent to collect sensitive data in the first place and for making it very clear to them what exactly is being recorded, what it is required for, how it is being processed and how its confidentiality will be safeguarded.

This has a moral dimension too. Do educational institutions really need to know this information about their students? Would it make any difference to a predictive algorithm to be aware of a student's political beliefs? Even if it did have a marginal impact, is it anyone else's business and should institutions not draw the line somewhere on what is acceptable data to collect and use for learning analytics? The main ethical justification of collecting such data would be to avoid prejudicial treatment of people based on particular attributes that may be integral to their identity. Some of this information is used to help ensure that institutions are not treating particular minorities differently, or, if they are, it is for assisting disadvantaged groups.

Other types of data that do not fit into a strict legal definition of sensitive data may also be open to abuse and again require learners' consent for their use: location data is one example. With attendance monitoring systems increasingly prevalent, GPS-enabled smartphones held continuously by almost all students and the logging of Wi-Fi use from mobile devices on campus, it is possible to monitor the location of individuals continuously as they move around. Data on visits to the library, for example, attendance at lectures or even visits to sports facilities may correlate with measures of student success and is therefore of considerable interest to data scientists wishing to refine their predictive models. Again, though, safeguards need to be put in place to avoid misuse of this data. There may also be adverse impacts if a student's every physical move around campus (or even externally to the institution) is being monitored: will this lead to negative emotions and adverse effects on educational performance?

An additional potential pitfall that has been pointed out is that the compilation of student profiles from multiple data sources, which are themselves not particularly sensitive, could nevertheless produce data which does fall into one of the sensitive categories.[25]

## Publicly Available Data

Other data available to institutions about their students is often already in the public domain and has been harvested by some researchers for the purposes of learning analytics. Examples include Twitter and open Facebook profiles, which can be mined for sentiment analysis or comments on the courses being studied.

It can be argued that as students are posting this information in the knowledge that anyone can view it, there is no requirement on institutions to request their consent to use it. However, this new purpose for the data may not be within the reasonable expectations of its creators: students posting information about themselves socially would be unlikely to consider that it would be used by their institution for the purpose of predicting their academic success and could validly object to their data being exploited in this way without their knowledge or agreement. The logistical problems of integrating data from social networking tools outside the institutional walled garden, such as knowing their usernames on other systems, make use of this data difficult anyway. However, much learning activity takes place in these systems and researchers continue to try to find ways to integrate it into their algorithms.

It may be appropriate to collect data without consent from physical public spaces where there is a reasonable expectation of observation by strangers. However, tweets, while readable by anyone with internet access, are individually attributable, which makes them fundamentally different from observations on aggregated populations in a physical space. Twitter users can expect a level of 'anonymity of the crowd' to help manage their privacy.[26] Meanwhile, the institution has no control over the multiple and varied data protection policies of external social networking sites and it may be impossible to authenticate the student properly.[27]

## MOOC Data

Massive open online courses (MOOCs) provide considerable opportunities for learning analytics. Some institutions claim that the ability to monitor participants' learning through MOOCs and thus to be able to refine their understanding of online learning, is their primary reason for providing them. Agencies such as Coursera or Udacity, which host MOOCs for universities, also have a strong interest in collecting data on MOOC users for a range of learning analytics purposes, including monitoring the effectiveness of particular teaching methods.

By definition, MOOCs generally have large cohorts of students, carrying out multiple learning activities online, with the consequent accumulation of potentially useful big data. Some early MOOCs were carried out in the public domain and learners were made fully aware of the fact that their forum postings would be both publicly visible and subject to analysis. Many participants are themselves educationalists and happy for their data to be used in this way for the furthering of understanding about online learning. However, the current prevailing model is more akin to traditional courses with defined (if very large) cohorts of students and discussion forums and content available only to subscribed users in closed online environments. In many ways these learners can be regarded as equivalent to paying, registered students. It is hard to argue that they should be treated in any way differently regarding consent to the use of their data. Providers of MOOCs often fail, though, to make it explicit to participants what data is being collected and how it is being used.

If the forums of a MOOC are visible to the public, as well as to enrolled participants, there may be a greater acceptance that user activity and comments are subject to scrutiny and analysis.[28] However there is a registration process in most MOOC platforms, for example, and non-participants cannot view forum postings and other data on learners, so there would appear to be a greater responsibility on those MOOC providers to steward the data appropriately.

## Anonymisation

The ethics and the legal situation alter considerably when student data is anonymised, removing any personally identifiable information from the dataset. The possibilities for misuse of the data and invasions of privacy are dramatically reduced, particularly when data is presented in aggregated formats. As more data subjects are included, the safety of the anonymisation process improves. Thus stating that 20% of students at a university are from a particular racial group and 62% of those have a low income, is highly unlikely to lead to the identification of an individual. However, publishing the information that visually impaired students on a low-population course obtained higher grades than the average might inadvertently allow the identification of a single student.

Anonymisation can be achieved through various techniques. However none of these is foolproof. The effectiveness of a technique can be assessed on the basis of whether:

- an individual can still be identified somehow;
- records relating to an individual can still be linked; or
- information relating to an individual can be inferred.[29]

However, the size of the datasets and the number of different sources drawn on, can make 're-identification' of individuals easier[30, 31] and there is growing scepticism that personal data can ever be properly anonymised. Pseudonymised data, where the student's name or identifier is altered consistently across their records, is not equivalent to anonymised data and is subject to the same protections as personal data in European law.[32]

The UK's Information Commissioner pragmatically suggests that

> the issue is not about eliminating the risk of re-identification altogether, but whether it can be mitigated so it is no longer significant. Organisations should focus on mitigating the risks to the point where the chance of re-identification is extremely remote. Organisations using anonymised data need to be able to demonstrate that they have carried out [a] robust assessment of the risk of re-identification, and have adopted solutions proportionate to the risk. This may involve a range and combination of technical measures, such as data masking, pseudonymisation, aggregation and banding, as well as legal and organisational safeguards.[33]

## Restricting Access to Student Data

In a survey conducted by Draschler & Greller, the majority of respondents thought that only appropriate staff members should be allowed to view student data on a 'need-to-know' basis.[34] Decisions need to be made on who can access the data.[35] Should teaching staff be given access to data collected on other courses for which they are not responsible, for example?[36] If so, should the identity of students for whom they are not responsible be masked?

Each institution will have to decide its own policies in these areas. At Oxford Brookes University there is a hierarchy of permissions for analytics data, which is passed up through various levels of the administration with individuals unable to be identified except by those directly responsible for teaching or supporting them.[37] At Charles Sturt University the policy is to control access by roles and to set privileges based on the individual's position and how sensitive the data is. Audit trails are expected to be kept on who has accessed what data.[38]

Despite the restrictions on access, how learning analytics systems are used in practice can potentially infringe students' privacy. At the University of Michigan, academic advisors were regularly sharing dashboards designed for their own use with individual students. However, the screens showed data about other learners, which could potentially be viewed by the student. A button was hastily added by developers so that advisors could hide the data about other students when required.[39]

## External Access

Another issue that has both a legal and ethical dimension is whether outside parties should be given access to personal student data and analytics. Students who are assured that their data will be held within the confines of their institution may develop greater trust in and acceptance of learning analytics. However, this may not always be feasible. Circumstances where analytics might need to be transferred externally include:

- cloud-hosted systems where data is nevertheless under the control of institutions;
- requests from external organisations such as educational authorities and security agencies;
- students taking their analytics with them when they transfer to other institutions;
- giving employers access to student learning data and analytics;
- sharing anonymised student data and analytics with other institutions in order to help with benchmarking and educational research;
- commercial exploitation of the data.

Some of these practices may be morally questionable and illegal and could require the consent of the student.

Institutions need to be careful that the data protection procedures they put in place internally are understood and followed by any external partners to which they subcontract data hosting or processing services. These organisations may be driven primarily by commercial motives, implying a greater incentive to use the data to target individuals for marketing their products and services. In the US the use of student information by third-party vendors is permitted without the express consent of the student when an institution uses educational records for predictive tests or enhancing learning. However, the data must not be released to outsiders and should be destroyed afterwards. The arrangement must be subject to a written agreement between the institution and the vendor.[40]

Meanwhile some institutions are wary about requests from government agencies about their students (perhaps those being monitored as potential security risks) and have put in place procedures to assess whether to comply with the requests. Employers, too, may increasingly request that they can track the progress of students while they are studying. Perhaps they will find that a student's engagement in their studies may be an indicator of how engaged they are likely to be in the workplace. This information could become part of job applications, allowing employers to compare applicants with each other.[41] Already Statewide Longitudinal Data Systems in the US store data about individuals' education from early childhood until they join the workforce; these are of increasing concern to privacy activists[42] and could be more intrusive if learning analytics data is included in the future.

## Data Ownership

Pardo & Siemens have asked who owns the data for learning analytics: institutions, students or the companies that might use them to enhance their products?[43] Ownership is linked to issues of control and responsibility. As the intellectual property rights (IPR) in the data relating to a student have been collected and possibly enhanced by the institution, it can claim to own these rights. However, in Europe at least, it must ensure that the data is accurate or that it can be deleted by request of the student. At any time the individual can ask for a copy of their personal data, though the IPR remains with the institution, which may prevent the student further transferring it. This has implications for the portability of learning analytics as students move from one institution to the next, taking their own data with them.[44]

## Student Access to their Analytics

Giving students access to the data collected about them and the analytics performed on it, is another area that needs to be considered from a legal and ethical perspective. There is likely to be little or no moral justification for withholding data or analytics about students from them, particularly if they are adults. Susan Graham, Records Manager at the University of Edinburgh, argues that, as well as being essential in complying with UK data protection legislation:

> we should be empowering [students] as independent learners and making the data we hold about them transparent ... an effective way of supporting the student and enabling them to work independently.[45]

One issue which might arise is that the analytics present a serious danger to the student. However, as Dragan Gašević points out:

> we are still to discover any serious incident that has happened with learning analytics due to privacy violation or anything with students. So we don't really detect whether students are pregnant or not and then accidentally feed that information back to their parents.[46]

The logistics of giving access to individuals about the data held about them can be complex, given the number of systems in use by universities and colleges. The Open University aims 'in the near future ... to provide basic aggregated results to students who request this information'. However, the institution states that there are still technical and organisational impediments to giving the students access to their data securely and transparently.[47]

One issue here for institutions is that the vast amount of data assembled on every electronically captured interaction the institution has about an individual would be overwhelming and meaningless. Do we, therefore, ensure that we give students copies of the summarised data with our interpretations and visualisations instead of or as well as the raw data? I asked Susan Graham if UK legislation required that universities need to make the data comprehensible to students or if a dump of everything we know about them would suffice. She responded:

> It is a requirement that it be ... comprehensible to the student. This includes things like ... if there's some form of coding in the data ... you need to provide the student with a key so that they can understand what the code is. A dump that's utterly incomprehensible would not be acceptable.[48]

## Data Stewardship

Some data, such as names, courses studied and grades obtained, may need to be retained by the institution permanently, both for logistical purposes and to meet the expectations of government agencies.[49] However, learners should be able to progress without records of past experiences 'becoming permanent blemishes on their development history'. Such data should have an agreed lifespan and expiry date and students should be able to request the deletion of data relating to them according to agreed criteria.[50] It would seem that most learning analytics data is unlikely to be regarded as appropriate for permanent retention.

The key dilemma for institutions in this area is that ensuring that personal data is deleted will build trust among students, however keeping that data allows institutions to refine their models, track performance over multiple years and cohorts and assist with quality assurance processes.[51] Applying big data techniques to large datasets regarded as worthless could result in valuable insight to the institution.[52] Arguably, though, many of these functions could still be carried out using anonymised data, minimising risks to privacy.

It may not in fact be possible for institutions to discover all the information they hold about a student, or to be absolutely sure that they have deleted all data relating to that person. As data is increasingly distributed it is difficult too to prove that it has been completely erased. Other issues include:

- as soon as data has been presented to an individual's eyes or ears in an analogue way, it can be 're-digitised';
- rogue computer programs may also obtain data and copy it illegally elsewhere;
- metadata may be stored separately and thought of as fundamentally different but could also be used to identify individuals.[53]

Perhaps we should stop trying to ensure that data can actually be deleted completely and assume that as soon as data is created it is permanent. One US agency argues that policy should concentrate on controlling the use of data rather than its collection. The emphasis, it argues, should be on preventing inappropriate use of the data rather than resorting to anonymisation.[54]

## References

1 Johnson, B., 2010, Privacy No Longer a Social Norm, says Facebook Founder, *Guardian*, 11 January.
2 Greenwald, G., 2013, Revealed: How US and UK Spy Agencies Defeat Internet Privacy and Security, *Guardian*, 6 September.
3 Richards, N. M. & King, J. H., 2014, Big Data Ethics, *Wake Forest Law Review*, 19 May.
4 Zetter, K. & Barrett, B., 2016, Apple to FBI: You Can't Force Us to Hack the San Bernardino iPhone, *Wired*, 25 February, https://www.wired.com/2016/02/apple-b rief-fbi-response-iphone/ (accessed 9 October 2016).
5 Kelion, L., 2016, Students Hit by University of Greenwich Data Breach, *BBC News*, 17 February, www.bbc.com/news/technology-35587529 (accessed 9 October 2016).
6 President's Council of Advisors on Science and Technology, 2014, *Big Data and Privacy: A Technological Perspective*, https://www.whitehouse.gov/sites/default/files/microsites/ostp/PCAST/pcast_big_data_and_privacy_-_may_2014.pdf (accessed 9 October 2016).
7 Information Commissioner's Office, 2014, *Big Data and Data Protection*, https://ico.org.uk/media/1541/big-data-and-data-protection.pdf (accessed 9 October 2016).
8 King, J. H. & Richards, N. M., 2014, What's Up With Big Data Ethics? *Forbes*, 28 March, http://www.forbes.com/sites/oreillymedia/2014/03/28/whats-up-with-big-da ta-ethics/ (accessed 9 October 2016).
9 Richards & King, 2014, Big Data Ethics.
10 Ibid.
11 Schwartz, P. M., 2010, *Data Protection Law and the Ethical Use of Analytics*, The Center for Information Policy Leadership.
12 Kay, D. *et al.*, 2012, *Legal, Risk and Ethical Aspects of Analytics in Higher Education*, Jisc Cetis.
13 Information Commissioner's Office, 2014, *Big Data and Data Protection*.

14 'K.N.C.', 2014, Withered inBloom, *The Economist*, 30 April, www.economist.com/blogs/schumpeter/2014/04/big-data-and-education (accessed 9 October 2016).

15 Balkam, S., 2014, Learning the Lessons of the InBloom Failure, *The Huffington Post*, 24 June, www.huffingtonpost.com/stephen-balkam/learning-the-lessons-of-t_b_5208724.html (accessed 9 October 2016).

16 Bogle, A., 2014, What the Failure of inBloom Means for the Student-Data Industry, *Slate*, 24 April, www.slate.com/blogs/future_tense/2014/04/24/what_the_failure_of_inbloom_means_for_the_student_data_industry.html (accessed 9 October 2016).

17 K.N.C., Withered inBloom.

18 Gross, A., 2014, A Brief History of Education's Big Data Debate, *Education Dive*, 7 May, www.educationdive.com/news/a-brief-history-of-educations-big-data-debate/258602/ (accessed 9 October 2016).

19 Podesta, J., 2014, Findings of the Big Data and Privacy Working Group Review, *The White House*, 1 May, https://www.whitehouse.gov/blog/2014/05/01/findings-big-data-and-privacy-working-group-review (accessed 9 October 2016).

20 Singer, N., 2014, Microsoft and Other Firms Pledge to Protect Student Data, *The New York Times*, 7 October.

21 European Commission, 1995, Directive 95/46/EC of the European Parliament and of the Council of 24 October 1995 on the protection of individuals with regard to the processing of personal data and on the free movement of such data, *Official Journal of the EC*, 23(6), pp. 31–50.

22 International Working Group on Data Protection in Telecommunications, 2014, *Working Paper on Big Data and Privacy: Privacy Principles under Pressure in the Age of Big Data Analytics*, http://dzlp.mk/sites/default/files/u972/WP_Big_Data_final_clean_675.48.12%20%281%29.pdf (9 October 2016).

23 European Commission, 2014, Progress on EU Data Protection Reform now Irreversible Following European Parliament Vote, *Press Release Database*, 12 March.

24 Gibbs, S., 2016, Google to Extend 'Right to be Forgotten' to All its Domains Accessed in EU, *Guardian*, 11 February.

25 International Working Group on Data Protection in Telecommunications, *Working Paper on Big Data and Privacy*.

26 Rivers, C. M. & Lewis, B. L., 2014, Ethical Research Standards in a World of Big Data, *F1000Research*, https://f1000research.com/articles/3-38/v1 (accessed 9 October 2016).

27 Slade, S. & Prinsloo, P., 2013, Learning Analytics: Ethical Issues and Dilemmas, *American Behavioral Scientist*, 57(10), pp. 1509–1528.

28 Esposito, A., 2012, Research Ethics in Emerging Forms of Online Learning: Issues Arising from a Hypothetical Study on a MOOC, *The Electronic Journal of E-Learning*, 10(3), pp. 315–325.

29 International Working Group on Data Protection in Telecommunications, *Working Paper on Big Data and Privacy*.

30 Bolllier, D., 2010, *The Promise and Peril of Big Data*, https://www.emc.com/collateral/analyst-reports/10334-ar-promise-peril-of-big-data.pdf (accessed 9 October 2016).

31 President's Council of Advisors on Science and Technology, *Big Data and Privacy: A Technological Perspective*.

32 International Working Group on Data Protection in Telecommunications, *Working Paper on Big Data and Privacy*.

33 Information Commissioner's Office, *Big Data and Data Protection*.

34 Draschler, H. & Greller, W., 2012, The Pulse of Learning Analytics: Under-standings and Expectations from the Stakeholders, *LAK12: Proceedings of the Second International Conference on Learning Analytics and Knowledge*, pp. 120–129.

35 Campbell, J. P. *et al.*, 2007, Academic Analytics: A New Tool for a New Era, *EDUCAUSE Review*, 42(4), pp. 40–57.

36 Pardo, A. & Siemens, G., 2014, Ethical and Privacy Principles for Learning Analytics, *British Journal of Educational Technology*, 45, pp. 438–450.

37 Sclater, N., 2014, *Learning Analytics: The Current State of Play in UK Higher and Further Education*, Jisc.

38 Charles Sturt University, 2014, *CSU Learning Analytics Strategy v1*, www.csu.edu.au/__data/assets/word_doc/0006/1350978/2013-05-following-ILSC-CSU-Learning-Analytics-Strategy-v1-3.docx (accessed 9 October 2016).

39 Aguilar, S. *et al.*, 2014, Perceptions and Use of an Early Warning System During a Higher Education Transition Program, *Proceedings of the Fourth International Conference on Learning Analytics and Knowledge*, pp. 113–117.

40 Sun, J. C., 2014, Legal Issues Associated with Big Data in Higher Education: Ethical Considerations and Cautionary Tales. In: *Building a Smarter University: Big Data, Innovation, and Analytics*, SUNY Press.

41 Reilly, M., 2013, *Further Education Learning Technology: A Horizon Scan for the UK Government Foresight Horizon Scanning Centre*, Ariel Research Services.

42 Sun, Legal Issues Associated with Big Data in Higher Education.

43 Pardo & Siemens, Ethical and Privacy Principles for Learning Analytics.

44 Kay *et al.*, *Legal, Risk and Ethical Aspects of Analytics in Higher Education*.

45 Sclater, N. 2016, *Learning Analytics and Giving Students Access to their Data*, Jisc [Podcast].

46 Gašević, D., 2016, *The Future of Learning Analytics* [interview by author], 9 February.

47 Open University, 2014, *Ethical Use of Student Data for Learning Analytics Policy FAQs*.

48 Sclater, *Learning Analytics and Giving Students Access to their Data* (transcript of podcast), https://www.jisc.ac.uk/sites/default/files/learning_analytics_and_giving_students_access_to_their_data_v2-transcript.pdf (accessed 9 October 2016).

49 Prinsloo, P. & Slade, S., 2014, Educational Triage in Open Distance Learning: Walking a Moral Tightrope, *International Review of Open and Distance Learning*, 15(4).

50 Slade & Prinsloo, Learning Analytics: Ethical Issues and Dilemmas.

51 Pardo & Siemens, Ethical and Privacy Principles for Learning Analytics.

52 President's Council of Advisors on Science and Technology, *Big Data and Privacy: A Technological Perspective*.

53 Ibid.

54 Ibid.

# 23  Expert Thoughts on Deployment

## Organisational Culture

Shane Dawson mentions a significant barrier to the adoption of learning analytics: lack of understanding about what learning analytics is:

> the speed at which the research is being performed ... and some fantastic journal articles [are] coming out now in the learning sciences ... it's out-stripping the reality of where organisations can go in the short term ... We're really going to have to work hard to keep senior managers – the leaders who are making decisions around policy around learning analytics for an institution – informed and integrated with this community. Otherwise we'll ostracise ourselves.

There has been somewhat of a 'revolt against the quantification of education' at Stefan Mol's institution, the University of Amsterdam, which is struggling to define learning analytics:

> One of the more senior people said 'we can spend 100,000 Euros on this or we can spend 40 million Euros on this'. Within the university it's not yet fully understood what LA can contribute or how to calculate a return on investment.

Institutional culture is mentioned by a number of the interviewees as being a serious barrier to the development of learning analytics. Bart Rienties sums up the primary challenge:

> If I'm really honest it's not data or technologies, it's people.

Even if you can identify where learners are getting stuck, he says:

> how can you then convince students and teachers to change whatever they're doing, either starting later or taking a different route ... Even if you provide hard evidence to the teachers there's a problem of how can you convince them to change.

Bart notes that there is a fundamental challenge in that there are big financial benefits for institutions in retaining students who are at risk of attrition, yet there is no system of incentives in place for individual instructors to use the analytics to keep those students in the system.

Josh Baron has also experienced difficulties in getting faculty to do things differently. He reports working with some faculty members to roll out early adaptive learning software in mathematics, reducing the number of lectures:

> I think instructors like the idea but when it comes to 'OK, now my whole role is going to shift and everything I'm used to is going to change' there is resistance to that.

According to Alan Berg, the problem of adoption of the new tools is exacerbated in some institutions by the Not Invented Here Syndrome – unless the technologies are developed within the institution itself, people are unwilling to adopt them. The broad scale adoption of learning analytics can only be achieved, suggests Shane Dawson, by it being built into all aspects of an organisation's operation:

> its incentives, its promotions, its probation, its work performance. I've not actually seen any organisation that has that in place yet. But it'll come.

The situation is often not helped by data ownership issues, as Cathy Gunn notes:

> Like any form of organisational change, the guardians of data will resist because they are risk averse ... The commercial world is moving fast while education finds obstacles at the starting line ... Part of the problem is a lack of mutual understanding among the key stakeholders. Institutional managers, data and IT specialists, learning designers and teachers are not used to collaborating in the way this requires.

Mark Milliron thinks change will be facilitated by moving from a 'culture of blame to a culture of wonder' in the use of data to optimise the student experience. Doug Clow, too, suggests that learning analytics requires a complete change in institutional thinking about running experiments on students and he draws parallels with the realisation in late twentieth-century medicine that rigorous trials needed to take place with patients to see if treatments actually worked:

> Experts with sincere, deeply-held and well-articulated beliefs are usually right but not always.

Before we get to that point, though, he says, institutions need a shift in thinking about data and to be able to work with it, enabling the earlier identification of problems with students and more rapid interventions.

Attitudes towards openness in the teaching process are another aspect of institutional culture that may need to be overcome. Timothy McKay points out that faculty are not used to having data about their teaching exposed – or about what is happening with their learners – and it opens them up to examination in a way that has not been possible before:

> I think for a long time a lot of higher education has had a sense that what happens in the classroom is the business only of the faculty member and the students who are in the classroom – and there's a point to that, there are certainly places where that might be quite true – but there are other places where it really shouldn't be.

## Data Literacy

Understanding the data is also a huge concern, particularly, as Alyssa Wise says, if learning analytics will be used across the institution to make informed decisions. Doug Clow notes that data literacy varies dramatically depending on the subject background of the individual:

> Show a huge number of graphs to the Science Faculty and they'll go 'oh that's interesting', whereas, the people who don't come from those sort of backgrounds, you just show them a whole lot of completely incomprehensible pictures which mean nothing to them, and you have to tell them a story about that. I think the number of fields in which it's possible to be a successful academic with zero data literacy is going to get less and less.

Leah Macfadyen, responsible for deploying learning analytics in a large faculty of arts with 26 different programmes and departments, is used to dealing with a huge span of different skillsets among her colleagues:

> There's a very large proportion of my audience who either have very poor data skills or who fundamentally reject the idea that data can tell you about human behaviour. I think I've done a pretty good job of generating mostly visual reports on things like course evaluation scores … but I have faculty members phone me up regularly to say 'What is this graph with dots on it? What is standard deviation?'

The challenge at all levels of the institution, suggests Mark Glynn,

> whether you are the CEO of a college or whether you are a lecturer [is] how to filter out what's good data and what's bad data, how to understand and not make the wrong assumptions on the basis of the data.

Simon Buckingham Shum notes that data literacy is not required simply for staff and faculty but for students too. His institution, the University of Technology Sydney, is attempting to make data literacy and numeracy a core competency in every course but, beyond that, to make learning dispositions an explicit topic of learning conversations. Even if you're data literate, he says, you also need the mindset to engage with it:

> We want the students to become a. data literate and b. able to take increasing responsibility for their learning, otherwise they will stay passive responders who submit the assignment because it's been given to them, but aren't developing the sort of lifelong learning curiosity, agency, sense of finding an interest in being able to chase it down etc. That's what's going to get them their jobs in the future, because they're actually passionate about something. So if those are the qualities we're trying to develop then we are very much talking about feeding back data to the learner as well as to the educators, and having the learners try and make sense of it.

Before the analytics even hit end users however, there may be a lack of skills in the institution available to *prepare* the data. Josh Baron reports that:

> A lot of institutions we work with kind of assume that someone with an advanced software engineering background can very easily do the data scientist stuff because when you look at it from a distance it's very technical work – it's using business intelligence tools, it's using the software – but they don't yet realise that there is a science behind this. If you don't have that data science skillset at your institution, I think that's going to be a big barrier.

While understanding of data science is clearly essential, Stefan Mol points out that it is not the only requirement for involvement in learning analytics:

> Learning analytics is currently inhabited by data scientists or people with a data science background, and there's at least a hundred years of research in pedagogy and educational psychology that has yielded pretty strong theory with regard to the learning process. I think just looking at data and identifying trends therein is very dangerous and, in order to fully understand what is going on, we need to test theories. One way of gauging the validity of our research is to evaluate the extent to which the empirical realm is in accordance with the theoretical realm.

## Leadership

Commitment is particularly important, Dragan Gašević suggests, at senior management level, as senior managers are the major sponsors:

> You may have many champions inside institutions that are at the level of faculty members or IT support but if there is no clear vision from the senior management then nothing much will happen.

John Whitmer reports never seeing a learning analytics initiative succeed without substantial support, if not requirements, from the top. He recounts a story of working with three similar institutions that were piloting *Blackboard Analytics* and *Analytics for Learn*. One of the institutions had strong support from senior management and a high level of trust with their faculty, who believed that the administration was 'not out to get them'. The different culture at another institution meant that there was significant suspicion and resistance.

Kirsty Kitto notes that those making decisions in institutions often do not understand data or technology in enough detail and is concerned that this could have adverse consequences:

> so you'll have a particular set of people who want sophisticated measures and metrics and then other people who just want to save time, and to know how many students are passing or what was the satisfaction score, and everything will just collapse down to some boring measure that will actually have really perverse effects on the institution.

Mark Milliron believes a fundamental change is required in leadership now that the age of analytics has arrived:

> Twenty years ago when advertisements for new presidents or principals went out, at the very bottom would be something that said 'understands uses of technology in education'. Now we're starting to see 'understands the uses of analytics in education'. It will rise up and up and up in terms of the requirements. I think we're probably one of the last sectors to be hit by that ... analytics is the new hot thing across business and industry.

He also suggests that most use of analytics to date has been of 'accountability analytics', getting data to boards or administrators rather than to faculty and students:

> Accountability analytics often cause the immune system of higher education to react and shut it down, as opposed to action analytics which helps faculty and students do their everyday job, and treats them like professionals by actually giving them the data.

### Funding

Moral support and leadership from the top is clearly important. However, adequate allocation of funding is also considered to be essential. Mark Glynn notes the opportunity cost of involvement in learning analytics:

> If I'm working on this, what am I not working on ... A lot of institutions [are] under-resourced, and they're being reactive rather than proactive ... people are just treading water, trying to keep on top of their day job at the moment, where if they had the time and effort to research into

learning analytics … So it needs somebody in an institution, somebody high up, to say 'this is a priority, this is what we're doing, this is the amount of staff we need'.

He says that the money saved by reducing dropout rates can easily cover the costs of a learning analytics initiative. Josh Baron reports that community colleges in the US could potentially benefit the most from early alert systems but have serious budget problems and are struggling to work out how they can finance them.

Financial restrictions are not, of course, unique to poorly funded institutions. As the person responsible for driving forward the use of learning analytics in her faculty at the University of British Columbia, Leah Macfadyen would like to see integrated data, better access policies and better resourcing:

> I'm very in demand all day every day but I haven't got enough money to really move ahead so I'm just stuck turning out stuff on demand. If I had a team … I need someone who can write me scripts and I need my database guy and I need a statistician and I need a couple of people who can help me with these projects – to pursue looking at network analysis of our MOOCs and I just don't have the resources and capacity to cover it all.

Leah is unsure what it will take to convince the senior management to put more money into analytics, but argues that if there was a retention problem at her institution it might be easier:

> It's not that there aren't challenges here, it's just that they tend to be more localised and they're not system-wide.

Mark Milliron makes the point that an educator's purpose is to help students learn and to complete their studies:

> If we can keep on purpose and focus analytics on those things I think we have huge potential. Which is why I get so frustrated with the mechanistic and money metaphors where it's like we're mining for this and there's tons of ROI in that. We have a lot of ridiculously talented students for whom education is a ceiling effect. It's just they're not being pushed. If we can identify that, push them up to the next level, some really exciting things could happen. I think if we do this right we could end up with incredibly expansive learning opportunities for a wide variety of students from the top of the top to the students who are really struggling.

## Ethics and Legal Issues

Ethics, data rights and privacy are mentioned frequently by the experts as presenting challenges to implementation. Stefan Mol suggests that:

what you are allowed to do under law is not necessarily what you should be doing ... You can under this umbrella term 'learning analytics' go in all sorts of directions, both evil and good. I think as a field we have a responsibility to be clear about the outcomes for all stakeholders.

Alyssa Wise suggests that institutional ethics boards are 'behind the game' when it comes to learning analytics. These were set up to give ethical consideration for research projects and are likely to be less suitable for authorising learning initiatives aimed at changing learning and teaching practice across the institution. Stefan's experiences with asking students for their consent to use their data for learning analytics, for example, are informative:

> We found working with full informed consent and running randomised control trials ... to be rather unfeasible ... When we asked our students for consent that led to a huge decline in participation, and I don't think necessarily because they didn't want to, but because it was something that was being asked of them, that they needed to put effort into. So I think 'selling' LA to key stakeholders will be a key challenge – both institutionally, but also to the students themselves.

## The Need for Systemic Deployment

Kirsty Kitto points out that many current developments are small scale and that this is holding back learning analytics from having the impact it should be having:

> If I talk to decision makers at universities at the moment they are all talking about 'oh well it hasn't really done much yet has it?' Well no it hasn't because we need systemic uptake. You actually need that kind of thing that you guys are providing [Jisc's national learning analytics architecture]. But at the moment it's really piecemeal. There's a whole heap of universities now diving into the field who have no idea about [existing research in learning analytics] so they're all going to repeat all of those early mistakes again.

# Part VI
# Future Directions

# 24  Emerging Techniques

In Chapter 9 I examined some of the methods used to predict student success. Additional techniques are now emerging to analyse various aspects of learning. These are potentially of use in applications such as early alert and student success, course recommendation, adaptive learning and curriculum design. Each of the emerging methods draws from existing disciplines and applies them to learning contexts. Some of these are already longstanding and respected research fields, with existing applications in areas outside education. In this chapter I discuss three of the main techniques that are being applied in educational settings: discourse analytics; social network analysis; and sentiment and emotion analytics.

## Discourse Analytics

Engaging in discourse enables learners to explore ideas together, to develop skills in argumentation, to identify disagreements and to solve them. During discussion, learners can absorb new information and perspectives and receive feedback or reminders. They can check their understanding or identify gaps in their knowledge and give or request information or advice. Contributions can be an indicator of their learning, showing how they engage with others' ideas and how they justify their own points of view. Discourse can take place in forums, blogs, wikis, synchronous chat tools, audio and video conferencing systems and through a variety of social networking sites and apps. The affordances of these tools shape the way that learners can communicate and learn collaboratively.[1, 2, 3]

Participation in discourse can be measured by counting the number of posts to discussion forums, the number of responses made or even the number of posts viewed by lurkers. Metrics such as 'posted at least once', 'contributed multiple posts in two or more weeks' and 'created a thread' have been devised to provide crude measures of engagement.[4] There is a growing interest, though, in attempting to evaluate the *quality* of learners' engagement, rather than using simple quantitative metrics of how active they are. Techniques for the automated analysis of writing, such as latent semantic analysis, have been used for many years, examining, for example, the sophistication of the vocabulary used and the sentence structure.[5] Such methods can produce reasonable predictions of students' final grades, with greater accuracy than the number of contributions or the word count of their posts.

---

### Assessing the Quality of the Language Used by Students in Forums at a Large For-Profit University

Ming & Ming used probabilistic latent semantic analysis to assess the quality of student contributions to forums. The less successful students tended to use more general language, addressing concepts superficially, for example:

> That's a good thought about the zebras and horses. Well, if you think about it, it makes sense why there are the different types of horses too. There's small, stocky horses and then there are the ponies and then the big, gigantic horses. So, I'm sure their surroundings probably played a role in their physical appearance over many hundreds of years.

Meanwhile, posts with more technical wording tend to address course concepts at a deeper level, for example:

> We know that an example of a r selected species in plants is the dandelion, how does the strawberry plant compare to the dandelion. Does the strawberry plant have numerous offspring? Does its traits contribute to high population growth? Is the strawberry found in variable, temporary or unpredictable environments, where the probability of long-term survival is low? Is it non-competitive?

Overall the researchers found that technically proficient use of language was correlated with higher grades. They suggest that such techniques can enable the flagging of students who are likely to perform poorly at the end of the course and to suggest actions that could help them. As well as being able to intervene with specific students, instructors could be made aware of the depth of the concepts being discussed and whether the learning was taking place as expected.[6, 7]

---

Researchers are now attempting to delve deeper than measuring the sophistication of the language used and to develop systems to assess the quality of the ideas that learners are presenting.[8] Measuring the depth of students' thinking is not trivial, though. Messages in forums can be threaded by subject, comments can be anchored to a particular part of a document, and postings can be tagged. These tend to be descriptive rather than analytical: there is no indication of what the key issues are and whether they are supported or not. To ascertain these, it is generally necessary to read all of the dialogue, including any accompanying 'noise'.[9] One method deployed manually by some researchers is to classify each 'dialogue act', such as asking a question, agreeing, disagreeing or giving feedback. They might also be examining whether the post displays phenomena such as critical thinking or the negotiation of ideas.[10] Such non-automated approaches are, however, expensive and not scalable beyond small research projects and are not therefore suitable for learning analytics.

## Cohere: Having Learners Make Sense of Their Own Posts

An innovative approach is attempted in the Cohere system, which encourages learners to tag their own posts with icons describing the type of contribution, for example providing an idea, opinion or theory and presenting a point against, or a point in favour, of the idea. The icon is shown in a visual representation of the interactions between the different users.

The system also enables students to draw semantic connections between their posts and those of others – for example 'is an example of', 'is inconsistent with', or 'improves on'. This provides a new way to browse and to make sense of the discussion. Additionally, automated analytics built into the system can facilitate the identification of aspects such as:

- what learners focus on;
- the problems and questions they raise;
- who they agree or disagree with;
- the ideas they support;
- their interactions with others;
- the most discussed topics.

Cohere classifies semantic link types as 'positive' – for example 'supports', 'agrees with' and 'improves on'; negative; and neutral. This can provide an indication of the learner's attitude towards the task. It may then be possible to correlate particular stances with grades. For example, maintaining a positive stance during a dialogue may indicate higher levels of engagement. On the other hand it may demonstrate a lack of independent thought.

The system could also potentially be used for assessment. Thus if a learning goal is to share online resources, the users' tagging of their posts as 'data' or 'illustration' may help to assess their performance in this task. Meanwhile, if a learner connects an idea to that of another student, this could indicate reflective thinking, which may be an assessment objective. The researchers suggest, too, that different post types have different impacts on others. Questions, in particular, appear to have a greater 'discourse power', by triggering responses.[11]

There are skills involved in using a forum to learn and further skills are required to use tools such as Cohere, which may mean that achieving wide-scale adoption among students and faculty will prove difficult. Another issue is that students may use forums differently as they develop understanding of their subject area and their learning skills and familiarity with the tools improve. The progression of their skills can potentially be validated through analytics on the forums.[12]

While the above example shows a way of understanding contributions to asynchronous forums, the analysis of synchronous chat sessions is more difficult. The identification of threads is complex, with multiple interwoven conversations taking place, single contributions often remaining isolated in the broader dialogue and wide gaps sometimes between utterances that connect to each other. Developing ways of classifying these is likely to remain a challenge for some time.[13] Learning is, however, complex, unpredictable, non-linear and inherently difficult for an outside observer or system to understand fully.[14] The measurements deployed in discourse analytics, as with other metrics in learning analytics, are proxies for learning and will never represent the entire picture; however, we can expect that technological advances in this area will enable us to achieve ever greater insight into many aspects of the learning process.

## Social Network Analysis

Social network analysis is a technique used in a wide variety of fields, including sociology, anthropology, biology, economics and geography, to evaluate the properties of a network. It draws on fields such as network theory and graph theory and is increasingly being applied to learning contexts.[15, 16] Being part of a network of contacts is vital for personal development, sense of identity and providing professional opportunities. *Weak ties* are held with acquaintances whereas *strong ties* exist in long-term friendships and memberships of communities. Both of these can be important for learning; however, weak ties with competent people can be more effective than strong ties in inward-looking communities that fail to absorb new information. Strong inner cores in networks, or *cliques,* can also prevent those on the fringes from full participation.[17]

Information overload requires learners to develop competences in filtering and navigation: social networks can help individuals to reduce the time for this and to focus their attention. New visualisations can assist them in building a network and maximising the usefulness of their contacts. Developing these skills will be increasingly important as education transitions from a curriculum based on absorbing and regurgitating a central corpus of knowledge, towards a greater emphasis on the development of skills to deal with complex, distributed information sources. Meanwhile, timely knowledge transmitted through contacts is becoming increasingly trusted, building learners' awareness of the importance of relationships and discourse.[18]

Given this context, Ferguson & Buckingham Shum propose that the analysis of social interaction and the co-construction of knowledge should feature highly within learning analytics.[19] However, until recently there has been little attention given to the ways in which academic success is influenced by different patterns of engagement in social networks.[20] Better understanding of the ways students are interacting with each other and how the community is evolving should help educators to monitor the effectiveness of their learning design, to facilitate more democratic and structured discussions[21] and to intervene with socially isolated or disengaged students who may be at risk.[22]

Social network analysis provides a range of metrics to measure aspects of the network. Many of these are potentially useful in networked learning contexts. Some refer to the group as a whole, for example:

- *centralisation* is the degree to which the network centres around a few individuals; in a decentralised network most individuals have a similar number of links;
- *clustering coefficient* measures how likely it is that two people connected to each other through someone else are also connected directly to each other; networks with high clustering tend to be cliquish and are known as cliques if everyone is connected directly to everyone else;
- *structural cohesion* is the minimum number of members who would disconnect the group were they to be removed from it.

Other metrics are used to analyse the connectedness of individuals, such as:

- *centrality* indicates an individual's 'social power', based on how well connected they are;
- *closeness* shows how close a person is to others in the network and reflects the ability to access information through them;
- *degree* is how many ties an individual has to others in the network.[23]

The network viewed from the perspective of an individual is known as an *ego network*.

## Analysing Aspects of Network Activity and Their Relation to Academic Performance at a Large Canadian University

Dawson wished to analyse network behaviour in order to guide educators in how to facilitate online networked activities. His assumption was that a student connected to others in a network of experienced, knowledgeable individuals should be able to use these connections to enhance their academic success. Instructors who could identify less well-connected students might then be able to take appropriate interventions. Specifically he wanted to know:

- if there are significant differences in network composition between high- and low-performing students;
- whether the size of students' networks is related to their academic performance;
- to what extent the presence of an instructor in the network affects the group;
- whether appropriate visualisations can assist pedagogical practice.

He applied social network analysis to logs of the discussion forums to ascertain aspects of the network complexity, who the main actors were and what relationships emerged. The top 10% and bottom 10% of students, based on academic performance, (n = 207) were analysed. High performers developed larger social networks and were inclined to connect to peers of a similar academic capacity. Low-performing students also tended to form relationships with students performing similarly.

Teaching staff were positioned in 81.7% of the high-performing networks and 34.61% of the low-performing groups. Dawson points out that if attention needed to be focussed on those most at risk then this certainly was not taking place. Visualisations that draw the attention of educators to how much time they are spending with differently performing groups, could help them to refocus on those who need the most assistance, as well as attempting to ensure that their students are connected to each other effectively. What was actually happening was that high-performing students were posting more conceptual questions, which the instructors felt required greater assistance. The high-performers were thus benefitting most from the interventions.

Dawson notes some potential limitations of this approach, in particular that it draws data solely from the forums and therefore misses the many other ways in which individuals are potentially connected and can interact. He also suggests that academic competition may reduce students' inclination to share and collaborate. While some more altruistic, high-performing students may be willing to build ties with less able students, many will focus on their own performance and develop connections that provide them with the maximum personal benefit.[24]

## Extending Social Network Analysis to Multiple Groups at the Open University of Catalonia

Hernández García and her colleagues point out that most applications of social network analysis to learning have focussed on small groups in single courses. To address this they decided to analyse the behaviours of students and teachers in ten concurrent instances of an online course in finance. Each instance had more than 60 students and several instructors.

Two different networks were created from the data: one containing only post-reading activity, the other containing only those students who had posted replies. They then examined two scenarios: one that included all interactions, the other removing teacher-related interactions.

A moderate relation was found between *centrality* and academic performance, when measured across the whole population. However, there were mixed results when the data was analysed for individual classrooms. Because of this, they express reservations about social network analysis being used as the sole predictor of academic success but believe it is relevant in certain circumstances. They also consider the visualisations to be powerful aids to teachers in identifying disconnected students or experts, for example.

Meanwhile, at a higher level, it is possible to draw conclusions about the impact of different teacher behaviours on group performance. Inactive teachers appear to increase withdrawal rates, while 'hyper-active' teachers may inhibit learning by posting too frequently.[25]

The use of social network analysis in learning contexts can still be regarded as in its infancy and is mostly taking place on a small scale, often within research projects. It remains to be seen to what extent it can be rolled out effectively across an institution. For this to take place, the data and visualisations will need to be in easily understandable formats and encourage reflection among practitioners.[26] They may also have to be trained in how to interpret and act upon the visualisations.[27]

The composition and interactions among a network are likely to evolve as the course progresses. A sociogram, displaying the connections between participants, may display a facilitator-centric model initially, when a tutor is initiating the discussion. Later their position may change to that of a co-collaborator as students gain more confidence in the learning task. Animated visualisations can show how the network is evolving, across multiple courses as well as within a single cohort. If the intention of a forum is to encourage the co-construction of knowledge among learners, then a facilitator-centric approach throughout is unlikely to be appropriate: the sociogram can highlight if the group's activity is taking place as planned. Meanwhile the development of cliques, which exclude some learners, can also be spotted early and participants assigned to new groups if required, or activities introduced to encourage sharing across cliques.[28]

As well as having useful visualisations of group activity at hand, instructors can undertake analysis of the ego-networks of individuals. Those with strong ties to similar students are likely to be exposed to less diversity than those with weaker ties, who may gain access to increased knowledge and resources. Encouraging the development of weak ties between different types of participants, for example medical and nursing students taking a course in clinical ethics, may be to the benefit of all. Ego-network analysis also enables an evaluation of how instructors are interacting with individual students.[29]

Social network analysis is likely to be of use to students, too. They may benefit from being able to see how their ego networks are evolving over time,[30] how they are learning from others and which patterns of engagement are correlated with greater academic success. However, in many circumstances learning activities using forums and other communication tools have been poorly designed and there is little incentive for students to engage with each other in this way. Given the increasing importance of effective online interaction with others in the workplace and other aspects of society, it may be desirable to build communication into assessed activities.

Dawson & Siemens propose that students could be assessed on the *process* of learning rather than the consequence of it. Skills in building relationships and participating in networks may ultimately be more critical to future success than ability to perform in traditional forms of assessment such as exams. These skills could be readily assessed through social network analysis metrics.[31] For this to work, institutions will need to move from a results-driven culture to one that values engagement in social learning. Student success would thus be reconsidered as being well connected to the learning resources and other actors in a social network.[32]

## Sentiment and Emotion Analytics

The importance of academic achievement for progression in the workplace and society and the personal investment made in it by individuals, mean that undertaking a programme of study at a university or college is likely to be an experience filled with different emotions of varying levels of intensity. Emotions are, in fact, an integral part of the learning process. They can affect students' motivation, their ability to think and concentrate and their learning strategies. The ability to emotionally self-regulate is key to successful academic achievement. Emotions also impact on mental and physical health, in turn affecting learning. They are differentiated from moods, which are regarded as being of longer duration, while emotions tend to be more episodic and intense.[33, 34]

Researchers have found that virtually all human emotions are experienced by learners as they progress through their studies. Rienties and his colleagues identify, in a literature review of more than a hundred studies, approximately one hundred separate emotions, which may affect attitude, behaviour or cognition.[35] Pekrun *et al.* list a number of 'academic emotions', including enjoyment of learning, pride in academic success and test-related anxiety. In their research they find that students experience positive emotions about as frequently as negative ones. Anxiety is reported most often and, not surprisingly, is often related to taking exams. However, anxiety also occurs in classroom situations or while studying at home. The pressure to achieve and the expectation of failure can also have a strong effect on emotions. Other frequently reported emotions are enjoyment of learning, hope, pride, relief, anger, boredom and shame.[36]

Emotions change over time. Alsmeyer *et al.* found that anxiety and relief are the ones that are subject to the largest swings of change during an academic experience. Boredom, hopelessness and anger are less likely to vary. Their research suggests, somewhat depressingly, that a student who starts off being bored is likely to stay that way, whatever is done to change the learning context.[37] However, educators have long been aware of the impact of emotions on students' ability to learn. They may intervene with learners who are frustrated by providing a clearer explanation of the topic they are struggling with, or presenting a more challenging task to an enthusiastic student.[38]

### Analysing Emotions in Student Writing at a Distance Education University

One of the ways in which learners' emotions can be identified is through examining their writing. To give an idea of the kinds of emotions that can be found in student writing, the work of Cleveland-Innes is illuminating. She and her colleagues labelled the emotions apparent in written responses to questions by students and in transcripts of their discussion forums, reaching agreement on the categories after multiple passes through the text. They identified the following emotions: appreciation, delight, desire, disappointment, dislike, emphatics, enjoyment, excitement, fear, frustration, happiness, hope, humour, irony/sarcasm, like, passion, preference, pride, surprise, thankfulness, unhappiness, wonder and yearning. The researchers recognise that this is only a subset of the entire array of human emotions and suggest that it is possible that some emotions are more common during learning than others.[39]

Emotions can be classified as negative (e.g. boredom, jealousy, anxiety, shame) or positive (e.g. excitement, pride, relief, gratitude).[40] A learner's happiness is likely to be founded on positive emotions and this is clearly a factor in increasing the likelihood that they will stay at an institution and complete their studies. Happy students may also be inclined to fill out student satisfaction questionnaires more positively. These are important considerations for institutions, which are increasingly going to great lengths to improve the overall experience for their learners, attempting to provide excellent campus-based or online learning environments. However, negative emotions may actually have positive impacts on learning: a student determined to avoid the shame of failure, for example, may be motivated to study harder. Similarly, some positive emotions, such as pride at earlier success, can engender negative study behaviour, such as laziness and a false sense of security.

The critical importance of emotions in the learning process suggests that understanding academic emotions and being able to help students to affect and control them, will increasingly be of interest to institutions. Analytics that simply examine student attributes and activity, but ignore emotion, are diminished in their diagnostic and predictive power. Identifying and measuring student emotions, however, is not trivial. Researchers have developed a number of techniques for attempting to do this, including self-reporting, multimodal data collection and inferring emotion from learning activities.

With self-reporting, participants are asked to describe how they are feeling using a list of words, or to respond to statements that summarise an emotional state without explicitly mentioning it. One drawback of this approach is that the researcher is restricting the analysis by providing a limited set of emotions for the learner to report on. They may also report experiencing an emotion simply to please the researcher.[41] As emotions can vary so frequently, it may be that the student's current emotional state is different from the one being reported on: while basking in the glory of excellent results, for example, a student asked to state how she felt before an exam might have forgotten just how anxious she was at that time. Frequent sampling of student emotions with the use of emoticons is one way that institutions have attempted to address these issues. They are still dependent on students being honest in their assessment of their own emotions and on their willingness to self-report in this way in the first place.

---

### Use of Emoticons for Assessing Student 'Wellness' at the University of New England, Australia

Every student at the University of New England is provided with a set of emoticons and a text box for more detailed comment on their online student portal page. They can note how they are feeling each day (happy, neutral, unhappy, or very unhappy), based on their current module. Those who record a negative emotion are contacted within 24 hours by a support team.

The University's 'Automated Wellness Engine' takes data from multiple sources, such as assessment scores, engagement data and the emoticons. The various triggers are combined to produce a score indicating whether intervention may be required. The 'unhappy' or 'very unhappy' emoticons are the most heavily weighted indicators in the overall metric.[42]

---

Measuring emotions in isolation from other data is unlikely to be particularly informative. Using social network analytics in addition to emotion analytics, for example, may help to understand which learners are actively engaging and which are relatively isolated and therefore potentially subject to more negative emotions.[43]

---

### Correlating Emotions with Learning Activity Data at Brigham Young University, Utah

Correlating self-reported emotions with learning activity data can bring particular insight. Henrie *et al.* asked students to complete a survey of Likert-scale and open-ended questions a number of times during the semester. They consider that the learning activity data helps to measure students' 'cognitive energy', which includes their attention, effort, cognitive strategy and metacognitive abilities. 'Emotional energy', however, can be measured by analysing the surveys. They suggest that it is the dynamic between cognitive and emotional energy that impacts learning outcomes.

The researchers also asked students to rate their learning experience using emoticons that signified 'awesome', 'good', 'okay' or 'awful'. They were asked to do this, throughout the semester, after face-to-face activities, online activities and a practical session. On visualising the data it was found that students who rated an assignment as good or okay tended to view pages more and for longer than those who considered it awesome. Boredom may have accounted for some of the additional time and page views. Starting and stopping an assignment repeatedly may also be a sign of lack of motivation – or lack of understanding of what they were supposed to do.

Early exploration of different features of the LMS, such as the syllabus, forums and quizzes, not surprisingly, tended to correlate with greater levels of success than concentration solely on the assignment. The more successful students also viewed assignment details earlier and much more frequently, suggesting that they were putting much greater effort into planning how they were going to tackle the assignment and were therefore better prepared – an indication of cognitive energy.[44]

Other methods of ascertaining emotional state include researchers observing and coding students' facial expressions.[45] This is clearly impractical for anything other than small-scale research projects. Different approaches have included using webcams, measuring skin conductivity and monitoring the pressure in objects such as the mouse and the chair.[46] In one study, videos of learners were coded by a researcher according to: changes in facial expression (e.g. frowning, smiling, touching the face etc.), changes in body language or posture (e.g. sitting up, fidgeting) and changes in speech (e.g. intonation, speed, long pauses).[47] Automation of such monitoring may become increasingly feasible as the technologies improve, although there is a strong possibility that learners will consider such monitoring overly intrusive, or that it will subconsciously impede the learning process.

Inferring emotional state from low-level activity data is also possible. At the Universidad Carlos III de Madrid the emotions of 334 learners in a programming course were monitored by Leony *et al.*, with a focus on happiness, frustration, confusion and boredom. A confused learner, the researchers suggest, may attempt to program by trial and error, while bored students' attention may be observed to be wandering as they browse web content unrelated to the task. Automated analysis shows the instructor when a learner is experiencing an unusual emotion and this may consequently enable them to adapt the learning task.

Much of the literature around emotions describes educational research in small-scale studies involving traditional methods such as interviews with learners. The labour-intensive nature of such data collection means it is likely to be unsuitable for learning analytics. A major issue with all assessment of emotions, as was discussed above, is that they may be recorded inaccurately: the window into a learner's head can never be entirely transparent. There can also be, for example, significant discrepancies between observers' perceptions of students' emotions and those of the learners themselves.[48] In addition, learners may wrongly report their emotions, or may be subject to complex emotional states that they find difficult to analyse. Furthermore, the analysis of emotions may not translate simply between languages, with words having subtly different meanings across linguistic and cultural contexts.

An assessment of emotions can enable the learning design to be manipulated in order to attempt to improve engagement[49] with the current or subsequent cohorts. Another benefit in foregrounding emotions in this way may be for the students themselves to develop their own metacognitive strategies or their meta-emotions – their feelings and understanding of the emotions they are experiencing. Feeling angry because of anxiety about exams, for example, has been suggested to be helpful in finding ways to cope with feeling anxious.[50] Emotions data is potentially useful for all of the applications of learning analytics detailed in this book, including early alert, course recommendation, adaptive learning and curriculum enhancement.

## Conclusion

This chapter has considered three techniques that are being applied in learning contexts: discourse analytics, social network analysis, and sentiment and emotion analytics. Each of these methods has developed in its own right, sometimes over many years, but has only recently been brought into learning analytics. None of them is yet mainstream in education and consensus has not even been reached over how to delineate them and what to call them. Ferguson & Shum, for example, use the term *social learning analytics*, grouping together methods such as 'social learning network analytics' and 'social learning discourse analytics'. They suggest that these techniques should focus on how learners co-construct knowledge and that tools should be provided for learners themselves to reflect on how their relationships and interactions affect their learning.[51]

Social network analysis visualisations and other tools are beginning to be included in systems, such as the analytics functionality increasingly found within LMSs. The true power of these techniques may emerge, however, when they are combined to build more complete pictures of individuals and groups. Bakharia & Dawson point to a limitation of the social network analysis tool, SNAPP, which does not analyse message content.[52] Future systems that combine the analysis of discourse in student assignments and interactions, their participation in social networks and their emotions, with the other techniques outlined in this book, will provide ever more sophisticated analyses of how students are learning. This will help educators to improve their courses and furnish learners with new ways to understand and enhance their own education.

## References

1 De Liddo, A. *et al.*, 2011, Discourse-Centric Learning Analytics, *LAK11: Proceedings of the First International Conference on Learning Analytics and Knowledge*.

2 Milligan, S., 2015, Crowd-Sourced Learning in MOOCs: Learning Analytics Meets Measurement Theory, *LAK15: Proceedings of the Fifth International Conference on Learning Analytics and Knowledge*.

3 Knight, S. & Littleton, K., 2015, Dialogue as Data in Learning Analytics for Productive Educational Dialogue, *Journal of Learning Analytics*, 2(3), pp. 111–143.

4 Milligan, Crowd-Sourced Learning in MOOCs: Learning Analytics Meets Measurement Theory.

5 Ming, N. C. & Ming, V. L., 2012, Automated Predictive Assessment from Unstructured Student Writing, *Paper presented at the First International Conference on Data Analytics*.

6 Ming & Ming, Automated Predictive Assessment from Unstructured Student Writing.

7 Ming, N. C. & Ming, V. L., 2015, Visualizing and Assessing Knowledge from Unstructured Student Writing, *Technology, Instruction, Cognition and Learning*, 10(1), pp. 27–44.

8 Ming & Ming, Automated Predictive Assessment from Unstructured Student Writing.

9 De Liddo, A. *et al.*, Discourse-Centric Learning Analytics.

10 Ezen-Can, A. *et al.*, 2015, Unsupervised Modeling for Understanding MOOC Discussion Forums: A Learning Analytics Approach, *LAK15: Proceedings of the Fifth International Conference on Learning Analytics and Knowledge*.

11 De Liddo, A. *et al.*, Discourse-Centric Learning Analytics.

12 Milligan, Crowd-Sourced Learning in MOOCs: Learning Analytics Meets Measurement Theory.

13 Knight, S. & Littleton, K., 2015, Discourse-Centric Learning Analytics: Mapping the Terrain, *Journal of Learning Analytics*, 2(1), pp. 185–209.

14 Milligan, Crowd-Sourced Learning in MOOCs: Learning Analytics Meets Measurement Theory.

15 Kosorukoff, A., 2011, *Social Network Analysis: Theory and Applications*, www. asecib.ase.ro/mps/SocNet_TheoryApp.pdf (accessed 9 October 2016).

16 Dawson, S., 2010, 'Seeing' the Learning Community: An Exploration of the Development of a Resource for Monitoring Online Student Networking, *British Journal of Educational Technology*, 41(5), pp. 736–752.

17 Haythornthwaite, C. & de Laat, M., 2010, Social Networks and Learning Networks: Using Social Network Perspectives to Understand Social Learning, *Proceedings of the Seventh International Conference on Networked Learning*.

18 Ferguson, R. & Buckingham Shum, S., 2012, Social Learning Analytics: Five Approaches, *LAK12: Proceedings of the Second International Conference on Learning Analytics and Knowledge*.

19 Ibid.

20 Dawson, 'Seeing' the Learning Community.

21 Dawson, S., *et al.* 2010, SNAPP: Realising the Affordances of Real-Time SNA within Networked Learning Environments, *Proceedings of the Seventh International Conference on Networked Learning*.

22 Ibid.

23 Kosorukoff, *Social Network Analysis: Theory and Applications*.

24 Dawson, 'Seeing' the Learning Community.

25 Hernández García, A. *et al.*, 2015, Applying Social Learning Analytics to Message Boards in Online Distance Learning: A Case Study, *Computers in Human Behavior*, 47, pp. 68–80.

26 Dawson, Bakharia & Heathcote, SNAPP.

27  Hernández García *et al.*, Applying Social Learning Analytics to Message Boards in Online Distance Learning.

28  Bakharia, A. & Dawson, S., 2011, SNAPP: A Bird's-Eye View of Temporal Participant Interaction, *LAK11: Proceedings of the First International Conference on Learning Analytics and Knowledge*.

29  Ibid.

30  Dawson, S. & Siemens, G., 2014, Analytics to Literacies: The Development of a Learning Analytics Framework for Multiliteracies Assessment, *The International Review of Research in Open and Distributed Learning*, 15(4), www.irrodl.org/index.php/irrodl/article/view/1878/3006.

31  Ibid.

32  de Laat, M. & Prinsen, F. R., 2014, Social Learning Analytics: Navigating the Changing Settings of Higher Education, *Research and Practice in Assessment*, 9, pp. 51–60.

33  Pekrun, R. *et al.*, 2002, Academic Emotions in Students' Self-Regulated Learning and Achievement: A Program of Qualitative and Quantitative Research, *Educational Psychologist*, 37(2), pp. 91–106.

34  Rienties, B. & Rivers, B. A., 2014, *Measuring and Understanding Learner Emotions: Evidence and Prospects*, Learning Analytics Community Exchange.

35  Ibid.

36  Pekrun *et al.*, Academic Emotions in Students' Self-Regulated Learning and Achievement.

37  Alsmeyer, M. *et al.*, 2007, Getting Under the Skin of Learners: Tools for Evaluating Emotional Experience, *Proceedings of AIED 07: 13th International Conference of Artificial Intelligence in Education*, pp. 153–161.

38  Leony, D. *et al.*, 2015, Detection and Evaluation of Emotions in Massive Open Online Courses, *Journal of Universal Computer Science*, 21(5), pp. 638–655.

39  Cleveland-Innes, M., 2012, Emotional Presence, Learning and the Online Learning Environment, *IRRODL: The International Review of Research in Open and Distributed Learning*, 13(4), pp. 269–292.

40  Pekrun *et al.*, Academic Emotions in Students' Self-Regulated Learning and Achievement.

41  Alsmeyer *et al.*, Getting Under the Skin of Learners: Tools for Evaluating Emotional Experience.

42  Leece, R. & Hale, R., 2009, *Student Engagement and Retention through E-Motional Intelligence*, University of New England.

43  Rienties & Rivers, *Measuring and Understanding Learner Emotions: Evidence and Prospects*.

44  Henrie, C. R. *et al.*, 2015. Exploring Intensive Longitudinal Measures of Student Engagement in Blended Learning, *International Review of Research in Open and Distributed Learning* , 16(3), pp. 131–155.

45  Blikstein, P., 2011, Using Learning Analytics to Assess Students' Behaviour in Open-Ended Programming Tasks, *LAK11: Proceedings of the First International Conference on Learning Analytics and Knowledge*, pp. 110–116.

46  Leony *et al.*, Detection and Evaluation of Emotions in Massive Open Online Courses.

47  Alsmeyer *et al.*, Getting Under the Skin of Learners: Tools for Evaluating Emotional Experience.

48  Ibid.

49 Henrie *et al.*, Exploring Intensive Longitudinal Measures of Student Engagement in Blended Learning.

50 Pekrun *et al.*, Academic Emotions in Students' Self-Regulated Learning and Achievement.

51 Ferguson & Shum, Social Learning Analytics: Five Approaches.

52 Bakharia & Dawson, SNAPP: A Bird's-Eye View of Temporal Participant Interaction.

# 25  Expert Visions

The final question I put to the 20 experts concerned what their ideal future scenario would be for learning analytics and where they would like to see the field developing over the coming years.

## Exploring New Data Sources

Dragan Gašević considers the most useful data sources to be unstructured or related to discourse and believes that these often come from social networks. He suggests that such data can help us to understand social processes, giving us ideas about the extent to which students trust each other or are worried about their learning, for example. Simon Buckingham Shum conceptualises the texts produced by students as a 'window into the mind of the learner'. A particularly interesting area, he believes, is the intersection of research into composition and writing with natural language processing. Shane Dawson says of textual analysis:

> I think we're still only just touching analytics around unstructured data and trying to get feedback to learners, particularly in writing contexts. I know there's been a long history in argumentation theory and natural language processing … I think there's a lot in the writing field we can work on more, and I think that does show promise and could have a large impact.

As the technologies develop, analytics may increasingly be carried out on things produced by students, other than text. Alyssa Wise discusses 'artefact analytics', which use natural language processing and other techniques. Other data sources for learning analytics are emerging, too, from applications not necessarily designed for learning contexts. Doug Clow discusses the 'quantified self' and points to Oral Roberts University in Oklahoma, which now requires its incoming freshmen to track their fitness levels using Fitbits, potentially providing interesting data for learning analytics:

> Do you learn better if you went for a run this morning or are you better off doing your learning and then going for a run afterwards? I don't

know – but we could find the answer with that amount of data. That's the other thing that's really exciting about learning analytics: there's a lot of questions like that, that as an educator you wonder about. We have all this data, we can get close to a first stab at an answer just by having so much data that enough natural experiments will have occurred in that data.

## Analytics as Normal Practice

Dragan Gašević sees analytics as enabling institutions increasingly to make decisions based on information and for them to develop much better understanding of what processes are driving learning and what kinds of learning strategies are most effective. This should become normal practice for learners and instructors, so that, as Cathy Gunn puts it:

> use of analytics data to inform learning and course design is a matter of routine.

Jeff Grann also foresees a future where

> learning analytics becomes as common as a chalkboard is to a classroom today.

This is John Whitmer's aspiration, too: that carrying out learning analytics becomes an ordinary part of working in higher education, 'like having email'. He would like applications to incorporate detailed analytics as a core feature, enabling institutions to demonstrate the impact of the software product. John also wants to see the fostering of a culture of exploration, where algorithms are continually adapted and refined in a collaborative effort between researchers and providers:

> It's not like you check the box and it's done – we continue to keep this as evolving because we should and we can.

This would help to address Siemens' concern that researchers can often be isolated from vendors or end users, resulting in a mismatch between empirical research and implementation.[1]

## Personalisation

Many of the interviewees return to the theme of greater personalisation as a future aspiration. Alyssa Wise would like to see students being given more opportunities to be in the driving seat of their learning, setting goals for their university career, for example, being able to monitor their progress better and then to make changes based on data-informed reflection.

Bart Rienties builds on intelligent tutoring systems for his ideal scenario:

> Imagine a knowledge tree ... every route you can take on that tree is completely personalised, and you get feedback and opportunities to work with people who are on a similar path ... Analytics can identify the shape of every module, every tree, every learning programme, and knows exactly which kind of path students have to take, and then provides a completely personalised path for our students.

Doug Clow has a similar dream of learning being continually refined as people learn, based not just on what is appropriate for others, but on what has worked for the individual to date. Despite continual advances in artificial intelligence, he would like to see people built into the process, as he believes that 'a machine-human hybrid system is often more capable than just a machine'.

The vision of highly personalised learning is further outlined by Josh Baron, who envisages a future where students manage their own learning in ways that they cannot currently do because they cannot visualise it, receive alerts, or know where they are in the learning process. He would like institutions to move away from the current situation where credit is awarded for sitting in class and engaging in highly formal, structured learning experiences:

> I think learning analytics can really give us these tools to allow us to break out of that very traditional kind of mould and give students the ability to do the formal but also informal learning, and collect it all together in terms of the data that's being produced ... Capturing all dimensions of learning, not just the formal stuff that we do today, I think can be a real game changer.

One mechanism to help achieve this could be the emergence, says Jeff Grann, of:

> a comprehensive learner record – a digital asset the student controls, containing the key academic evidence of learning that institutions have gathered for that student, who could share a document like that with other institutions [so the students can] continue a personalised learning pathway for themselves; they could share it with a hiring manager to advocate for career positions that they seek.

Kirsty Kitto, too, envisages students having personal learning record stores:

> I will take my data with me for life and I will be able to make sense of it in multiple institutions and in different scenarios. That would be amazing. I'll have tools for understanding my learning, thinking about what I want to learn next, ways of matching jobs with my current skills and capabilities – working out what the gap is, and how I can enhance my skills and capabilities to get that thing that I want. This is going to be

very important given the way that all of our jobs are about to disappear and everybody's going to be spending an inordinate amount of time retraining. This is something that learning analytics can really help society with – that's where the really big wins will be from.

Shane Dawson wants to see analytics being used as soon as students commence their studies, with suggested pathways and opportunities provided to them from the outset, rather than a blanket curriculum given to all. Continual feedback would nudge them into being independent, effective, self-regulated learners. He would like assessment tasks to be set every day that the student comes onto campus:

> So you're doing good in this, well, forge ahead. You're not doing so good in this area, here's some other opportunities for you to develop in that space, so we're going to focus on that. How critical is it for your degree, how critical is it for your employability? I'm doing glass-blowing on my elective course because I just want a little bit on the creative side. Does it really matter then that I just get 50% or 51% in my class? Probably not. But if … I'm doing chemistry and I can't do a titration, that's probably a hell of a lot more of a problem.

For Stefan Mol, while learning analytics potentially offers a better match between individuals and the workplace, there are other benefits:

> If we can tailor our educational process to teaching students that which they need in their job, there will be room left to do all sorts of other stuff around good citizenship and appreciation of culture, and what have you. I think if we can define these outcomes … that which lies beyond education, this might be used not only to help students but also to optimise curricula.

Timothy McKay also focusses on personalisation when I ask him what he thinks the 'end game' of learning analytics is:

> I don't know that 'end game' is quite the right word for it because nothing like this is really going to end but I do have a kind of goal here to spend my time here in the next few years thinking about ways in which we can meaningfully and effectively, and with impact, personalise education. So I would really like the education that our students have five years from now – if I asked a student 'how did we use technology to personalise education for you' – they should really see it. And when they get to that point that they're regularly interacting in ways that they find valuable with personalisation systems. There's almost none of it right now. The students go to the University website and they see the same website everyone in the world sees. They go to the *New York Times* and they get a unique page. There's a long way to go but I think we're ready to make some substantial steps in that regard. So if they can see personalisation being a

valuable and important thing and recognise that we put a lot of energy, effort into doing that – and I hope that we will be ahead of what other people are doing – that I think would be a success for us.

Rebecca Ferguson hopes that students will appreciate all the efforts that are being put into enhancing their learning experience by harvesting and analysing their data,

> reaping the benefits of that and saying, 'Oh yeah because you've pre-sented me with this data in this way and with these recommendations, that has changed my learning experience for the better'. And teaching staff could turn around and say, 'Yes you're giving me information about my teaching, about my students, and I can use that to affect their learning and improve my teaching.'

## Linking Research to Practice

Another challenge may be a mismatch in the field between research and practice. Kirsty Kitto suggests that research into learning analytics at institu-tions rarely results in innovations that are usable:

> PhD students don't get their PhD by solving some small problem that would be really useful to an educator. They get it by building the new latest greatest classifier or recommendation algorithm that doesn't do anything useful educationally … and if you actually go and talk to educators they just want to know who watched their video (which is actually worth knowing as well). So there's very few attempts to engage with the people who use the stuff, and find out what they actually need, and you don't see these systemic adoptions because people are trying to drive the state of the art of the research and not really pushing up at that practitioner level.

There is a warning, too, from Rebecca Ferguson, who criticises some researchers in the area for concentrating on 'sexy' areas, with an attitude of:

> 'We want to get involved in this; this is new and exciting' and not neces-sarily thinking 'OK, why do we want to go into these areas, what will this tell us and how will that help?' I was talking to Dragan yesterday and he was talking about the University of Edinburgh, saying 'we were imple-menting learning analytics but then we had to step back and think why were we implementing learning analytics, because', he said, 'we don't have a retention problem: our students stay, they want to be there. So analytics which have been designed for retention, which most of them are, are not the analytics we wanted.'

Rebecca wants to see people thinking more carefully about why they are doing the research and not just because there is an easily available dataset. She believes there need to be links into practice:

So to me learning analytics is very much that cycle that Doug describes: you come up with a question, you get some data, you do some analytics, you feed it into practice and then you reflect on it, and you keep going round. And to me if you don't engage with that cycle you're not really doing learning analytics, you are doing some sort of statistical research, educational research, data research but if you haven't influenced learning or teaching or the environments in which they take place, how can you claim that you're doing something that is new rather than what we were doing ten years ago?

Mark Glynn would like to see learning scientists speak more to learning analytics specialists and believes that collaboration, both inside and between institutions, is essential if the field is to progress. Jeff Grann notes that, while there is a society for research into learning analytics, there is no professional society for practitioners and that this could help move the area forward, particularly in helping to define the competencies required among staff and faculty.

Simon Buckingham Shum is inspired by the potential linkages between learning analytics and learning design, in particular:

My ideal outcome looks much more like intentional learning design to achieve certain outcomes which are gathering data, which will tell us whether those are happening or not. The dream scenario is that that is going on in what we would call an 'improvement science methodology' – that's a whole discipline that's coming now – educational improvement science – and that the students are part of that process as well ... learning design and analytics dancing well together, and it's one where data literacy on the part of the students as well as the educators is part of what it means to be literate in the future. The analytics technologies will always be imperfect. Let's make that a feature: it's a learning opportunity for students to push back and critique the analytics as much as to take what they're saying as gospel truth.

As well as ensuring that the technologies are more pedagogically driven in their design, Dragan Gašević suggests that we may have to redesign our courses in order to motivate students to communicate more. Most courses he says that are available in learning management systems (LMSs) are built on poor pedagogical principles. This is an important point for learning analytics in general: in order to collect the most useful data to ascertain whether students are learning or not, institutions will have to develop courses and learning activities that require the use of systems designed to gather that data. Traditional lecture-based courses will not provide enough fine-grained information about how students are learning.

John Whitmer envisages ever greater use of academic technologies by students, with institutions increasingly requiring their use, too. This in turn will help to 'instrument' learning:

We're getting an increasing number of relevant data points across the student experience, across the student lifecycle that it just behoves us to use – and to me we're really in our infancy, but the amount we're able to discern, understand, glean from the existing data – just doing clicko-metric frequency work – imagine what we'll get in two years when we're actually moving to looking at content evaluation and subject matter evaluation, and we have more instrumentation.

Finally, Bart Rienties reminds us that despite huge advances in recent years, these are still early days for learning analytics:

I think we're still so much on the frontiers of learning analytics – it's all uncharted territory. There are massive opportunities.

## Reference

1 Siemens, G., 2012, *Learning Analytics: Envisioning a Research Discipline and a Domain of Practice*, ACM, pp. 4–8.

# Index